TRANSFORMING RUSSIAN ENTERPRISES

TRANSFORMING RUSSIAN ENTERPRISES

From State Control to Employee Ownership

Edited by
John Logue, Sergey Plekhanov,
and John Simmons

Contributions in Economics and
Economic History, Number 168

GREENWOOD PRESS
Westport, Connecticut • London

Library of Congress Cataloging-in-Publication Data

Transforming Russian enterprises : from state control to employee
  ownership / edited by John Logue, Sergey Plekhanov and John Simmons.
      p.   cm.–(Contributions in economics and economic history,
  ISSN 0084–9235 ; no. 168)
    Includes bibliographical references (p.   ) and index.
    ISBN 0–313–28748–1 (alk. paper)
    1. Privatization–Russia (Federation). 2. Business enterprises–
  Russia (Federation) 3. Business enterprises–Russia (Federation)–
  Case studies. I. Logue, John. II. Plekhanov, Sergey.
  III. Simmons, John. IV. Series.
  HD4215.15.T73 1995
  338.947–dc20   95–6666

British Library Cataloguing in Publication Data is available.

Library of Congress Catalog Card Number: 95–6666
ISBN: 0–313–28748–1
ISSN: 0084–9235

First published in 1995

Greenwood Press, 88 Post Road West, Westport, CT 06881
An imprint of Greenwood Publishing Group, Inc.

Printed in the United States of America

The paper used in this book complies with the
Permanent Paper Standard issued by the National
Information Standards Organization (Z39.48–1984).

10 9 8 7 6 5 4 3 2 1

Copyright Acknowledgment
Slightly different versions of Chapters 11, 12, and 15 first appeared in the EDI Working Paper, *Restructuring for High Performance: Transforming Russian Enterprises*, edited by John Simmons. Copyright ©
1994 by the Economic Development Institute of the World Bank. Reprinted by permission.

To our children—
Karen and Anne Marie Logue
Vasya and Lisa Plekhanov
Kevin, Erica, and Ian Simmons
—and to the world they will help shape

Contents

Illustrations

Preface

◆ A central feature of the initial phase of Russian privatization has been the transfer of ownership of the means of production from the state to the employees of the enterprises being privatized. More than 70 percent of all Russian firms privatized to date have done so through majority employee ownership.

The success or failure of employee ownership in the Russian privatization process is crucial to the type of Russian society that will develop in the post-Soviet era. Will it be one of relative economic equality and efficiency? Or will it be one of concentrated wealth with the economic inefficiencies and social unrest that flow from it?

This book focuses on employee ownership in the Russian process of privatization and economic reform. What are the determinants of success for implementing employee ownership, management reform, and high-performance work systems in individual Russian firms? Part I traces the development of Russian economic reform efforts beginning with Nikita Khrushchev's efforts to reform the planning and control system, continuing with Mikhail Gorbachev's cautious, incremental effort to promote a kind of market socialism, and culminating in Boris Yeltsin's near revolutionary transition to capitalism through "shock therapy" and mass privatization. Part II examines the empirical changes within firms as they have privatized using employee ownership; specifically, we examine the experience of six Russian enterprises which were pioneers in this process. Part III distills some useful lessons from the wealth of Russian and American empirical experience with employee-owned firms.

Since the Russian debate about privatization and employee ownership has been intensely ideological, it is well to say a word about the underlying premises of the editors and authors of this book. The reader who starts at the back of the book will see a significant eclecticism in the list of contributors: it includes American Soviet scholars of long standing, American practitioners, Russian managers, and Russian scholars. We share, however, two common denominators.

The first is a simple assumption about methodology: facts count. We are less interested in the grand theoretical constructs which have characterized the Russian debate during both the Soviet and post-Soviet periods than we are in what has actually happened in Russian firms.

The second is an assumption about the good society: broadly dispersed ownership of property by the many is preferable to the concentration of great wealth in the hands of the few. While the editors can speak only for themselves, we share fundamental beliefs that, first, an economic system based on widespread property ownership provides a greater degree of social and economic justice and, second, that Thomas Jefferson was right in arguing that political democracy and broadly dispersed ownership of productive assets go hand in hand. And we share a sense that it would be a tragedy were the productive assets created at the cost of such sacrifice by the Russian people over many decades to serve in the end only to "propertize the nomenklatura"–that is, to enrich the old political and managerial elite, to pass into the hands of the mafia, or to be sold at fire-sale prices to foreign firms.

In short, we see employee ownership in Russia not simply as a shortcut to speed privatization or as a brief transitional form of ownership until the "real" owners appear. Rather, we see it as a form of ownership compatible with high levels of economic efficiency, at least among the firms analyzed here. They dramatically outperformed the rest of the Russian economy between their privatization, beginning in 1987, and the completion in 1993 of the empirical chapters in Part II.

In the time that this book has been under way, circumstances in Russia have changed dramatically. Privatization and direct employee ownership of the means of production were still experimental Soviet policies at the time our research began; by the time we drafted this preface, half the economy had been privatized, much of it through some form of employee ownership, and the Soviet Union itself had vanished. The speed of change has tended to date the case studies quickly, particularly as the Russian economy has declined, plunging even the best-managed firms into crisis. Capital goods producers like KEMZ and Krasny Proletary were particularly hard hit by the collapse in capital spending in 1994–95. At KEMZ, with most of the workers laid off, general director Vadim Vrachev, previously a hero for his work collective, survived a recall vote by a 60–40 margin, and took a part-time job teaching. At Krasny Proletary, renting out office space in company facilities replaced production results as the first item on the board agenda. Similarly, the rapid fall in the value of the ruble has rendered the early salary figures quaintly amusing; the ruble has fallen from about 30 to the dollar to about 4,500 to the dollar during our work on this volume. Consequently, we have tried to benchmark the ruble figures cited to the average industrial wage of that particular time.

The collapse of law and order took its toll as well: Alexander Mironov, the general director of MOVEN, was assassinated in January 1995. His murder, which remained unsolved as this book went to press, was believed by many to have been caused by his refusal to pay protection money.

As any book nears publication, the list of those to whom the authors and editors owe thanks grows to frightening length. Each of the editors owes intellectual debts to his coeditors, and each has his own debts—intellectual and otherwise—to acknowledge.

John Logue appreciates the assistance, comments, criticism, insight, and support of Dan Bell, Joseph R. Blasi, Rudolph Buttlar, Carol Cartwright, Richard Celeste, Bob Clawson, Richard Duval, David Ellerman, Tim Frye, Yakov Keremetsky, Byron Lander, Olga Maiboroda, Lowell Marshall, Ron Phillips, Corey Rosen, Karen Schwartz, Victor Supyan, Oleg Tikhonov, and Valery Varvarov during this project. The financial support of Kent State University and of the John D. and Catherine T. MacArthur Foundation made his work on this book possible, and the hospitality of many Russian friends turned work into pleasure.

Sergey Plekhanov expresses his thanks to Valery Varvarov, Vladimir Patrikeyev, and Vyacheslav Kamenetsky for involving him in the study of employee ownership in the United States and Russia.

John Simmons appreciates the comments of Maria Kamenskaya, Michael Shandler, David Binns, and Sally Craig on earlier drafts of his chapters and notes his great debt to Russian colleagues who have helped him begin to understand the Russian management landscape, including Yakov Keremetsky, Arcady Prigozhin, Andrei Voronkov, Maxim Iliin, Elena Kishinets, Yuri Kirillov, and Svyatoslav Fyodorov. Simmons acknowledges with gratitude the encouragement of Wade Greene and the financial support of Rockefeller Financial Services and IREX.

The authors and editors also owe a number of common debts of gratitude: to the managers and employees of Kazansky Elektromekhanichesky, Krasny Proletary, MOVEN, Saratov Aviation, Stroipolymer, and Veshky who took the time to answer many questions about their experience; to Vilius Pogozhelskis for the translation of the chapter on the BUTEK experience and for designing many of the graphs and figures; and to our editors at Greenwood for their patience with our many delays.

Terminology

◆ A word about the organization of the Russian firm and the terminology we have used in English may be useful.

All the personnel of the enterprise—managers, salaried employees, and hourly workers together—make up the *trudovoi kollektiv*. This group in its entirety has substantial rights under Russian law, including—crucially for the discussion in this book—the right to determine which privatization option is chosen. The English terminology of "personnel," "employees," or "staff" simply does not convey the sense of a decision-making unit, though those terms include the same group. In their original drafts, our authors variously spoke of this group as the "work collective," "workers' collective," "collective of the enterprise," and "labor collective." We have standardized the term throughout as the *work collective*.

In the period discussed, ultimate authority over the firm—and over its management—formally rested with the work collective's annual meeting (*yezhegodnoye sobraniye trudovogo kollektiva*). The work collective elected a representative conference (*sobraniye predstavitelei*) to exercise its oversight function between annual meetings. The authority of the representative conference vis-à-vis the general director varied dramatically with the situation and with the leadership ability of the general director.

The *soviet direktorov* performs the functions generally associated in the United States with those of the board of directors: it hires the general director, approves capital expenditures, and develops long-term plans for the firm. We have translated it as *board of directors*. In closely held companies, the board is larger than the average American board of directors, meets more frequently, and is more likely to be consulted on operational decisions. Public firms privatized under Options 1 and 2 are required to have a smaller board of directors (for a discussion of the privatization options, see Chater 3); outside directors must make up two-thirds of the members even when the employees own the majority of the shares.

The *direktsiya*–the senior management group–provides the firm's daily leadership. It is composed of the top management of the firm, including the general director–equivalent to our chief executive officer–and the directors of individual plants and departments. Typically it is made up of the top five to twenty managers in the company and meets with regularity–once a week or more–to make operational decisions. We've translated that as *management team* or *management board.*

PART ONE

REFORMING THE RUSSIAN ECONOMY: HISTORICAL AND THEORETICAL PERSPECTIVES

1 Introduction: Employee Ownership and Russian Economic Reform

John Logue, Sergey Plekhanov, and John Simmons

♦ RUSSIA has embarked upon an experiment in economic transition that is unprecedented in scope and speed. It is a dual transition: from central planning to a market economy and from state to private ownership. If the transition is successful, there is reason to hope that economic prosperity will nurture the fragile Russian experiment with political democracy. If it fails to improve the living standards of the majority of the population, there is little reason to believe that the Russian transition to a democratic political regime will succeed either.

Since 1991, the administration of President Boris N. Yeltsin has undertaken a wrenching economic transformation of Russia that makes Mikhail S. Gorbachev's reforms of the 1985–91 period seem halting experiments by comparison. The Yeltsin economic reform team, in addition to dismantling the state planning system that administered prices and production, has freed enterprises to set their own prices and undertaken privatization of state enterprises on an unparalleled scale. The state economic planning agency (Gosplan)–that pervasive integrative feature of Soviet economic life–has simply ceased to exist. Most prices were freed in January 1992 to seek their own levels. They shot heavenward, and the queues that had been such a characteristic of Soviet daily shopping vanished along with consumer buying power and the overhang of household savings which reformers had feared as a source of inflation. In 1993–94, the gradual steps toward the creation of a private sector that had begun in 1986–87 gave way to massive privatization according to the Russian government's program that set privatization targets which rivaled the most ambitious of Gosplan's goals.

Key to rapid privatization has been the sale of state-owned enterprises primarily to their employees for vouchers issued under the June 1992 privatization law. While numerous exceptions (for leased enterprises, independent privatization legislation in some of the component republics of the Russian Federation, and the special presidential decree of December 29, 1991, for the city of Moscow's separate program) make all generalizations fraught with qualifications, the process has usually involved the conversion of state or municipal enterprises into joint-stock companies and the subsequent sale of majority shares to employees and outside owners.

The foundations for this policy of privatization through employee ownership were laid under Mikhail S. Gorbachev. From the first hesitant steps in 1986 toward perestroika–the restructuring of the sclerotic planned economy left after the "years of stagnation" of the latter part of the Brezhnev era–Gorbachev's economic reform efforts targeted greater decentralization and enterprise independence within a general system of "socialist self-management." Reforms in 1987–88, most notably the Law on State Enterprises which went into effect in January 1988, systematically increased the rights of the work collective(*trudovoi kollektiv*)–the personnel of the enterprise–and its representative structures vis-à-vis the enterprise general directors and the government ministries, while it introduced the principle of greater enterprise independence and increased the scope for enterprise financial independence. Simultaneously in 1987, the encouragement of cooperatives and the first contracts leasing the assets of state enterprises to their work collective since the New Economic Policy of the 1920s represented tentative steps toward privatization and experiments with quasi-market prices. (For a chronology, see the Appendix to this chapter.)

Although some of the more radical of these measures, including the direct election of enterprise general directors by the work collective, were repealed in the June 1990 revision of the Law on State Enterprises, experimentation with privatization accelerated with the passage of the Law on Leasing in 1989, the Council of Ministers' decree in 1990 permitting enterprises belonging to the BUTEK Association to buy their assets from the state, and special ministerial decrees for individual enterprises (such as Saratov Aviation in 1991). All of these measures focused on a transition from state control to ownership by the work collective.

The modest experimentation with privatization of the Gorbachev period was overwhelmed by the events of 1991. The struggle inside the Soviet government between conservatives and reformers threatened to block continued reform. The deepening conflict between the dual centers of power in Moscow–the Soviet government under Gorbachev and the

Russian Federation under its directly elected president, Boris Yeltsin—saw the Russian Federation legislate its own radical version of rapid privatization in July 1991. This legislation, which was premised on the distribution of privatization vouchers to all Russian citizens, provided special privileges in privatizing the Russian Federation's state and municipal property to work collectives.

The abortive hardline putsch against Gorbachev in August 1991 sounded the death knell of the Soviet Union. With its collapse in December 1991, power in Moscow passed exclusively to the Russian Federation's government, which was itself increasingly torn by internal conflict between Yeltsin's young, neoliberal economic reform team under Yegor T. Gaidar, who joined the cabinet in November 1991, and the increasingly recalcitrant majority of what had been the reformist Russian parliament. Much of this struggle was fought out in the spring of 1992 over the draft privatization program.

Although employee ownership had been accorded a key role in the Russian Federation's privatization law of July 1991, in December 1991 Gaidar's economic team proposed a more modest role: employees were to receive a minority interest of up to 25 percent of the shares of privatized enterprises without charge and without voting rights, and could purchase an additional 10 percent at a concessionary price; top management could purchase 5 percent. Caps which related wages to value of shares granted ensured employees a far smaller portion in the more capital-intensive industries. Lease contracts that permitted employees to purchase 100 percent of their firms were to be abrogated retroactively. Gaidar's proposal brought what privatization had been occurring among leased companies under the 1991 law to a screeching halt.

The government's privatization proposal was the subject of an acrimonious debate throughout the spring of 1992. The eventual compromise, passed in June, let each company's work collective choose between two basic privatization options which both involved employee ownership; a third option in the legislation had very restricted utility. In the first option, which was essentially the government's December proposal, employees received a minority interest of up to 25 percent in nonvoting preferred stock free from the government with an option for managers to buy an additional 5 percent and for employees, an additional 10 percent; the controlling ownership would be sold in subsequent voucher auctions which were open to employees as well as outside bidders. In the second option, employees received no stock free but could purchase up to 51 percent of the voting shares in a closed subscription using vouchers primarily and could subsequently bid for a portion of the remainder in voucher auctions. More than two-thirds of the firms targeted for privatization under the program selected the second option.

While the two options were seen as dramatically different, according to a survey of some two hundred privatized firms done for the State Property Committee by Joseph Blasi (1994b), insiders ended up controlling a majority of shares even under the first option; on the average, employees and managers held 66 percent of company stock (including 8 percent going to top managers), 21 percent was sold to outsiders, and the government retained the remaining 13 percent.

The June 1992 law also permitted leased firms to privatize under the contractual terms of their lease agreements, which typically provided 100 percent employee ownership.[1] Leased enterprises were quick to use their reinstated right to buy before this part of their contract was again abrogated.

Thus between the passage of the Russian Federation's first privatization law in July 1991 and the end of the "voucher privatization" process in July 1994,[2] the principal tool of privatization was the sale of a majority interest to employees. Although the Gaidar team opposed this outcome ideologically, it grudgingly accepted the possibility of majority employee ownership—at least as a transitional phase—as the price for rapid privatization.

Curiously, the Russian experience with employee ownership in leased and privatized enterprises from the Gorbachev period was ignored in the economic reform process under Yeltsin. Yeltsin's reform team showed a striking disregard for what actually had happened in previously privatized firms.[3] In a televised debate with John Simmons in March 1992, Anatoly Chubais, who as deputy prime minister and head of the State Property Committee was in charge of the privatization process, bluntly dismissed the utility of even visiting employee-owned Russian enterprises which were making significant progress; he had no need to, he said, because he had visited a collective farm. Equally symptomatically, a ranking official of the State Property Committee in July 1993 responded to a suggestion by one of the coeditors that a study of the experience of privatized firms might have positive consequences for privatization rules by insisting that the committee was concerned only with meeting privatization quotas; the subsequent performance of the privatized firms was not its concern. When the State Property Committee finally sought data, it commissioned an American adviser, Professor Joseph Blasi of Rutgers University, to collect them.

Thus the privatization process, like Russian economic reform efforts in general, seemed to be driven more by politics than by economics. Frequently, government statements reflected the primacy of its neoliberal ideology, which bordered on unrestrained market romanticism. One is reminded that the only precedent for an economic transformation of this magnitude in Russian experience is a disturbing one: the collectivization of agriculture and the introduction of the Five Year Plan at the beginning of Josef Stalin's rule. It was with this in mind that some critics of Gaidar and Chubais spoke of them as "neo-Bolsheviks" (Arbatov 1992).

This book explores the process of privatization through employee ownership under Gorbachev and Yeltsin and how it has worked in practice at the level of the company. Only part of the discussion is about ownership, however. As the reader will quickly note, the transformation of state-owned enterprises within a planned economy into employee-owned, market-directed firms requires more than just a change of owners. It requires a complete reorientation of the firm toward the market, and that, in its turn, demands a radical reconstruction of management through decentralization and democratization.

The first section of the book places employee ownership of individual Russian enterprises in the broader context of economic reform in the post-Stalin period. Robert Clawson traces the major efforts to reform the Soviet industrial economy and its planning system between Stalin's death and Gorbachev's assent to power. Privatization was not on that agenda, but the themes of decentralization, flexibility, and management responsibility continue to resonate. Sergey Plekhanov takes up the story with Gorbachev as the "years of stagnation" at the end of the Brezhnev period led reformers to go beyond reforms *within* the system to attempt reform *of* the system. He analyzes the evolution of Russian privatization policies as they collided with the realities of the Soviet heritage in industry and society. Finally, Valery N. Varvarov examines the experience of the largest-scale privatization effort under Gorbachev: the BUTEK experiment in 1990–91.

The second part of the book deals with the experience of six firms which were early starters in the privatization process and the transition to a market economy. Oleg Tikhonov surveys MOVEN's experience, John Logue and Olga Maiboroda examine Kazansky Elektromekhanichesky Zavod (KEMZ), Victor Supyan traces Stroipolymer's development, Yakov Keremetsky analyzes Veshky, David Binns discusses Saratov Aviation, and John Simmons, David Hanna, and Yuri Kirillov detail Krasny Proletary's evolution. These firms privatized under a variety of different legal forms—as cooperatives, as leased enterprises with a right to purchase, as BUTEK members, or under special ministerial decree, or under Option 2 of the 1992 privatization law.

These firms are atypical in that they made an early commitment to privatization, to employee ownership, and to management reform. They embraced the reform process and tried to make it work. Their experience traces the development of privatization from its onset in the middle of the Gorbachev years through the mass privatization of 1993. These case studies, which were completed in 1993, overrepresent the "premature privatizers" which were first out of the starting gate in the privatization process. Precisely this fact gives them a sufficient duration of experience to permit analysis of the postprivatization development of Russian enterprises and to be instructive to those which followed.

This section of the book is about microeconomic reform—about reform within the firm. However, macroeconomic policies form the context for the experience of the firms from January 1992 to the present. Virtual chaos at the macroeconomic level created a context that has made rational decision making at the level of the firm difficult. Indeed while all the firms that are the subject of case studies in Part II were still flourishing when the final touches were put on the studies in 1993, the continuing Russian economic crisis—now worse than the Great Depression in the United States if measured by fall in production—had severely affected even these well-managed firms. The capital goods producers were particularly hard hit: by March 1994, for example, KEMZ was operating with a skeleton crew primarily doing repair work, and Krasny Proletary had most of its workforce on layoff. Even consumer product firms like Veshky were working short weeks and piling up inventory. These case studies, therefore, are snapshots of the proverbial moving target.

The final part of the book begins with reflections by John Logue and John Simmons on the American experience with employee ownership and management redesign and its relevance to Russian conditions. The American experience with both employee ownership and reengineering management has played a significant role in the Russian privatization debate. There is, of course, a historic irony in Russians turning to Americans to learn about direct worker ownership of the means of production, but it is in fact true that, since 1974, the United States has become the principal arena for experimentation in the West with employee ownership, and many of those firms have been remarkably successful compared to their conventional competitors. The context of the American experience, of course, is very different: the market economy and private ownership are well established. Still, there are also substantial similarities, including a predominance of Taylorism as a management ideology and an alienation of Russian workers from managers *very* similar to that which American employee-owned firms struggle with in making the transition from conventional ownership to high-performance employee ownership. We conclude with a chapter discussing what lessons can be drawn from both the Russian and American empirical experiences.

Is employee ownership in Russia only a transition to the concentrated ownership of conventional capitalism? That has seemingly been the goal of the Russian privatization agency, and it certainly is the hope of many Russian general directors who would like to own their plants outright. Opinion polls revealed that an overwhelming majority of the Russian population feared that it was: by July 1993, a survey revealed that while only 11 percent thought that ownership would be widespread, fully 74 percent thought that privatization would lead to ownership by a small group of people.[4] As economic circumstances have worsened, the likelihood of this prognosis proving true has increased.

Microeconomic reform at the level of the firm ultimately has macroeconomic consequences. Without its success, macroeconomic reforms are doomed to failure. To be blunt, Russian economic reform stands or falls on the basis of its success at the level of the enterprise. It is at the micro level that people earn their incomes, buy their goods, make their decisions. The interaction of the macro and micro levels will determine the ultimate distribution of wealth and economic power in the new Russia.

NOTES

1. Similarly, in the special Moscow city privatization program for municipal retail and service enterprises in 1992–93, typically 100 percent ownership initially passed to employees, though managers were often quick to buy many of the employee shareholders out.

2. The voucher privatization program was originally supposed to end in December 1993. But privatization lagged the plan, and many vouchers remained outstanding, so the program was extended to June 30, 1994.

3. For a review of some of the issues in the privatization discussion, see John Simmons (1991, 1992a, 1992b) and Simmons and John Logue (1992).

4. Fifteen percent had no opinion. *Ekonomicheskiye i Sotsialnyie Peremeny: Monitoring Obshchestvennogo Mneniya*, no. 5 (September 1993): 23.

APPENDIX
Toward Privatization: A Chronology of Reform

March 1985. Mikhail S. Gorbachev becomes general secretary of the Communist Party of the Soviet Union (CPSU).

February 1986. At the CPSU's Twenty-seventh Congress, Gorbachev stresses worker participation and "socialist self-management in the economy." This congress establishes the foundations for reform.

October 1986–February 1987. Various Council of Ministers' decrees permit the formation of workers' cooperatives in the service sector, in production of consumer goods, and in recycling. Cooperatives become prominent in restaurant sector, especially for foreign press.

November 1986. Law on Individual Labor Activity permits small-scale provision of services and consumer goods by private enterprise for first time since the 1920s; only individual owners and members of their families can work in these businesses, and hired labor remains prohibited.

June 1987. The Law on State Enterprises is adopted by the Central Committee and the Supreme Soviet to take effect January 1, 1988. It provides for far-reaching changes in enterprise management, including the election of managers and of councils of workers, and in enterprise independence, including replacement of Gosplan targets with state orders, enterprise self-financing, new latitude in price and wage revisions, and greater freedom to engage in international trade.

1988. Work collectives begin to lease assets of some service and light industrial enterprises from the state or municipalities on a contractual basis in the Russian Federation. Capital improvements made during lease period are the property of the work collective, not the state.

January 1988. Law on State Enterprises implemented.

May 1988. Law on Cooperatives adopted as one of the most radical economic measures taken in the first years of Gorbachev's reforms. By 1990, nearly 200,000 cooperatives were formed in the USSR.

1989. Economy sputters throughout the year.

January 1989. Reforms of 1987 are extended to entire economy and begin to disrupt supply relationships.

July 1989. Major coal miners' strike: 400,000 walk out across the four major coal fields. Large-scale independent trade union organization among miners. The official All-Union Central Council of Trade Unions begins to move toward collective bargaining.

*August 1989.*The government's bill banning strikes for fifteen months is rejected by parliament. In October of 1989, the Law on Strikes bans strikes in strategic sectors of the economy and introduces a set of procedures for settlement of labor disputes.

August 1989. Entrepreneurial Association BUTEK (*Budushchee tovarnoi ekonomiki*) formed.

October 1989. Leonid I. Abalkin's program calls for gradual transition from state to other forms of ownership and development of market-oriented financial system.

December 1989. Law on Leasing legalizes previous contractual system but restricts leasing generally by raising lease prices.

1990. Economy passes from stagnation to decline.

January 1990. BUTEK experiment sanctioned by Council of Ministers' decree, and work collectives of BUTEK enterprises are permitted to buy the assets of their firms from the state. BUTEK is given special privileges during 1990 to encourage enterprises to participate.

June 1990. New Law on State Enterprises reverses some of the governance reforms of the previous law. Direct election of managers abolished.

August 1990. Stanislav Shatalin presents reform program which calls for market determination of prices and output.

December 1990. Russia's Supreme Soviet passes the Law on Enterprises and Entrepreneurial Activity which further strengthens the rights of the work collective in the Russian Federation.

December 1990. Formation of Union of Work Collectives to represent workers' councils within larger enterprises.

1991. Decline in production continues while inflation rises from about 5 percent in 1990 to about 90 percent in 1991.

March 1991–fall 1992. Process of experimentation with privatization is impeded as interest rates rise, conflict between Russian Federation and Soviet Union grows, and the victorious neoliberal reformers in the Russian government seek to reduce preferences for work collectives in privatization.

June 1991. Boris N. Yeltsin wins popular election as president of the Russian Federation with 58 percent of vote. Power struggle between Yeltsin and Gorbachev intensifies.

July 1991. Passage of Russian Federation's laws on privatization. These laws call for sweeping privatization of enterprises controlled by the Russian Federation and its component units with ownership preferences going to the work collectives and all citizens receiving privatization accounts.

August 1991. Abortive putsch against Gorbachev. Balance of power shifts decisively to Yeltsin, who rallies Moscow against the coup.

November 1991. Yegor Gaidar enters Yeltsin's cabinet and becomes chief architect of economic reform policy.

December 1991. Dissolution of the Soviet Union. It is replaced by the Commonwealth of Independent States.

December 1991. Draft Russian privatization program for 1992 reduces work collectives' advantage in the privatization process.

1992. Production decline accelerates. Industrial production falls about 18 percent from the depressed level of 1991. By the end of 1992, the gross domestic product has fallen to 64 percent of 1989's level.

January 1992. Price liberalization launched as the centerpiece of economic reform. Prices jump 350 percent, and will rise by about 2,600 percent for the year.

Spring 1992. The city administration in Nizhny Novgorod (formerly Gorky) starts selling retail outlets in weekly public auctions under the auspices of the International Finance Corporation, a World Bank affiliate. City of Moscow embarks on mass transfer of small service-sector enterprises to their work collectives.

June 1992. Compromise Russian privatization program enacted. It establishes procedures for large-scale privatization outside the defense and natural resource sectors through issuance of vouchers to all citizens. This program gives work collectives certain preferences in privatization.

Fall 1992. Transformation of state enterprises into joint-stock companies begins as a step toward privatization. Privatization gets under way.

1993. Inflation for the year declines to about 900 percent. Industrial production for the year falls a further 16 percent.

1993–July 1994. During "voucher privatization" period, work collectives opt overwhelmingly for majority employee ownership. State Property Committee grudgingly accepts worker ownership as a transitional phenomenon "until the real owners appear" and crafts implementation rules to make it difficult to keep shares inside the enterprise. More than 14,000 large enterprises are privatized through voucher privatization.

May 1994. Industrial output is down 26 percent for the first five months of 1994 from 1993's depressed levels. One-quarter of large Russian factories are reported shut down for all or part of May; more than half of these are capital goods producers. Inflation falls to 8.1 percent for the month, the lowest rate since price liberalization in January 1992.

July 1994. New privatization decree by Yeltsin provides for the second stage of privatization: direct sale of shares to investors for cash with minor preferences to work collectives.

2 Post-Stalin Efforts to Reform the Soviet Industrial Economy, 1953–1985

Robert W. Clawson

◆ OBSERVING the economic dynamics of post-USSR Russia in the early 1990s, it is all too easy to assume, erroneously, that the Soviet system of industrial administration had always been characterized by permanent deadening inertia. It would be an additional mistake to conclude that the various experiments were simply tinkering. From the beginning of Lenin's leadership in 1917 to the death of Konstantin Chernenko in 1985, Soviet industrial administration was the subject of a continuing series of reorganizations ranging from major overhaul to minor adjustment. There are few generalizations that can usefully be made about those efforts. For instance, while it is accurate to say that there was an overall tendency toward centralized control of industrial production, in several noteworthy periods there was only a kind of semipassive magnetic pull that seemed to draw major experiments in decentralization back toward Moscow. Although most reform experiments were eventually undercut, they should not be ignored; they present a wide variety of possibilities, some of which, had they been carried further consistently and without bureaucratic sabotage, might have yielded a dramatically different result than the system now characterized as "stagnation."[1]

The history of Soviet industrial administration from 1917 to Josef Stalin's death in 1953 featured periodic reorganization, innovation, and reform. The pre-Stalin periods were characterized by a variety of orientations with only a hazy set of ideological principles to guide experiments. Following Stalin's accession to power in the late 1920s, the reorganizations began to take on the nature of personal whim based on a set of assumptions about human political and economic behavior that could not bear any significant degree of decentralized, unregulated activity. Stalin and his associates built a pseudo-ideological framework to explain agricultural collectivization and their unique form of state-capitalist industrialization, but it never achieved the status of a truly independent guide in any but the most simplistic sense. When war came in 1941, a set of major emergency modifications was very quickly put in place, contributing fundamentally to victory over Nazi Germany and the postwar emergence of the Soviet Union as a major force in world affairs. The industrial economic system established after the war was a combination of retreat to the prewar model and of significant changes based largely on technology received and developed in the effort to defeat Hitler.

By the time of Stalin's demise, his postwar system of central planning and industrial administration had seemingly outlived the utility it had previously demonstrated, even in the rebuilding of the devastated postwar economy. The positive aspects of a single-minded industrialization strategy and a crash recovery effort had, by the early 1950s, been offset by the disadvantages of rigidity, overcaution, departmentalism, and empire building on the part of the powerful industrial branch ministries and central planning agency (Nove 1961: 68–69; Azrael 1966). The fact that the post-Stalin years were characterized by a power struggle that lasted well into the 1960s guaranteed that the question of industrial reform would be a central element in the politics of succession (Conquest 1961: 346–394). Stalin's system of industrial administration did not long survive his death, partly because it depended on the force of his personality, but principally because the system was vulnerable to problems of maturation. At the Soviet economy's stage of development in the mid-1950s, it could no longer afford the inflexibility and other disadvantages of the old centralized scheme (Nove 1972: 324–350).

A bewildering series of decentralizing industrial administrative reforms characterized Nikita Khrushchev's leadership (1955–1964). The subsequent Brezhnev-Kosygin recentralization of the system did not actually result in a total restoration of the classic Stalinist model, as convenient as that label is for present-day reformers in the former USSR. However, by once again centralizing industrial administration and by trying, against the results of previous experience, to make central planning and industrial administration work, the Soviet leadership guaranteed the persistence of inaccurate information feedback, inflexibility, overcaution, departmentalism, empire building, and all of the other disadvantages of the old system; it would eventually require major, if not comprehensive, reformulation. In any event, truly effective reform never emerged during the Brezhnev years, despite several important, if half-hearted, efforts. Failure by the regimes of Brezhnev and his immediate successors to take seriously the need for fundamental industrial administrative reform surely created the economic environment for the shattering events of the Gorbachev and Yeltsin periods (Hewett 1988: 303–391).

THE DEVELOPMENT OF SOVIET INDUSTRIAL ADMINISTRATION

The initial period of Bolshevik rule was characterized by radical experiments with worker participation in the administration of industrial production. At first, virtually all of the means of production were nationalized, and within that framework a variety of local initiatives were undertaken. A chaotic mixture of everything from direct and continuous worker management to centralized control of key sectors ultimately caused sufficient confusion to require the imposition of a fairly tight system of administration until the new regime felt secure enough to worry about rebuilding the devastated economy. This period, known as "War Communism" (1918–21), is best known for the imposition of mandatory agricultural deliveries, but it had important industrial dimensions as well (Ulam 1976: 25–58).

Following the civil war and intervention, Lenin and the Bolshevik leadership concluded that the only practical way to consolidate political power, and thus get on with building what they imagined to be communism, was to restore the devastated economy to at least prewar levels. In an illustration of how even fanatics can be practical when their power is in jeopardy, Lenin allowed much of industrial and agricultural production to be returned to private hands. Labeled the New Economic Policy, or NEP (1921–1928), this seeming sacrifice of basic Marxist principles allowed a significant proportion of the economy to be organized around an essentially free market. It produced an economic revitalization that lifted industrial and agricultural production statistics toward prewar figures. However, through the concentration of economic strength in potentially hostile hands, it also created groups of independent businessmen and farmers that were inevitably perceived as direct threats to post-Lenin Bolshevik political power. The usually accepted maximum figure for private control of the NEP economy is about 80 percent; it is also generally understood that the "heights," or the key elements of industrial production, were retained under direct state control (Seliunin 1988).

As originally devised by Lenin in 1917, the postrevolutionary Soviet state-owned economy was administered generally on a territorial basis, with the exception of certain large-scale industrial units. The country was divided into large economic administrative areas; each was run by a council known as a *sovet narodnogo khozyastvo* (national economic council) or *sovnarkhoz.* The *sovnarkhozs* were responsible to a central organization in

Moscow known by its Russian initials as the *VSNKh* (Supreme National Economic Council). This top organization not only coordinated the work of the regional *sovnarkhozs* but directly ran the exempt industries (the "heights") through industrial branch trusts. The Moscow *VSNKh* supervised the *sovnarkhozs* through republic-level institutions also known as *VSNKh*s. Thus, during the NEP period, the privatized industrial economy was coordinated in a decentralized fashion. The exempt industries were run directly from Moscow with no republic participation (Yampolskaia 1965).

By 1928, Stalin had garnered enough personal political power to begin to transform the independent economies in both industry and agriculture. Using the occasion of a grand debate on the future of Soviet economic development, Stalin attacked first the market-oriented proponents of light industrial development and then the radicals pushing for a quantum jump into some kind of pure industrial communism; eventually able to label both groups as illegitimate "opposition," Stalin eliminated them first politically and then physically. The power struggle did seem to be almost entirely over Stalin's drive for total personal political power but once it was resolved, he embarked on a series of policies to bring the national economy completely under his single-handed control, continuing the process of creating Soviet totalitarianism. While committed to eliminating most vestiges of private agriculture and to imposing a virtually confiscatory system of collective farms, Stalin began a crash industrialization program to lay the base for a unique new form of state capitalism. The Stalinist system of industrial administration was increasingly controlled by an army of government bureaucrats in Moscow. The newly burgeoning working class subordinated to Stalin's state apparatus were told that because it was a "workers" state, they "owned" the means of production. While Stalin did devote some scarce resources to convincing the workers that the state always acted in their best interest, he was not reluctant to imprison those who disagreed. In his drive to create a secure personal dictatorship, Stalin created a gigantic concentration-camp system that provided seemingly cheap labor for his massive construction and mineral extraction projects (Ulam 1976: 88–112).

As Stalin had begun to take power, the decentralized system of administration created by Lenin had been subject to experimental modification. In 1932, following Stalin's consolidation of his personal dictatorship, the *VSNKh* was finally abolished and all industrial production was placed in the hands of Moscow-based "commissariats" (renamed ministries in 1946). Branches of industry judged critical to national security—and to Stalin's own position—were directly subordinated to central commissariats without even token regional participation. Those industries deemed to have lower priority were administered through a system of commissariats shared between Moscow and the republics. A central state planning agency, Gosplan, was charged with coordinating and controlling production throughout the entire system (Nove 1972: 188–224).

Between 1932 and 1957 the peacetime Soviet economy grew at relatively high rates and, though plagued by numerous problems, the commissariat (ministerial) system and central planning did get effective, if expensive, results. As is now well known, the devastating costs to the environment, to the natural resource base, and to human health and welfare had been completely ignored. However, even by the time of Stalin's death in 1953, it was widely assumed that the old system was in need of major revision because the economy had begun to slow down and the continued profligate application of massive inputs of energy, labor, and natural resources could no longer easily overcome the disadvantages of an increasingly ineffective system of overcentralized planning and administration (Grossman 1976: 213–244).

Although the impetus for the decentralization reforms enacted in 1957 had key political components, powerful economic pressures were starkly evident. Normal relations between industries in the same geographic region were widely assumed to be poor or nonexistent because the branches of production were administered by different ministries. All communication between them had to go through Moscow. The system had been largely responsible for the problems of supply caused by unnecessarily long haulage distances and unreliable delivery; the lack of local integration of different industrial branches was at the root of that problem. Moreover, construction was split up among many ministries, resulting in what Soviet observers felt was wasteful duplication of facilities, materials, and equipment in the same geographic area. The enormously bulky ministries swallowed large numbers of well-trained and talented specialists who, under a different organizational scheme, might have been put into productive work at the enterprise level. From the very beginning, the ministries had engaged in empire building because of continual shortages of supplies, inefficient coordination among branches, and virtually no regional cooperation. Thus, each ministry sought to become independent from the rest of the economy; for example, every industrial ministry produced its own paint, not wanting to rely on the ministry actually charged with manufacturing paint for the entire economy. Finally, because the enterprise manager was not responsible to anyone locally, the regional government, Communist Party, and trade union organizations had only marginal influence over industry in their region; thus, industrial production was divorced from local conditions with what seemed to be obviously negative results (Khrushchev 1957a).

All of these problems were cited in 1957 by Khrushchev as evidence of the pressing need for major decentralization of industrial administration. Had these been the principal reasons, the reorganization might have had a different outcome. But economic variables played only a partial role in shaping the content of the reforms. Caught up in the post-Stalin succession struggle, the 1957 return to decentralized administration of the industrial economy was shaped as much by political as by economic motives; the reforms were doomed from the beginning.

THE SOVNARKHOZ REFORMS OF 1957

In February 1957 Khrushchev announced that important changes in the economy would soon be forthcoming. In May, following widespread public but guided discussion, the system of industrial administration was restructured and decentralized. The Moscow-based industrial ministries were forced to yield control to local comprehensive territorial organizations. The new scheme created slightly more than one hundred regional economic councils whose primary mission was to administer virtually all industrial production in their areas. The councils were once again called *sovnarkhozs*. In February Khrushchev had made a special point that he was returning to the true Leninist scheme of industrial administration. The *sovnarkhozs* roughly corresponded to the government and Communist Party *oblast* (provincial) level of government and party organization. Khrushchev made it clear that the *oblast* party secretaries especially would play a greatly increased role in directing the industrial economy (Khrushchev 1957b).

The process of de-Stalinization, Khrushchev's battle with the "anti-party group," and the defeat of that coalition of conservative hardliners were intertwined with the decentralization reforms. The new system of administration seemed to give Khrushchev's *oblast* party secretary allies major influence over industrial production and thus significantly increase their local political importance. The reforms also had the effect of reducing and diluting the strength of the Soviet governmental apparatus in Moscow. While the "heights" (defense and key heavy industries) were exempt from decentralization, as they had been under Lenin's scheme, the reforms did dilute the centralized power of a very significant portion of Stalinist industrial administration. At the same time, centralized communication links within the Moscow industrial administrative community were disrupted if not destroyed.

In short, the reform scheme promulgated in May 1957 sought to provide partial solutions for two sets of problems. First, the changes were supposed to address the afflictions of a Soviet system that was slowing down under the inflexible rules of an overcentralized economy; most of the Soviet economists and administrators whose comments were published during the open discussion between February and May 1957 advised decentralizing to about fifty large, locally controlled economic districts. They argued that a significantly larger number would result in dysfunctional fragmentation (Koroyed and Kugukalo 1957). Second, Khrushchev's political problems were becoming critical in early 1957 and he needed outside help in his struggle to achieve a stable hold on the entire top leadership; he sought to broaden his base by making his natural—beyond the Kremlin—constituency, the *oblast* party secretaries, more powerful. That required the creation of more than one hundred *sovnarkhozs* corresponding to the *oblasts*. The result was the sacrifice of economic administrative rationality and effectiveness to the needs of political survival. Undoubtedly, Khrushchev assumed that there would be little difference between the effectiveness of one hundred or fifty economic councils. But there was indeed a difference; the ensuing fractionalization of industrial administration quickly proved to be as troublesome as prereform ministerial overcentralization (Bruce and Clawson 1977: 198).

To emphasize the decentralizing nature of the reforms, politically and economically, the *sovnarkhozs* were made administratively responsible directly to the republic councils of ministers and only through them to the central USSR Council of Ministers in Moscow. At the same time, local light and food-processing industries were subordinated directly to regional government councils: local soviets (Mamutov 1961).

The *sovnarkhoz* reforms also included a cautious attempt to make the industrial incentive bonus scheme more effective. The problem, not high in Khrushchev's priorities, was that bonuses, previously based on gross production, had resulted in generations of factory administrators schooled to maximize simple gross output regardless of quality, range, or even basic demand. Reform of the bonus system, put in place in 1959, still used gross output but only as a preliminary target; then industrial managers were supposed to concentrate on cost reduction. This innovation was not very sophisticated but it did seem to be a first step toward changing the Soviet economy from one in which any and all industrial output was assumed to be positive, to one in which the growing complexity of the maturing economy was addressed by a system of increasingly complex success indicators. Progress along this line was to prove slow and difficult (Hewett 1988: 225).

Within the first year of operation, the *sovnarkhozs* were being accused of pervasive autarkic behavior, acting just as many had predicted. They were neglecting their economic commitments outside of their own "economies" and diverting resources, supplies, and funds to regional enterprises. In addition, local officials were actively seeking to influence the central allocation of funds, supplies, development projects, and other resources in their favor (Swearer 1963).

During the first year it had also become clear that under the previous system of central ministerial direction a surprising amount of informal, regional integration across ministry lines had in fact existed. When those regions were divided among different *sovnarkhozs*, regional cooperation was disrupted. Where important but informal large, multibranch, industrial complexes had existed, as in the Urals, their fragmentation meant substantial economic dislocation. The basic reasons for the quick emergence of rampant localism are self-evident, that is, many locally experienced administrators ended up in *sovnarkhoz* executive positions; they could hardly be expected to have anything other than a local perspective. However, largely overlooked in this whole equation was the fact that most new top *sovnarkhoz* management positions were filled by former ministry officials long experienced in the art of empire building. Away from Moscow, seemingly having to prove themselves all over again, the "exiles" did what came naturally. More than one hundred separate economies began to emerge. Relations among them were hampered by the rapid development of a new kind of mercantilist culture. While a set of informal and often illegal methods of obtaining scarce resources did begin to evolve, it was a time-consuming and only partly successful process (Grossman 1963: 32–40).

One of the most critical controversies that arose during the first year of operations, and one that regularly recurred during the entire period of decentralization, concerned the role and function of the republic and USSR planning agencies. There were numerous changes in the planning units' structures and chains of command, and throughout the period there were important uncertainties concerning the spheres of operations of these various organizations. There were serious doubts and questions about the role that Gosplan should play in helping to bind the fragmented economic regions together. Experience showed that the typical *sovnarkhoz* administrator perceived the republic-level Gosplan office as the prime time-waster and principal obstacle. At the same time, the republic Gosplan officials complained that their *sovnarkhozs* were always trying to pass administrative problems upward, avoiding responsibility at the cost of cluttering the planning process (Clawson 1969: 213–219).

As the effects of localism became widely appreciated, the industrial growth statistics seemed to indicate immediate failure. Initiated in order to deal with declining growth figures, decentralization seemed instead to be accelerating the slowdown. For example, real per capita consumption rates, while fluctuating in the late 1950s and early 1960s, did so around a lower average than in the period immediately prior to the reforms of 1957. Although the central cause of the problem—fragmentation due to political considerations–had been repeatedly and publicly identified by Soviet economists and administrators, no serious attempt was made by Khrushchev to fix the basic flaws in the reforms until it was clearly too late. Instead, beginning in 1960, a dizzying series of patchwork remedies were devised (Hewett 1988: 226).

In July 1960 three republic *sovnarkhozs* were created, one each for Russia, Ukraine, and Kazakhstan. The other republics, with the exception of Uzbekistan, already had just a single *sovnarkhoz* apiece. This revival of yet another Leninist institution from 1917 was designed to solve the problem of localism. Also in the early 1960s an additional series of modifications resulted in the division of the USSR into eighteen "large economic regions" where councils for coordinating the activities of the numerous *sovnarkhozs* were created. By late 1962 the whole thing had been jury-rigged to the point where the resulting administrative confusion could scarcely get much worse. The demand for a basic reformulation of the 1957 system was irresistible (Mamutov 1964).

THE REVISED SOVNARKHOZ REFORMS: 1962–1963

The dimensions of the massive reforms, introduced in November 1962, today seem almost surreal. Khrushchev sprang them on the Soviet Communist Party with very little warning or preparation, thus supplying his insider enemies with potent evidence of his "adventurism" and "harebrained scheming." The party, he announced, would be split into two branches, one specializing in industrial administration and one focusing on agriculture. Party members would have to go back to school to learn the skills necessary to become branch specialists who would actively participate in the management of the national economy. There would be no more enlightened amateurism and no more adherence to the hallowed Leninist rule that party workers should stay above day-to-day administration. Conditions demanded an end to the waste of party talent. The elite would have to pitch in, to get their hands dirty. The Communist Party would have to prove itself capable of actually dealing face-to-face with the major economic problems facing the country. The reforms were formulated to put an end to the party's habit of making policy and then sitting back and complaining that state bureaucrats were not properly carrying out their orders. Modern, well-trained party officials would lead the country into a whole new way of running the socialist economy: hands-on Communist Party management. This concept of party activism was justified ideologically by some freshly discovered bits of Lenin's thought produced from the nearly thirty thousand unpublished memos, notes, and other material housed in the Lenin archive, waiting for just such an occasion (Khrushchev 1962).

Addressing the compound problems plaguing his hodgepodge system of industrial administration, Khrushchev declared that the *sovnarkhozs* would be reduced in a ratio of 2½ to 1, thus aiming for the seemingly contradictory result of liberating them from the *oblast* party organization at a time when the party was supposed to be taking a more activist role in administration. The new number of regional economic councils was much more in line with what some Soviet economists had continued to argue was a potentially workable number, producing an effective scale for regional operations. Khrushchev stressed that newly trained party specialists would be sent out to lead the effort.

Those smaller industries that had been assigned to the local soviets and that had proved generally successful were to be transferred to the new *sovnarkhozs*. Officials had argued that they could hardly be expected to make the new system work if those more effective enterprises were kept out of the scheme.

In addition, the new 1962 decrees stated that the formerly rather insignificant but growing system of industrial state committees would be given increased control over the entire economy; inevitably that would exert a strong centralizing force upon the whole system. The state committees, originally designed to coordinate rather than administer, increasingly engaged in direct economic management. Between 1962 and the reversion back to branch ministerial administration in 1965, the state committees gained significantly more influence over the administration of the industrial economy. In fact, they became ministries in everything but name.

The republic-level *sovnarkhozs* also were allocated additional power under the 1962 reforms. It was clear they were anticipating that the system of decentralized administration would be strengthened by the more rational number of approximately forty new regional economic councils.

Needless to say, the whole fundamental attack on party tradition and practice was virtually stillborn. By the time that Khrushchev was relieved of his responsibilities as party leader in October 1964, very few changes had actually been made. Middle-level party bureaucrats knew very well how to drag their feet in the face of such basic challenges to their role and privilege. Khrushchev, with his efforts at shaking up the system, had taken on deeply entrenched party interest; it was an adversary that he could not possibly overcome, even if his economic reform had been a good, well-thought-out idea.

Immediately after Nikita Khrushchev was dismissed, the previously glacial movement toward implementing the 1962 reforms came to a complete halt. The new leadership group, represented in economic matters by Alexei Kosygin, soon began to publicize its profound displeasure with the whole *sovnarkhoz*-based system. The state committees were also attacked as inefficient and ineffective; the planning agencies were likewise subjected to strong criticism. The whole unfortunate business was portrayed as having been Khrushchev's exclusive brainchild. With him gone, the others could get down to serious and rational economic reconstruction.

The ideas of reform-minded economists such as E. G. Liberman, V. S. Nemchinov, L. M. Gatovsky, and others—whose advice to devolve significant decision-making power to the enterprise level had been ignored in 1962—were revived. This time their emphasis on redefining the basic incentive system did find its way into the reform process, in theory if not in subsequent practice (Zaleski 1967: 66–93).

THE KOSYGIN REFORMS OF 1965

No significant element of Khrushchev's *sovnarkhoz* system could long survive his departure from power. The bifurcation of the party had never really taken place. The initial impulse of the successor leadership was simply to restore the Stalinist scheme featuring ministerial control by industrial branch. But at least the Kosygin faction of the new group realized that the basic economic problems that the 1957 reforms were supposed to address, however imperfectly, still existed and could not be completely ignored during the process of recentralization. In the early days of the new collective leadership, Kosygin prevailed (Zaleski 1967: 141–183).

While the *sovnarkhoz* reforms were designed to change who supervised the system, they did not challenge the basic nature of the system itself. After Khrushchev's dismissal but before the promulgation of the 1965 reforms, a noteworthy set of public discussions took place, challenging key features of the old Stalinist model (Hewett 1988: 227).

The proposals made by Professor E. G. Liberman and his associates were essentially recommendations for a fundamental change in traditional management incentives (Liberman 1962; Hewett 1988: 227–228). Under the old model, enterprise directors could expect bonus premiums if they fulfilled and overfulfilled the output and cost plans. They were rewarded for efficiency on the basis of various indicators, such as increasing labor productivity, staying within the wages fund allotted, introducing successful innovations, improving quality of output, and so on. But in order even to qualify for rewards based on the indicators, management had to assure that the basic output plan was fulfilled. The general operating efficiency of the enterprise was based on a ratio of planned profits to actual profits. This bore no relation to total investment or total sales. These bonuses and premiums were the targets of continual criticism in the press, with good reason.

The traditional system induced managers to hide productive capacity in order to be responsible for an easy output plan target. Traditionally, Soviet management also tended to hoard capital goods to ensure having the equipment on hand to increase production whenever it might become necessary. They could do so without real penalty because none of the bonuses were based on any ratio involving fixed capital. Further, there was a general disincentive to innovate because of the possibility of failure or, at least, some slowdown to make required changes. The decrease in production that might accompany any attempt to innovate was usually not considered worth the risk. The fact that exact specifications could not be given for everything within the plans (due to sheer volume) meant that the managers had to have some latitude in the quality of goods produced. Thus, those whose indicators were based on length (e.g., wire) might make the product thinner than qualitatively sound or preferred by end users.

The Liberman arguments can be summarized as follows: First, all plans such as cost, labor productivity, and wages fund, normally labeled "enterprise plans," would be wholly prepared by the firms themselves. Volume of output, goods assortment, and delivery schedules would be determined from above but largely drawn up by the enterprises primarily with regard to anticipated demand.

Second, a single fund for all types of material incentives would be created, dependent upon profitability. Incentive premiums per ruble of investment, which would rise as the profit rate increased, would help to encourage management to reveal true capacity. Planned scales of incentives would be carefully determined and confirmed, and established on an individual industrial branch basis. Enterprises would no longer hoard capital goods because management's bonuses would be computed from a profit rate given as a percentage of the total fixed and working capital. That is, it would be best for managers to have as much of their total fixed capital actually working, not rusting or waiting for some possible change in the plans.

Third, and possibly most suggestive, was Liberman's point that profits would not be earned in the old manner. This had long been done by reaching a *planned* profit target—which was, in effect, a planned *output* figure. The method proposed by Liberman would count production only if it were actually sold. Rejections for poor quality, which had never previously reduced planned profits at all, would be considered unsold goods.

Finally, in a practical vein, Liberman suggested that the central planners should not be anxious to readjust targets upward upon successful introduction of some production-increasing or efficiency-enhancing innovation. He also advised that the production of obsolete goods be made less attractive simply by making it less profitable through the planned pricing system (Hewett 1988: 228–229; Zaleski 1967: 66–80).

The other public discussions preceding the 1965 recentralization covered a number of points that would not have an immediate impact but would crop up again in the 1980s. The most noteworthy of them might best be characterized as proposals for the use of optimal planning techniques (Campbell 1961: 403–412; Hewett 1988: 229). Several groups of mathematicians, mathematical economists, and cyberneticists aggressively argued that the problems of the Soviet economy would best be addressed using what they characterized as optimal planning methods to produce meaningful prices for enterprises; the new pricing process would focus on minimizing costs associated with producing planned outputs. Control of the system would shift from bureaucrats to computers run by mathematical economists. They saw the generation and maintenance of an accurate and useful data flow as essentially a workable management problem (Fedorovich 1963: 95–106).

Other academics proposed specific changes: shifting focus, for example, to the control of certain key commodities and the development of a modern wholesale trade system. These ideas attracted somewhat less attention than did those of the managerial or planning reformers (Zaleski 1967: 103–107).

A few brave souls tried to blend proposed changes in management incentives with key arguments of the cyberneticists (Birman 1963). In the abstract, reconciliation of the two schools might indeed have been possible; in practice, they were fatally contradictory.

In September 1965 Alexei Kosygin announced the reform initiatives that would become briefly associated with his name (Kosygin 1965; Hewett 1988: 230–235). Administrative reforms included the reestablishment of the branch ministerial system of industrial administration and, thus, the recentralization of basic bureaucratic control. The *sovnarkhoz* system was completely dismantled and the newer branch state committees were subsequently also largely eliminated; a supporting group of centralized state committees and commissions was established along largely traditional lines (Schroeder 1968: 462–477).

To implement incentive reforms, the old method of establishing planned targets was to be changed and a new bonus system established. The measures announced went nowhere near as far as the managerial reformers had advocated, but they did at least seem to be designed to make it more difficult for the newly reestablished branch ministries to intervene in day-to-day enterprise operations. However, many features of the old Stalinist model were, in effect, revived. Despite gestures toward enterprise autonomy, the reestablished ministries and central planning agencies were given substantial control over production through continued domination of key performance indicators. Ministries also held practical power over the promotion and reward of managers within their jurisdictions and were held ultimately responsible for enterprise performance (Campbell 1968: 547–558).

Price reforms constituted a major portion of the 1965 changes; the power to set prices was put in the hands of a newly created state committee (Goskomtsen). This effectively centralized the previously dispersed–though Moscow-based–pricing system under one roof to provide a more coordinated effort. A comprehensive attempt at revision of the price structure was introduced in 1966–67. The most important ground rule of the new scheme was that it should be designed to make all enterprises profitable, thus maintaining the implicit assumption that it was possible to preserve the principal aspects of the traditional Soviet economic system while introducing modest incremental reforms. No enterprise would be closed for economic reasons; reform would be slow and evolutionary. Workers would not lose their jobs merely because their factories produced goods that nobody wanted (Hewett 1988: 233–234).

The Kosygin initiatives reflected the prereform debates only symbolically. The most fundamental proposals, those of the Liberman school, implying a profound reduction of central bureaucratic control over industrial management, could hardly have come at a less propitious time. The assertions of the cyberneticists were also unpersuasive. Although they pointed to theoretically more effective central control, the implication that computer networks would replace bureaucrats was not an argument likely to please the industrial administrative elite, one of the Brezhnev-Kosygin leadership's most important constituencies. At the same time, it was also clear to informed Soviet observers that the technological infrastructure required to achieve the computer networking essential to the cyberneticists' schemes was unlikely to be produced by Soviet technology in the foreseeable future. Realistic insiders knew that the degree of data accuracy necessary to support an effective national cybernetic control system was simply beyond conceivable reach.

Implementation of the 1965 Kosygin reforms was characterized by predictable bureaucratic behavior. Using the reforms as cover, the industrial administrative elite quickly reconstructed the old ministerial empires. From those new positions of authority, they successfully delayed or blocked implementation of major portions of the incentive and price reform packages. What could not be slowed or stopped was co-opted, absorbed, or hamstrung. The essence of the reforms was dead by the early 1970s, although an organizational skeleton remained intact through the Gorbachev years, and the ministerial system continued to exercise its deadening control largely unaffected by subsequent experiments (Schroeder 1970: 38–40).

Once reestablished and operating, the industrial branch ministries found themselves consistently opposed to those portions of the reforms that suggested enterprise autonomy or control by economic forces. Of course, the economic bureaucracy naturally sought to protect its position within the administrative hierarchy. But, in effect, the impact of the reforms was to put the ministries in an impossible position. They were supposed to reduce their interference in the production process but at the same time were ultimately responsible for results. It must therefore be said that although the top industrial administrative elite surely lobbied heavily to retain that responsibility in the face of modest enterprise autonomy, the centralizers surely knew that in the resulting confusion, they would ultimately triumph. On the other hand, once the scheme was in place, even well-meaning ministry personnel were forced to make a choice (Hewett 1988: 240–241).

After the new incentive system became even partially operational, managers worked hardest to achieve their most comfortably achieved targets, just as could have been expected. In the face of this rational behavior, the ministries and planners tried to restrict their options by devising new target indicators, attempting to corral enterprise management.[2] Industrial production that was supposed to be regulated, at least modestly, by economic forces was steadily corralled by administrative fiat.

Thus, the actual incentive system was steadily eroded to one in which the key determinant of bonuses was once again output. The reform indicators receded into minor importance, if not obscurity (Hewett 1988: 241–243).

REFORM IN THE BREZHNEV ERA

The Soviet government of the 1970s, dominated by Leonid Brezhnev, continued to generate episodic and ultimately inconsequential efforts to affect the industrial incentive structure. In addition, the conservative top leadership, itself little interested in the seemingly intractable problems plaguing the mature Soviet economy, let its industrial administrative *apparat* devise a variety of other measures to improve industrial performance.

The 1973 reforms were conceived as measures to merge enterprises into what was termed "production associations." In their efforts to increase efficiency, experiments run in the 1960s and early 1970s suggested that carefully designed mergers might provide the means to reduce ministerial micromanagement and autarkic behavior. Enterprises producing like products were to be gathered into what was thought to be a manageable number of production associations administered by all-union industrial associations (*vsesoyuznie promyshlennie obedinenie,* or VPOs). This scheme was designed to get the ministries to focus their efforts on planning and technology development (Hewett 1988: 246).

The VPOs, which were to control production associations throughout the USSR, were subordinated to the various ministries, but were more independent than previous middle-level industrial administrative units. They were to operate on a self-financing (*khozraschet*) basis.[3]

Ministries themselves were directed to devise merger plans, and, of course, they procrastinated. By the early 1980s about half of industrial production came from production associations of one kind or another. The other half was from still-independent firms, which were nevertheless administered by VPOs (Hewett 1988: 247).

In any event, many of the mergers took place more on paper than in actual operation. Individual enterprises often continued to work independently under cover of their parent associations. Also, since the VPOs were formed within ministries, a reconstituted ministerial autarchy quickly developed. Because the central authorities continued to hold branch ministries ultimately responsible for production, there was little incentive for the ministries to give up micromanagement and to grant real administrative power to the VPOs; the associations thus acted primarily as their predecessors had, doing the ministries' bidding.

While the reforms created yet another facade of change, the whole system continued to operate largely in the same old way. This was assured by the manner in which the whole thing was supposed to be implemented. Asking the ministries to design the operational side of the mergers, to do something that they would inevitably see as counter to their own basic interests, once again doomed reform from the very start. In addition, the fact that these 1973 measures were organizationally dictated from the supplier side drove them even farther away from any reliance on end user demand, actual profits, or other sales-related indicators (Hewett 1988: 248–250).

In 1979, the industrial administrative leadership again tried to address persisting problems in the incentive system through comprehensive action. The initiatives included in the various decrees were mainly based on disparate ideas announced but never implemented over the last decade. They included more measures designed to encourage the creation of more stable plans, including ten- and twenty-year versions, and counterplanning[4]; stable norms linking enterprise performance to bonus funds; bonus indicators that avoided direct use of gross output; and *khozraschet* conditions which could be forced farther up the industrial administrative hierarchy.[5] They also attempted to introduce some new— at least on the national level—incentive devices. For example, they tried to promote the use of a value-added index as a primary bonus-forming indicator for enterprises. While these 1979 efforts brought together a number of ideas that had been more or less free-floating in the industrial administrative environment for an extended period, there was little that was actually new. In any event, even these rather tepid initiatives got little support (Hewett 1988: 251–255).

The USSR entered the 1980s suffering from the worst economic performance since World War II (Schroeder 1985: 42–74). Few doubted that something had to be done. In November 1982 Leonid Brezhnev died; he was replaced as Communist Party general secretary by former KGB chief Iuri Andropov.

EXPERIMENTS UNDER ANDROPOV AND CHERNENKO

As Soviet economic performance continued to deteriorate and the challenge of Ronald Reagan's military buildup began to exert pressure on Soviet productive capacity, Andropov urged immediate action. He made it clear that he was dissatisfied with the whole dismal economic picture, but was particularly dismayed at the inability of the industrial economy to work efficiently to produce competitive goods. He called for innovative solutions and urged public debate (Hewett 1988: 258–260). Although his eighteen-month tenure was too brief to have a fundamental impact, he set the tone for reform—and he brought Mikhail Gorbachev into the reform process. In the last days of Andropov's life in 1984, under the direction of Gorbachev, experiments aimed at enhancing technical progress and product quality were launched.

Konstantin Chernenko, Andropov's successor, inevitably ran a short caretaker regime. Whatever his real interest in the health of the Soviet economy, he allowed Gorbachev to continue the 1984 experiments. Under Chernenko's permissive leadership, the debate widened and paved the way for Gorbachev's subsequent attempt to overhaul the system.

A detailed discussion of the 1984 experiments, started under Andropov and continued by Chernenko, would be tedious and unrewarding. Suffice it to say that the ministries and their VPOs continued to retain ultimate responsibility for output and so continued to interfere comprehensively in the industrial process at the production level. Just as it had done in earlier reforms, the central industrial administrative apparatus successfully blocked implementation of many aspects of those measures. Thus, the impact of these initiatives was restricted and the effect on ministry behavior was minimal.

The period between Andropov's accession to power in 1982 and Chernenko's death in 1985, though it featured only measured reform efforts, was characterized by an atmosphere of steadily expanding debate over the future shape of the Soviet economy. Encouraged by Andropov, some of the most imaginative thinkers of the day engaged in a substantive critique of the old system. Sociologist Tatiana Zaslavskaia argued that social conditions had changed so fundamentally that a relatively inflexible system designed in the 1930s to urbanize and industrialize a peasant population could hardly be expected to work in the 1980s (Zaslavskaia 1985). She urged those responsible to recognize contemporary reality. Reform-oriented economists such as Leonid Abalkin, Vasili Seliunin, and Abel Aganbegian, as well as many others who would become much better known in the second half of the 1980s, joined more cautious voices in a swelling debate over the future structure of the Soviet economy. Radical public-administration specialists such as B. P. Kurashvili joined the economists and sociologists arguing that unless radical and comprehensive reforms were implemented soon, the economic difficulties confronting the system would become critical (Hewett 1988: 279–302).

While it is not possible to say that the voices urging reform proposed obviously workable solutions to the most intractable of the Soviet Union's economic administrative problems, it should be noted that their arguments, along with the specific reform atmosphere initiated by Andropov and allowed to continue under Chernenko, set the stage for the Gorbachev period. The postwar era of Stalinist economic administration was rapidly drawing to a close.

CONCLUSIONS

The history of post-Stalin efforts to reform fundamental elements of the centralized industrial administrative system is one characterized by continued frustration. Part of the reason is relatively simple to identify. Right from the start, principal elements of the major post-Stalin reform efforts failed because basic economic goals were sacrificed to short-term political considerations. This was particularly true in the case of Khrushchev's various initiatives. They were, more than anything else, key elements in his struggle to gain and maintain a firm grip on political power. The Kosygin reforms were largely an attempt to recentralize the system to satisfy the demands of several major elite constituencies. The reinstitution of a comfortable, predictable–if flawed–centralized administrative scheme was crucial to stabilizing the party-state equation.

At the same time, many of the most promising possibilities were sabotaged by the ministerial personnel charged with actually implementing reform. In most cases those officials were the very ones responsible for designing specific operational details; their hands in the process helped assure that the actual, specific working regulations would be bureaucrat-friendly. Thus, in a majority of cases, the real impact was reduced to far below the intent of the reformers. Due to the key political status of the industrial administrative elite, only the most "adventurist" leader–that is, Khrushchev–could think it possible to leave them out of the policy process. The lessons of his fate and reforms was not lost on his successors, who were anyway a faithful, plodding auxiliary of that elite. But this is only the most obvious part of the answer.

Another reason for the continued frustration of reform initiatives had a more fundamental root: a persistent reluctance to address the major economic problems in an effective manner because of the obviously threatening implications. At least in the minds of the core Communist Party leadership, but also widely accepted throughout the Soviet population, there surely existed a kind of basic social compact containing a seemingly incontestable set of implicit assumptions.[6] The leaders all seemed to accept that their implicit deal with the Soviet people consisted of an agreement that the manifest disadvantages of the centrally controlled socialist economy would be made tolerable by the existence of a social safety net consisting of guaranteed full employment, free medical care, inexpensive housing, efficient public transportation, safe streets, and a cheap selection of basic foods, as well as protection against a seemingly inexorably hostile world. To undertake reforms that might, for instance, increase the system's sensitivity to consumer or even capital equipment user demands would imply the possibility that enterprises producing shoddy or unwanted goods might have to be retooled, their workforces trimmed, or, at worst, their plants shut down. Between Stalin and Chernenko, no Soviet Communist leader was willing to contemplate that kind of serious challenge to the social compact. Reform could be accommodated so long as it did not threaten to generate serious trouble for the status quo. Therefore, even if the ministry bureaucrats might have tolerated a diminution of their own personal power, no leader until Gorbachev was willing to challenge the basic set of assumptions that made up the bedrock of the Soviet system.

The traditional Stalinist approach, forming the foundation of the implicit social compact, persisted. The guiding tool was the plan as a basic document controlling decisions at the enterprise level and enforced most often by the industrial branch ministries. The primary operational feature was the joint system of plan indicators and bonuses. Improvements to the system were constrained to include only reform around the edges, such as spruced-up incentive systems involving new or fine-tuned indicators.

Quality control became important as the Soviet economy matured. But it was still unable to compete in world markets, especially when there was a key connection between science, technological development, and production. The Soviet leadership of the 1970s and 1980s wanted world markets and the same product quality as the West but were persistently reluctant to use those markets for discipline, fearing loss of control and market chaos. Instead, they tackled the quality control problem with the same old tools: new plan indicators and bonuses.

Another key root of the tenacious residual support for the existing system was that it exerted sustained if modest pressure toward social leveling. The term most often associated with this was *uravnilovka*, the tendency for everyone to earn the same income. This egalitarian effect, basic to the social compact, had a powerful hold on the Russian, if not the entire Soviet, political culture.

Having reviewed the principal post-Stalin reform initiatives prior to Gorbachev's accession to power in 1985 and suggested a select, though by no means exhaustive, list of the reasons for their frustration, we may now ask whether or not the system could have ever been reformed from within. It is tempting to speculate about what might have developed had the leadership not been so constrained by their unimaginative interpretation of the social compact. It is, however, instructive that the first Soviet leader seriously to attempt fundamental reinterpretation of the compact turned out to be the *last* Soviet leader. Without the legitimacy derived from the compact, as broadly understood, there was simply no reason for the Soviet system, with all of its other disadvantages, to continue to exist.

NOTES

1. This brief study outlining post-Stalin industrial administrative reform must necessarily be set at a macroeconomic level of description and analysis. In a few instances, examples from microeconomic institutional or behavioral experience are noted. However, in this context it would be inappropriate to try to combine an overview of the ultimately unsuccessful efforts to reform the Soviet socialist system with a detailed description of the evolution of the structure and function of the Soviet enterprise. The case studies in this book focus on the micro level and, wherever appropriate, note various facets of historical development. This chapter is an attempt to provide the larger experience from which the Gorbachev and Yeltsin phenomena emerged. The primary point of reference for this overview is provided by the comprehensive volume by Ed Hewett (1988).

2. Soviet enterprise managers of the late Khrushchev era, subsequently kept in place by Brezhnev's revival of the "respect for cadres" principle–which essentially granted a kind of civil-service status to senior bureaucrats–rarely felt comfortable operating under the constricting rules of the industrial branch ministries. Though pleased to be removed from the threat of Khrushchev's bold approach to industrial reform and provided with a certain buffer imposed by the ministries, Soviet managers chafed under the restrictions. Naturally, this generalization is most characteristic of managers in the smaller-scale light and consumer-goods industries and less so in the case of heavy industry and defense production.

3. The term *khozraschet* has sometimes been taken to mean "cost accounting," but in other instances it has suggested "working in a business-like manner." In the present case and in subsequent usage, it means "self-financing." Enterprises successfully operating in this mode would no longer receive centrally allocated operating or investment funds but

would utilize their above-cost income to cover those expenditures. Very few enterprises ever achieved this level of self-sufficiency because planning agencies and parent ministries consistently followed policies contradictory to the achievement of effective *khozraschet*.

4. Counterplanning refers to a suggested practice whereby managers would adopt more ambitious annual plan targets than those handed down from above. They were to be specially rewarded for meeting the upgraded objectives. In practice, this never worked well because the central planners could not resist raising the next year's targets to reflect the better figures achieved (see Hewett 1988: 252).

5. One effect of the slow and fitful progress toward enterprise autonomy was a marginal increase in financial independence. Companies were allowed to dispose of their above-cost incomes in a number of prescribed ways, including the building of day-care centers, polyclinics, apartment houses, and other social-welfare investments. Above-cost funds generated by successful companies and then not encumbered in an acceptable manner were subject to a kind of "confiscation." Central authorities then reallocated the funds to bail out less successful enterprises. It is hardly surprising that profitable companies were also seemingly the most socially conscious. Of course, such amenities had long formed a set of useful perks to attract and retain employees.

6. The assumption that a kind of implicit social contract existed between the Soviet Communist Party leadership and the population is rather widely held among Western specialists. There is less consensus on the question of whether or not the contract had effectively broken down by the mid-1980s. For a well-developed introduction to the basic issues, see Jan Adam's essay in his 1991 collection (Adam 1991). That a substantial number of post-Soviet disillusioned Russians now wish they could return to the conditions of the old contract, however imperfect, is widely confirmed by attitude surveys conducted by a number of Russian scholars. See, in particular, the work of Tatiana Zaslavskaia's All-Russian Center for the Study of Public Opinion. Of specific interest is the *Ekonomicheskiye i Sotsialnyie Peremeny: Monitoring Obshchestvennogo Mneniya* information bulletin series.

3 The Road to Employee Ownership in Russia

Sergey Plekhanov

◆ IN the center of Moscow, almost exactly at the midpoint between the Kremlin and the former Russian Parliament building, on the eastern side of Novoarbatsky Prospect, stands a restaurant called Ivushka (The Little Willow). When it first opened in 1968 as a showcase state-owned enterprise in a newly rebuilt, prestigious part of the city, it swiftly became a popular place: stylishly furnished, with good cuisine, reasonable prices, and unusually friendly service. As a frequent customer whose office was a five-minute walk away, I recall that early Ivushka with fondness.

After twenty-three years of operation, Ivushka lost much of its early luster. Management would change, new concepts would be tried, but just like every other state-owned Moscow restaurant, the place was gradually deteriorating. The city's notorious restaurant shortage still kept it very much afloat: the place was always full. But it was increasingly obvious that if Ivushka was to be revived, it would have to change not just its managers, but its owners, too. There was just no way the state could run a restaurant well.

In 1991, with the winds of economic reform blowing stronger than ever, it became the time for change. In February of that year, Food Kombinat, the state company owning Ivushka, decided to sell the bar on its first floor to a joint venture. In the old days, the decision would have been implemented without a hitch, but Russia was now in the midst of a democratic upheaval, and the restaurant's staff strongly protested against the sale, which had been enacted without their consent or even knowledge. The staff complained to the Moscow City Council and requested permission to lease Ivushka from the state. Citing the statement of the city council chairman that the fate of an enterprise could be decided only by the enterprise's work collective, restaurant workers wrote in their application, "We want to work at our own enterprise, and we will perform just as well as a joint venture."

While the employees' lease bid was slowly moving from one Moscow city office to another, Food Kombinat's executives were not wasting their time. In six months, they signed another joint venture contract: Little Willow was to be turned into Venus Seafood Place. Seventy-five percent of its stock was sold to a shoe company in Singapore, another 15 percent was bought by a company in Panama, and the remaining 10 percent was retained by Food Kombinat.

In November 1991, having heard a rumor about Food Kombinat's new move, Ivushka's staff, which still had not received any reply to their lease request, decided to buy out the restaurant under the new Russian Law on Privatization. In February 1992, the Moscow authorities responsible for privatization registered the restaurant as a limited liability partnership, owned by its employees. But Venus Seafood Place had already been registered, too—by the Russian Finance Ministry as a joint venture. The officials of Food Kombinat who were involved in the Russian-Singaporean-Panamanian deal were fully determined to break the resistance of the old restaurant's staff. In March 1992 they hired private guards to evict Ivushka's employees from the premises they "illegally" occupied. Having rebuffed the assault, the employees staged a round-the-clock vigil in the restaurant.

Moscow bureaucracies were firing paper shots at each other. "The rights of the work collective have been violated," asserted one department of the city government. "The joint-venture contract must be implemented," insisted another. Meanwhile, the restaurant's staff appealed to the United Nations Human Rights Commission, and the Singaporean shoemaker threatened to appeal to the International Court of Justice. Having dragged on for more than three years, the conflict is not over yet, and the cafe, located in the middle of one of Moscow's busiest areas, remains closed.

The long standoff around an eating place in downtown Moscow is symbolic of the messy, labyrinthine and unpredictable process of history's largest transfer of property from a state to private hands—the struggle of millions of Russians to become owners of the means of production.

Russia's desperate efforts to effect its transition from command to market economy will succeed or fail on this very issue. The processes of privatization are reflecting fierce struggles among social groups whose interests are involved in one way or another. The results of those struggles are visible in the drafting of privatization laws, in the changes in government policies, and, of course, in the way specific pieces of state property change hands.

But there is a powerful logic behind the mess, even if it is not always realized: capitalism can become a reality in Russia, if at all, only as one or another form of "people's capitalism," or economic democracy, providing for effective devolution of ownership rights to Russia's citizens.

Employee ownership fits the Russian conditions much better than any other form of private ownership proposed so far. Yet resistance to its implementation has been remarkably stubborn, and the progress toward employee ownership has been marked by zigzags, steps backward, and a tremendous amount of purposeful obfuscation.

This chapter examines the process of privatization, the political struggles that surrounded it, the role that employee ownership has come to play in it, and the strengths and weaknesses of this approach in political and economic terms.

GORBACHEV OPENS THE WAY

The road to employee ownership in Russia could not be easy, given the radicalism of the idea. A huge state with ancient traditions of dominance over society was expected to give up its ownership and control of productive assets. It would seem that by definition, such a fundamental shift in economic power could only be effected, if at all, through massive social upheavals with a high potential for violence. The fact that Russia has so far avoided violence in its privatization process is remarkable.

The trends toward employee ownership in the Soviet Union and then in Russia and other former Soviet republics were rooted in the general crisis of the Soviet system. Two aspects of that crisis were especially important.

One was the all but forgotten legacy of the October 1917 revolution. The Soviet state had long since become a bureaucratic monster run by the conservative nomenklatura, but the monster did owe its origins—and its legitimacy—to that revolution. The only way Mikhail Gorbachev and his supporters could approach the problem of reforming the Soviet system was by echoing the revolution's original promise, which included a heavy dose of straightforward economic populism. The idea of self-management had been there for decades as a socialist alternative to total bureaucratic control of the economy. It was practiced in Yugoslavia with seemingly more success than the Soviet model. Poland's Solidarity demanded worker control of the economy in its struggle with the government. Besides, there was the example of Western social democrats, whose thinking had a strong impact on the Gorbachev reformers. No less important, the idea of yielding partial economic control to workers as an incentive to greater productivity and a way of strengthening the regime's social base was acceptable to the state and party bureaucracy as a relatively safe concession, so long as the ownership remained with the state: after all, control could conceivably be taken back if the going got rough.

If the first aspect had to do with the things which made the 1917 revolution possible, the other stemmed from the reasons why capitalism was able to survive and defeat the Leninist challenge. After seven decades of trying hard to find an alternative to the market mechanism, Soviet leaders were now searching for ways to restore at least some elements of that mechanism in the Soviet economy. It was clear even to most conservatives that profit and loss incentives were a more efficient way to affect producer behavior than administrative fiat. The problem was how to fit such incentives into the state planning system. Previous attempts were not very successful: a viable compromise between the efficiency imperative and the power-preservation interests of the bureaucracy was elusive, and bureaucracy would invariably gain the upper hand. Gorbachev was determined to overcome bureaucratic resistance.

The Gorbachev economic reform attacked the monolithic system of state ownership and control of the economy on three fronts: (1) state enterprises were to get some economic freedom from branch ministries and the Gosplan; (2) workers were to get some leverage over managers; and (3) a new private sector was to be allowed to form and coexist with the state sector. The state would retain its command positions, but its management of the economy would become more flexible, while producers would be able to respond to market incentives.

In 1986–90, the Soviet government took a number of steps aimed at a "destatization" of the economy. The Law on State Enterprises gave such enterprises a measure of independence from central bureaucratic control and provided for certain forms of self-management within enterprises: establishment of work collective councils and election of managers by employees. The Law on Leasing set up a legal basis for gradual evolution of state ownership: work collectives could now lease enterprises from the state and run them as more or less private entities, according to the market logic. The Law on Individual Labor Activity and the Law on Cooperatives served to legalize some forms of private ownership and free enterprise for the first time since the 1920s. The Law on Property introduced collective ownership as an arrangement for the transfer of state enterprises to their work collectives.

Experimentation with new forms of ownership and management brought notable positive results wherever it was tried seriously. However, microeconomic advances were overshadowed by a rapidly worsening economic crisis and the absence of sound macroeconomic policies which would guide the processes of transformation.

By 1990 it became evident that the uncertain and contradictory steps from statism to economic freedom had only exacerbated the crisis of the

Soviet system. Increasingly bitter political conflict led to a polarization of views between free-market advocates and proponents of continued state control. Impelled toward a more and more radical challenge to the system, Russian democrats gradually abandoned the ideas of market socialism and mixed economy and began to argue forcefully for a rapid transition to capitalism. The Communist Party elite, led by Gorbachev, was responding with an increasingly conservative policy designed to preserve the system's foundations.

In December 1989 the Soviet government drastically weakened the provisions of the Law on State Enterprises concerning worker control of management. State enterprises were being pulled back under tighter central control. The new private sector was subjected to limitations and regulations which undermined its most productive elements and encouraged corruption.

After the election of the new Russian Parliament in 1990 and the emergence of Boris Yeltsin as its chairman and the leader of the radical democrats, the focus of the efforts to move the Soviet economy out of the bureaucratic quagmire shifted to the government of the Russian Federation. The rising Russian political elite wanted a clean break with state socialism, and remnants of perestroika like work collective councils, co-ops, or leased enterprises were not capitalist enough for them. The idea of making workers owners of enterprises they worked at also smacked of discredited socialism—despite the fact that it had never been tried under Soviet socialism. But radical democrats were not fully in control of government. Having put privatization high on their list of priorities, they needed the support of more moderate factions in the Russian Parliament and had to come up with proposals based on workable compromises.

The three Russian laws on privatization, adopted in July 1991, were products of that political process: the Law on the Basic Principles of the Destatization and Privatization of Enterprises (adopted July 1), the Law on Privatization of State and Municipal Enterprises, and the Law on Personal Privatization Checks and Accounts (both adopted July 3). The laws represented the first serious and systematic attempt at a policy designed to dismantle state control of the economy and create strong structures of private ownership.

The July 1991 legislation set targets for the process: by 1995, up to two-thirds of the Russian economy was to become privately owned. Three main methods of privatization were specified: an enterprise could be auctioned off to the highest bidder; it could be transformed into a joint-stock company, with shares then traded at a stock exchange (the company's employees would get a 30 percent discount); and a leased enterprise could be bought out by its employees. The privatization process was to be closely controlled by the Russian state. To give every Russian citizen a stake in the process, privatization accounts were to be opened in banks for all citizens of Russia, with equal deposits to be used to purchase stock in privatized enterprises.

Underscoring the importance of what was happening, KGB chairman Viktor Kryuchkov, who was at that very time plotting a hardline coup, openly and rather clumsily interfered in parliamentary debates. He sent a letter to the Parliament with a warning that if the privatization laws should pass, the Soviet economy would be destroyed. Kryuchkov claimed that KGB analysts had studied the American experience with employee ownership and found that it had mostly negative results. To the credit of Russian lawmakers, most of them would not be swayed by that combination of persuasion and intimidation, and the legislation was approved.

Of course, no one expected back in July 1991 that the Soviet Union would cease to exist before the year was out. But a month later, the failed coup delivered a mortal blow to the Soviet state. The democrats emerged victorious and the hardliners were defeated. But what the victorious democrats inherited was an economy in a tailspin and an absence of any workable mechanism for economic policy. To make matters worse, they were not prepared to govern: history thrust them into a position of responsibility for the post-Soviet mess without giving them time to grow.

In October–November 1991, Boris Yeltsin, now the freely elected president of Russia, launched his version of radical economic reforms, drafted by a group of young Russian economists who admired the free-market theories of Friedrich von Hayek and Milton Friedman and the ways those theories were put into practice in Poland and Czechoslovakia. The leader of the group, former *Pravda* economics editor Yegor Gaidar, was named first vice premier of the Russian government.

Egged on by the financial crisis of the Soviet system in the final stage of its demise, Yeltsin opted for what is usually referred to as "shock therapy"–a rapid jump to a free-market economy through price liberalization, tough monetary and credit policies, and encouragement of competition. Those measures were supposed to establish a measure of macroeconomic balance between supply and demand and turn the Russian ruble into real money.

The risks of imposing this combination of price decontrol and financial austerity on an economy almost totally owned and controlled by the state were obvious. To respond to "shock therapy" in a way which would make for financial recovery and then economic growth, the Russian economy had to undergo huge changes: demonopolization and privatization or at least commercialization (giving state-owned enterprises freedom to operate as private entities). Gaidar openly recognized that but maintained that there was no way Russia's "financial stabilization" could wait until the inevitably long and complicated structural changes were made.

The government started working on its first privatization program in November 1991. After many debates and modifications, the program was approved by the Parliament in June 1992–almost a full year after the passage of the privatization laws.

Why did it take the Russian government so long to come up with a privatization policy? In the highly partisan debates around the issue, several competing explanations have been offered:

1. The process is by definition so complicated that no one should have expected faster action.
2. Privatization was opposed by powerful nomenklatura groups which tried to bend the policy in their favor.
3. The confrontation between the president and the parliament turned privatization into an important arena of political conflict.
4. The government's own policy was guided by faulty assumptions and had to be repeatedly revised.

There is enough evidence to support each of these explanations, and the delays resulted from a combination of these factors. However, the government's own mistakes played a special role. Since Gaidar's game plan depended so much on rapid privatization, he was obliged to put forward an economically sensible and politically viable privatization policy–one that had to take full account of the social forces at play, including the nomenklatura. Conversely, if the government had no realistic plan for fast privatization, it had no moral right to apply "shock therapy." It was this glaring contradiction between the government's own intention to "shock" the economy out of its dependence on the state and its inability to help enterprises become free-market entities that produced most political battles around privatization. And it was as a result of those battles, rather than in spite of them, that a somewhat more realistic policy ultimately emerged and made it possible for the process to start.

THE GOVERNMENT POLICY

The July 1991 legislation was a significant step forward. But in order to become the basis for a vigorous privatization policy, it had to be improved.

First, it gave too much power over the process to the state, investing it with the power to decide whether a particular enterprise was to be privatized and how. For all the dangers of elemental privatization, the government's reliance on the traditional Russian method of "revolution from above" (especially at a time when the Russian state lacked an efficient and loyal bureaucracy to execute it), rather than on an attempt to build a consensus among the interest groups involved, led to a lot of chaos and corruption.

Second, even though the legislation did recognize the important principle that the state could not dispose of public property as if it were its own and that, indeed, it owed it to Russian citizens to return to them, through an egalitarian scheme, at least part of the property which they had collectively built up, the privatization laws still contained very little that would encourage the linkage of ownership with productive work. Promising a crumb of the national pie to every citizen, the laws made it excessively difficult for people to become owners of their workplaces. What looked like a great step toward economic democracy was in reality a choice of atomized absentee ownership over ownership firmly grounded where it really counts: at the production level.

In November 1991 Anatoly Chubais, another young neoliberal economist put by Yeltsin at the head of the State Property Committee (GKI), started drafting a privatization program for 1992–94. Meanwhile, Yeltsin signed a decree on December 4 providing for the transfer of all assets of state enterprises to the "full economic disposal" of their managers. Giving managers this type of economic freedom was the simplest thing to do before a full-fledged policy was in place. Also, it was aimed at winning the managerial class over to Yeltsin's side in his struggle against Gorbachev and Soviet Union bureaucracies: managers could now start their "elemental privatization," if they wanted. Actually, Yeltsin's decree only legalized a process which was already under way. Amid the ruins of the Soviet system, people who had wielded power in it were now busily recycling that power into new, capitalist forms.

By the end of the year, fundamentals of the privatization program were in place, approved by President Yeltsin's decree of December 29 "On Accelerating the Privatization of State and Municipal Enterprises." The preferred methods of privatization were chosen to be auctions and competitive bidding. The new Russian state was determined to sell state assets as dearly as possible.

Characteristically, the Russian government, now emerging as the most important caretaker of the vast Soviet assets, backtracked from the ideas of mass privatization. Use of privatization accounts, provided for in the July legislation, was put off until 1993. Workers at enterprises to be privatized were allowed to get 25 percent of the assets free of charge in the form of nonvoting shares and to buy 10 percent more at a 30 percent discount. Leased enterprises were not recognized at all. Thus, the main players in the great post-Soviet sell-off were to be government officials in the role of the sellers and big private investors, domestic and foreign, in the role of the buyers. The vast majority of citizens, their role as political supporters of the Russian democrats now much less needed, were assigned the role of passive onlookers who would wait for their free crumbs–non-voting shares and/or privatization checks (Russian Federation 1991).

The government's approach was deeply contradictory in several respects. First, although it proclaimed the goal of creating a substantial private sector, the program offered means which could not achieve that goal. Convinced that state ownership was inherently wasteful and an obstacle to the development of the Russian economy, Yeltsin's reformers were anxious to privatize as much and as quickly as possible. Yegor Gaidar and Anatoly Chubais were insisting on the creation of a "normal" Russian capitalist class by selling state assets to individuals who would then turn them into profitable enterprises.

Yet it was easier for the new government to order the state to withdraw from ownership than to find new owners who would fit the mold. "Real" domestic capitalists were too few, and most of them were not interested in sinking their money into open-ended, unpredictable, long-term business ventures, preferring short-term speculative deals with high profits. Most foreigners were too deterred by Russian chaos to consider long-term commitments. Thus, it became clear very soon that Russia had to either give up the idea of substantial privatization in the near future or find new owners for state enterprises in some way other than the "classic capitalist" one.

Second, the main goal the Russian government set for itself in 1992 was financial stabilization, which involved a drastic attempt at closing the budget deficit. Determined to reduce spending and to increase revenue, the government was planning to raise substantial sums through the sale of state enterprises. Obviously, the state was interested in selling the assets at the highest possible price. That interest dovetailed nicely with the ideological notion that the assets should be sold to the highest bidder–the people with real money–rather than be given away to work collectives or citizens at large through vouchers.

In reality, of course, regarding privatization as a deficit-buster was a self-defeating proposition. The buyers, whether they were work collectives or new millionaires, were interested in buying enterprises as cheaply as possible, and thus the government would be forced to choose between privatizing on the cheap or not privatizing at all. It could not have its cake and eat it, too–unless, of course, it would resort to compulsory sales rather than rely on a voluntary interest. In addition, the government's own price liberalization policy, which wiped out savings through inflation, undermined the fiscal approach to privatization even further. When incomes drop to, or even below, bare survival levels for 90 percent of the population, urging people to come and buy state assets sounds like a mockery.

Third, facilitating foreign investment was considered one of the most important ways of revitalizing the Russian economy. A major reason why foreign capital was extremely cautious toward the idea of investing in

Russia was the absence of a private sector. Privatization was supposed to create better conditions for attracting Western investors by offering them a chance to buy stock in privatized enterprises. This priority, just like the budget-balancing drive, made the notion of mass privatization decidedly unpopular with the government. Indeed, since foreign investors usually prefer full operational control of target enterprises, the Russian government expected that any serious democratization of ownership would scare potential investors away.

The problem with that logic is that social tension and political instability can be even stronger disincentives to foreign investment than absence of Western-style private ownership. On the other hand, an efficient, well-run enterprise can be much more attractive to a foreign investor even without a controlling interest than would a wreck with sullen and alienated workers that is available for a takeover at a bargain price.

In January–June 1992, the government worked out its three-year program for privatization of Russia's state and municipal enterprises. The process of producing the policy was marked by fierce debates and heavy political fighting over its contents. Various interest groups weighed in. The government stood its ground on some issues and gave in on others. Passions ran high, but the ultimate result reflected something like a baseline compromise on how to proceed.

One issue in the politics of Russian privatization was–and continues to be–the question of the role of the government in the process. Too little government control can lead to rampant plunder of state assets by people in power, while too much can strangle privatization and boost corruption. Since Yeltsin was engaged in building the new Russian state, an emphasis on the state role was inevitable, whatever the free-market protestations of his economic team. But the statist emphasis in the original version of the policy was too great.

In its review of the draft program in March 1992, a team of experts from the World Bank and the European Bank for Reconstruction and Development, led by Ira Lieberman, noted:

> Privatisation on the scale and the timetable being considered by Russia will require commitment of enormous resources and unprecedented cooperation among individuals, enterprises and agencies. The process cannot be driven "from the top down" by one or more bureaucracies. Experience in other contexts demonstrates that government agencies do not have sufficient resources, and will not receive critical support and information at the enterprise level. If, on the other hand, employees and management are given incentives to initiate, rather than obstruct, the process, then the results can be dramatic. (World Bank and European Bank 1992: 3–4)

The issue of the rights of the work collective became central. The original version of the privatization program viewed the state enterprise as an alien structure to be compelled, rather than induced, to reform either through a government order to privatize within a given time or through a decision by an outside investor to buy the enterprise at an auction whether its managers and employees liked it or not. Government-ordered auctions, at which state assets would be bought by people with "real money" from Russia or abroad, would satisfy both the government, which would profit from the sales, and the new owners; those currently employed at the privatized enterprises would just have to take the consequences.

This approach, naturally, caused strong protests across Russia. Moscow mayor Gavriil Popov, a leading reform economist and an important Yeltsin ally, had launched an alternative strategy of privatization in November 1991, worked out by economist Larisa Piiasheva. Piiasheva, a fervent disciple of Hayek and Friedman, insisted on the fastest possible transfer of state assets to private individuals—to be achieved through selling enterprises to their employees at hugely underrated official book value. Leased enterprises could become employee owned especially easily.

Piiasheva's interest in giving enterprises away to their work collectives did not reflect any belief in employee ownership. In her own words, she would have rather had state companies transferred to their present-day directors, but realized that it was impossible for political and social reasons (*Moscow News*, No. 42, 1992). Thus, workers were being invited to join in the privatization process not to become effective owners but to provide the right political climate for dismantling state ownership, with worker ownership being seen as a way station on the road to some "normal" form of capitalism.

President Yeltsin signed a special decree authorizing Moscow to proceed with the Piiasheva approach, which significantly deviated from the nationwide program. Lynn Nelson and Irina Kuzes (1994b: 48) conclude in their study of Russian economic reforms: "Thus, many workers in Moscow had a more attractive privatization opportunity than workers anywhere else. This example undoubtedly encouraged workers in other areas to press for benefits not provided under the proposed state program."

But even as the Moscow experiment helped workers throughout Russia get some control over their enterprises, it also hurt the cause of employee ownership by failing to demonstrate that this type of ownership was efficient. Given the purely tactical and destructive role that the Piiasheva policy was designed for, Moscow authorities did nothing to facilitate the empowerment of new owners. Thousands of Moscow enterprises, especially in the service sector, were bought out by work collectives under the Piiasheva program in 1992, and, predictably, the economic effect was zero, and in some cases even negative.

In the debates which followed, government spokesmen, led by Anatoly Chubais, tried hard to kill the idea of employee ownership as spurious. In an interview with the Moscow daily *Izvestia*, Chubais attacked the idea as "bolshevist":

> It has been etched into our heads that for some reason everyone must be an owner of his workplace. . . . And this is presented as the most sensible way of privatization? No, not everyone must be an owner of his workplace. But everyone must have a choice and decide for himself whether he will be an owner, especially in the entrepreneurial sense, or not. There is a mass of people—knowledgeable, skilled, strong, erudite—who cannot and will not play such a role. They do their job fine, but after they have done it, they forget about all job matters and happily plunge into their domestic, family, and other concerns in full accord with their interests. Are there many such people? Experts think that about 40 percent of employees will sell their shares. Why, then, should we impose on these people the status of an entrepreneurial collective?
>
> A person with an entrepreneurial potential is entirely different. He has a totally different mentality: he is happy when he gives himself to his business completely, when he takes full risk and responsibility for its results, when he has power over his capital. And he will fulfill himself whether he is included in the entrepreneurial collective or not. To turn the first social-psychological type into the second and, what is more, to hope to do it "in one step" is either naivete or purposeful deception. (*Izvestia*, February 26, 1992)

Telling people, most of whom had just lost their savings and purchasing power, that they now had a choice of becoming or not becoming private owners was adding insult to injury. Assuring them not to worry about ownership anyway because ownership is a burden that only people of the appropriate "social-psychological type" can bear and enjoy was a parody of social Darwinism.

In the spring and summer of 1992, Chubais's dismissals of worker ownership were publicly challenged in the Russian media by American experts John Simmons, a well-known Chicago management consultant, and John Logue, director of the Northeast Ohio Employee Ownership Center—both of whom were deeply involved as advisers in Russian privatization efforts. In April 1992, Simmons and Logue published an article in the leading Russian daily *Izvestia* titled "The 13 Myths of Russian Privatization." Warning that the government's program effectively prohibited workers and managers from buying out their companies and encouraged the concentration of wealth in the hands of a small number of very wealthy stockholders, the two authors analyzed the arguments put forward by the Russian government to justify its unwillingness to promote employee ownership (Simmons and Logue 1992).

The government's arguments centered around the notion that employee ownership was inherently inefficient. If workers are owners and play a significant role in management, the company's performance presumably suffers, because the workers will irresponsibly vote themselves higher wages at the expense of productivity. The government further argued that employee ownership would hinder the development of capitalism in Russia: both labor and capital markets would be constrained by the proliferation of firms having low labor-force mobility and relying primarily on internal capital resources. Finally, government officials asserted, employee ownership would discourage foreign investment.

None of those arguments was supported by existing data on Russian or foreign employee-owned companies. In fact, both Russian and Western firms offer impressive evidence in favor of the opposite conclusions. Giving workers real ownership and management rights in their companies usually generates powerful incentives in the labor force, because both success and failure of the company affect the interests of the employee-owner more directly and more strongly than they affect the interests of the employee who does not own any stake in the company. Employee ownership does make it more difficult for the management to fire workers (which is the essence of the labor market argument), but this is more than balanced out by stronger positive incentives inherent in the ownership status and by the peer pressures to work well or leave which worker-owners exert on each other within the firm. As far as the foreign investment argument goes, experience shows that well-organized employee-owned companies are attractive targets for foreign investors because they are more efficient and profitable than firms with hired labor. One of the most recent Russian examples was the purchase by the British company Illingworth Morris of 49 percent of the stock in Russia's largest clothing company, Bolshevichka, 51 percent of which is owned by the company's workers and managers (*Finansovye izvestia*, November 19–25, 1993).

Taking issue with the Russian unwillingness to involve workers in enterprise decision making, Simmons and Logue (1992) noted: "American law requires that employees vote their shares in public companies. When employees become owners, they expect to participate in helping solve a company's problems. The best management methods today are based on finding as many ways as possible to encourage employee participation, not reduce it, as the Russian law seeks to do."

This reasoning would be countered by yet another argument: in a country like Russia, where people lacked market skills and even the most elementary knowledge of how a market economy worked, employee-owned companies would fail because people simply would not be up to the test of private ownership. Nelson and Kuzes (1994b: 48–49) report from their extensive surveys of Russian attitudes to privatization: "The view that workers often lacked the skills necessary for ownership of enterprises was deeply rooted in the thinking of privatization planners at the federal level, and it was an important reason for their resistance to Piiasheva's proposal that enterprises throughout Russia be turned over to their employees."

But this "cultural" argument cuts both ways. If employees are unfit to become effective owners without generations of market experience, who can be considered fit for ownership? Managers of state enterprises and government officials certainly are more experienced in management, but most of that experience was gained in a nonmarket bureaucratic setting and thus is not of much use now. The new private entrepreneurs are usually more skilled in buying and selling than in running production. Foreign capitalists would conceivably be more efficient, but when operating in the Russian society, they have to deal with the same problems of lack of market traditions. In other words, if employees are unfit for capitalism, then Russia as a country is not fit for capitalism either. But then any plan for privatization becomes idle talk.

In reality, segments of the Russian workforce had already acquired considerable experience in working under market conditions by the time privatization started. A report by the Coordinating Committee for Economic Democracy, a Moscow-based nongovernmental group advocating employee ownership, stressed that

> acquisition of a considerable part of an enterprise's capital by its employees is not only an act of fair distribution of property rights. The experience of many existing work collectives at leased and cooperative enterprises shows that real worker ownership becomes a powerful incentive to increased efficiency at that enterprise and to economy in material and labor costs. Of course, managerial structures should not be viewed as something separate from the work collective, much less opposed to it. Everyone working at a company should get his share of the property. And it is important to emphasize that when employees own a large share of the capital, they are much easier to involve in economic decision making, especially at the middle and lower levels. (Coordinating Committee for Economic Democracy 1992)

The privatization strategy chosen by the Russian government in December 1991 was not only based on false assumptions about worker ownership, but was also patently untenable in the real Russian situation of 1992. It lacked a mass base; it was insufficiently related to the interests of the traditional Soviet managerial class, which continued to control the economy; and it did not contain real incentives for the workers.

Bowing to political reality, the government modified its approach, adding elements designed to win mass support for privatization. Anatoly Chubais submitted the new policy to Russia's Supreme Soviet in May 1992. Having recognized that it did not have effective power to compel Russian enterprises to privatize on terms unacceptable to either their workers or their managers—and that there were too few domestic and foreign millionaires anxious to buy state companies—the Russian government had to give some concessions to the work collectives to get them interested in privatization. They were now allowed to choose from a wider range of privatization methods, a change which gave employees and managers an opportunity to obtain majority stock on favored terms.

The privatization program was approved by the Russian Parliament on June 11, 1992. Its goals were defined as follows:

- Formation of a stratum of private owners, which would facilitate the creation of a socially oriented market economy
- Increased efficiency of enterprises through privatization
- Increased state funds to pay for social programs
- Facilitation of financial stabilization
- Creation of a competitive environment and demonopolization
- Attraction of foreign investors
- Preparation of the ground for expanded privatization

All Russian state assets were divided into several groups. The first group included strategic assets excluded from the privatization process: natural resources; gold and diamond reserves; assets of the armed forces, security ministry, and the police; broadcasting stations; general-use highways; the nuclear fuel industry; the Central Bank; and other assets considered strictly public domain.

Enterprises of the second group could be privatized only by decision of Russia's federal or regional governments: defense industries, power stations, mines, commercial banks, communications, wire services.

The third group included large enterprises which could be privatized only by decision of the State Property Committee of Russia (GKI): those which occupied dominant positions in their markets or those employing ten thousand people or more.

Authority over privatizing the fourth group of enterprises (municipal transportation, baths, laundries, pharmacies, etc.) was given to local governments.

The fifth group was defined as those enterprises which must be privatized, including (1) those whose operations had the greatest impact on the

formation of market relations (wholesale and retail trade, services, construction, producers of food and consumer goods) and (2) those operating
at a loss or mothballed.

The privatization program stipulated goals for all levels of state administrative bodies responsible for privatization, both in terms of numbers of
enterprises to be privatized and in terms of expected state income from
the sales.

Addressing the issue of funding privatization was a major reality check
for the government. According to their estimates, 21 percent of the funds
were to come from citizens' personal savings; 44 percent, from privatized
enterprises' own internal resources; 21 percent, from enterprises which
would buy other enterprises; and 14 percent, from foreign investors.
Having made a good count, Chubais realized that most of the money to
buy out state enterprises had to come from the enterprises themselves. For
1993–94, the program projected vouchers and enterprises' own privatization funds as the main sources of financing the buyouts.

The program provided for several methods of privatization:

1. Small enterprises employing fewer than two hundred people and
   with a fixed-capital book value of less than 1 million rubles (as of
   January 1, 1992) were to be sold through auctions or competitive
   bidding.
2. Large enterprises with more than a thousand employees and with
   the book value of fixed capital of more than 50 million rubles (as
   of January 1, 1992) were to be turned into open joint-stock
   societies.
3. With regard to all other enterprises, one of several options could
   be chosen: (a) turn them into open corporations and sell their
   shares to the public; (b) sell them through auctions or competitive
   bidding; (c) privatize leased enterprises through employee buyouts; or (d) sell the assets of bankrupt enterprises.

In a concession to employees of privatized entities, those employed at
the moment of sale, those who were retired after working at the enterprise
for at least 10 (men) or 7.5 (women) years, and those laid off after January
1, 1992, were entitled to certain advantages in the privatization process.

At enterprises transformed into joint-stock companies, employees had
a right to choose among three options: (1) Option 1–to receive gratis 25
percent of the stock in the form of nonvoting shares and to be able to buy,
at a 30 percent discount, another 10 percent of the stock, with the top
management having a right to buy up to 5 percent of the stock at face value;
(2) Option 2–to buy up to 51 percent of the common stock at prices set by

the government with the possibility of a closed subscription for shares; and (3) Option 3–to allow a group of employees, assuming responsibility for privatization, to buy 20 percent of the common stock, with another 20 percent available to the rest of the work collective at a 30 percent discount.

Creation of closed partnerships was specifically forbidden. The law also banned establishment of corporations on the basis of concerns, alliances, or associations of state enterprises.

The program authorized Russian commercial and foreign banks to provide credit to privatization deals without any limitations. Local governments could use their own budgets to facilitate privatization (Russian Federation 1992).

On July 1, 1992, President Yeltsin issued two decrees aimed at facilitating the privatization process: one on commercialization of state enterprises (replacing the decree of December 1, 1991) and the other on organizational measures to transform state enterprises into joint-stock companies. The main thrust of these measures was to compel state enterprises to privatize through turning themselves into joint-stock companies and being put in trust of individuals and firms. Interestingly enough, the decrees gave significant rights to work collectives: in a reversal of its previous attitude to employees, the government now clearly counted on them to press for a faster transformation of state industries. In particular, the president empowered employees to initiate privatization on their own in those cases when the management was reluctant to do so (*Kommersant,* August 4, 1992).

Having made concessions to enterprise insiders–workers and managers–the Russian government then revived its 1991 plan to give stakes in privatization to every Russian citizen. The decision was taken reluctantly and motivated by political considerations: the government's "shock therapy" was generating growing discontent in society, and the government realized that it might lose power unless something were given to the masses hit by the drastic reduction of their incomes.

President Yeltsin's decree of August 14, 1992, served to implement the July 1991 law providing for free distribution of Russian state assets to citizens. The new vehicle for this "people's privatization" would be the privatization voucher or check. Each citizen of the Russian Federation was entitled to one such voucher, which he or she would be able to exchange for the shares of the company one was employed at or any other company, or put into an investment fund, or sell on the open market. The face value of the voucher was 10,000 rubles ($61 at the then-current exchange rate)–the estimated book value of about a third of Russia's large industrial enterprises as of January 1, 1992 (that is, on the eve of price liberalization) divided by the number of Russia's citizens.

Distribution of vouchers began on October 1, 1992, which was also the deadline for enterprises that were to be privatized in 1992 to submit their transformation plans. January 1, 1993, was set as the date of the beginning of the exchange of vouchers for property, a process to continue for one year. Later, the deadline for voucher exchange was extended.

It was only after the Russian government took those two steps to involve the masses of the Russian society in privatization—extending to the work collectives the right to obtain controlling stock and introducing the voucher as the key vehicle for the buyout—that the privatization process could start in earnest. Russia now stood on the threshold of a real revolution. Still, the privatization program contained serious conceptual flaws which limited the effectiveness of the socioeconomic change being undertaken.

In late September, major Russian newspapers published an appeal by Anatoly Chubais, who explained the goals and methods of the privatization program. It was ironic that this major document of the campaign officially aimed at making every Russian a private owner put so much stress on the notion that ownership was a burden that common people should think twice about assuming. "No one intends to impose ownership on those who do not want to get it," announced Chubais to a nation which for generations had seen governments taking wealth away from citizens and now needed to be persuaded, if anything, that this time the process would be reversed. Chubais continued:

> In every country with a market economy . . . there are people who have their share of ownership of productive assets and resources, and much more numerous [are] those who do not. . . . Each citizen must now make a choice: to assume the rights of an owner and the concomitant responsibility for the future of his property; to transfer the disposal of those rights to those who are creating special firms, called investment funds; or to give up those rights and responsibilities by selling or presenting the privatization check to someone else. . . . Only such a freedom of choice, equal for everyone whatever the nationality, sex, age, position, or any other characteristics, makes it possible to enter the market economy. (*Izvestia*, September 28, 1992)

Commenting on Option 2 for joint-stock companies, which opened the widest opportunities for employee ownership, Chubais thought it important to warn: "It is desirable that employees who would choose this option first convince themselves about their company's profitability. It is possible that the State Property Committee may not authorize this option" (*Izvestia*, September 28, 1992).

It was obvious from the statements of Chubais and other Russian government officials that they regarded the distribution of ownership rights through employee buyouts and vouchers as a temporary, transitional, and tactical measure. Masses of Russians were invited to join the process of dismantling the system of state ownership, but most of them were considered a priori unfit to exercise their ownership rights intelligently and were encouraged to pass the ownership burden onto the shoulders of those who would dispose of it in an appropriate manner. Rather than try to forge strong links between ownership and work, the Russian reformers tried hard to facilitate their separation. Rather than try to build the structures of responsible private ownership based on one's control of one's workplace, they encouraged the ethic of the casino, largely irrelevant to the situation of most Russian citizens. In a remarkable passage, Chubais explained in his appeal:

> The stock market where shares circulate is essentially an exciting game, which has its own fascinating and complex rules. Rank-and-file shareholders, who do not work at stock exchanges, need not know those rules in detail. It is enough for the rank-and-file stockholders to be aware that they can either win or lose in this game, like in any other. . . . Sometimes, the dividends are so high that one can live off them without having to work. (*Izvestia*, September 28, 1992)

The Russians were being invited to make their bets in the exciting new "something for nothing" game. As far as making the formerly state-owned enterprises efficient and profitable private companies, workers and managers were left to their own devices.

THE SOVIET ENTERPRISE: FRIEND OR FOE OF REFORM?

The central issue in all reforms of the Soviet, and then the post-Soviet, economies has been transformation of the state-owned enterprise. Near total control of enterprises by branch ministries, the Gosplan, and the Gossnab (State Committee for Supplies) had long been seen as a major flaw of the Soviet economic system, and granting enterprises some freedom of action to respond to consumer demands and changing circumstances was recognized as the most logical and necessary kind of change. Enterprise managers formed a powerful pressure group trying to weaken central bureaucratic control.

Managers of Soviet state enterprises were often referred to as "commanders of production." Of course, some of them were just cogs in the giant bureaucratic machine, without talent or interest in change. But there was also a critical mass of "commanders" who did care about the conditions of their enterprises and of the economy as a whole, and who did try to overcome at least some of the irrationalities of Soviet central planning.

The managers had pressed, above all, for a maximum degree of economic freedom from the state bureaucracy so that they could reorganize production on efficient principles. They admired traditional Western management methods, and they wanted to get as close to that model as possible. Of course, the capitalist model attracted them not just for its perceived efficiency, but also for the much higher rewards it gave to those at the top.

One of the freedoms managers lacked in the Soviet system was the freedom to fire loafers and reward those who performed well. A yearning for a real market was combined in the thinking of many in the managerial class with a strong preference for an authoritarian style of management.

If in Stalin's times the totalitarian state enforced labor discipline in the most brutal fashion (and quite often punished managers with the same brutality), post-Stalinist liberalization of the Soviet system led to the emergence of a labor relations regime inside state enterprises that some researchers have characterized as "authoritarian-paternalist." As the authors of a British-Russian study of the transformation of Soviet state enterprises put it, "Soviet workers appear to have been powerful, in that managers had to make extensive concessions to enlist the workers' cooperation, but the workers were weak in that they were denied any effective representation and had no means of collective resistance" (Clarke, Fairbrother, Borisov, and Bizyukov 1994: 180).

Soviet labor relations were characterized by muted conflict. Neither management nor workers were free to pursue their interests and clash openly over terms and conditions of employment. The managers represented the state, which both limited and strengthened their authority. In the name of fulfilling plan targets handed down from above, the managers were expected to enforce strict discipline but also to guarantee the other part of the socialist bargain, job security and social benefits. The workers, of course, could not challenge the managers, for that would be inherently a challenge to the state. Labor unions were little more than the state's "transmission belts," strengthening control of the workforce.

British economist Simon Clarke described the situation as follows:

> The soviet enterprise is almost as different from the capitalist enterprise as was a feudal estate from a capitalist farm. Like the feudal estate, the soviet enterprise is not simply an economic institution but is the primary unit of soviet society, and the ultimate base of social and political power. The basis of soviet enterprise was not capital, but the productive activity of the labor collective [*trudovoi kollektiv*, which is translated in this book as "work collective"–Editor]. The public measure of its success was not its profit but the size of its labor force and the number of tons they produced, the houses it had built, the number of places for children in its kindergartens and in summer

camps, the sporting, medical and cultural facilities it provided, the number of pensioners it supported. (Clarke 1992: 7)

Gorbachev's Law on State Enterprises, which began to be implemented in January 1988, gave the managers considerable freedom from the state to set wages, decide on what to produce, reorganize production, choose customers, and finance operations through using portions of enterprise profits and bank credit. But the authoritarian proclivities of the managers were checked by the creation of work collective councils (STKs) within enterprises, through which workers would participate in management and even elect managers. In addition, as part of general political liberalization, labor unions obtained a degree of freedom unheard of in Soviet history, with strikes becoming a regular and powerful practice in Soviet industry from 1989 on. Thus, the Soviet enterprise regime was becoming more corporatist, in the sense that the enterprise as a unit was now more independent and its components depended more on each other than before, and less authoritarian, in the sense that managerial power within enterprises was now more constrained by counter-vailing pressures from the workforce.

Gorbachev's attempt to revive the moribund bureaucratic economy with the injection of market incentives and economic democracy, just like his overall policy of perestroika, was a success in undermining the old system but a failure in building a new one. The power of central bureaucracies was, indeed, drastically weakened. But no efficient market mechanism could spring up overnight to replace it. Transformation of state enterprises into market entities did move ahead, especially in the form of leasing: almost ten thousand enterprises were transformed into leaseholds by February 1992, accounting for 13 percent of industrial output and 8 percent of total employment (Frydman, Rapaczynski, and Earle 1993: 22). But the bulk of the economy was stuck between the old and the new. Having tasted their new freedoms, managers found that they were in many ways ephemeral in the absence of the market infrastructure they could rely on in charting their new strategies. When they sought to turn back to the state's protective fold, they discovered that the old state, which they had tried to free themselves from, was not quite there anymore.

Yeltsin's "shock therapists" were impatient with the heritage of perestroika and above all with its centerpiece, the half-reformed Soviet enterprise. The basic cell of the Soviet economy was subjected to a multipronged assault, designed to force it to transform itself into a regular capitalist enterprise or to disappear. Unregulated prices, privatization, the growth of private banks, and opening the economy would create the market infrastructure without which enterprises could not function on their own. Hard budget constraints would cut the subsidies and state orders which continued to tie enterprises to the state.

To most managers, it was a hostile posture, amounting to what they branded as a real war on industry. Conditions of production deteriorated, as the division of the USSR into newly independent states disrupted traditional economic ties, price liberalization sent inflation soaring, and "financial stabilization" began replacing state subsidies to enterprises with high taxes. While state enterprise managers had particularly acute grudges against Yeltsin's policies, many of their criticisms were fully shared by private producers as well.

Yeltsin's privatization policy reflected an intent to break up, or at least weaken, corporatist structures of the state sector. This was to be achieved by forcing enterprises to go private and open themselves to outside investors. First it was to be millionaires; later, when millionaires failed to show up, the masses with their vouchers. The attack on managers' positions in the state sector was motivated to some extent by the neoliberal economic orthodoxy that Yeltsin's reformers acquired from their Eastern European counterparts and Western advisers: according to that orthodoxy, insider takeover of state enterprises would perpetuate the Soviet economy's inefficient ways. Other considerations involved a desire to weaken the managerial class as a powerful rival group in Yeltsin's struggle for power, and an intention to make the state sector available for acquisition by foreign investors and new Russian private entrepreneurs, the rising class generally siding with radical democrats at that stage.

But the attack was doomed. The Russian government, barely established and without a solid social base yet, was no match for the deeply entrenched corporate structures of the Soviet economy. State-owned companies turned into pockets of resistance to the government's policies. In the old Soviet days, a manager would develop unusual skills to obtain better terms for his enterprise, cultivating connections with party bosses in Moscow and locally, lobbying in Central Committee departments and in the branch ministry, sending trusted people to obtain key supplies by whatever means possible, and skillfully getting around the law. It was a survival game no less tough than what the typical Western entrepreneur is accustomed to, and it worked as a natural selection process. After the collapse of Communism, managers applied their skills and experience to the new conditions with considerable success. They had many more weapons in their contest with the new state than did the state itself.

They would fight for government assistance to keep their plants running and their workers paid. They would form political coalitions like the Civic Union to press for a slower and more regulated transformation of Russia's economy. They would lobby in the Parliament and use the specter of politically explosive mass unemployment to intimidate the government into helping them survive. In a very real sense, they became the most important cushion against the blows of "shock therapy"—even as they contributed to the inflationary pressures by raising the prices of their products, cutting back production, and forcing the government to subsidize them.

If in the old days a manager's success at his survival game depended primarily on his adeptness at playing people at the top, conditions in post-Communist Russia have increasingly rewarded those who were good at building their home bases—at enterprises and in localities. Of course, there has been a whole spectrum of different ways to play the role of a corporatist leader standing firmly for the interests of the enterprise and the hometown against the pain-inflicting government. Some tried to be benevolent dictators, others pursued more consensus-oriented strategies, and still others experimented boldly.

The basic normative framework for all Russian companies, public and private, is the Law on Enterprises and Entrepreneurial Activity, adopted by Russia's Supreme Soviet in December 1990, at the height of Russian democrats' struggle against the top Soviet bureaucracy. The fact that the independent labor movement was a key force in that struggle is reflected in the substantial powers that the 1990 law gives to the work collective, including the election of the manager, the determination of the scope of his authority, and the right to amend the enterprise's charter.

Of course, the situation at state companies has been a far cry from real industrial democracy, with decisions being taken by the management and/or the state body responsible for the enterprise, and the work collective's consent being largely a formality. But on the other hand, existing legal norms did put some limits on the management's power as weapons of struggle available to those who would be pressed hard enough to use them. Just as important, the existence of a relatively democratic legal order within enterprises made it easier for managers and workers to form alliances to defend and advance company interests; that is, it gave state enterprises the inner strength to cope with an adverse economic environment and, in better cases, even to make companies more efficient.

Under such conditions, it turned out to be very difficult for Russian state managers to take over their companies directly as new private owners. It turned out to be quite natural for them to effect "work collective" buyouts.

Having compelled the government in the early months of 1992 into amending its original privatization blueprint to include Option 2, which allowed employees to obtain 51 percent of the stock, the managerial elite by and large accepted privatization. Among many other indications, a detailed survey of attitudes to privatization, conducted in 1992 in several large Russian cities, found that 43 percent of plant directors supported the privatization program "completely" or "to a considerable extent," 46 percent supported it "to some extent," and only 10 percent opposed it (1 percent had no opinion). Sixty-two percent thought privatization should proceed more quickly, while only 21 percent advocated keeping the present pace or slowing down. Seventeen percent had no opinion (Nelson and Kuzes 1994b: 208, 211). Boris Mikhailov, general director of Impuls, a large defense company in St. Petersburg, summed up in the summer of 1992: "Some think it will go back to the way it was. But that will never happen, and few managers want it to happen. Of course, Gaidar has made mistakes. But every military-industrial manager understands that privatization is inevitable. The arguments are over the approach, the pace, the methods" (*New York Times*, August 19, 1992).

Simon Clarke observed in his study of the evolution of the Soviet enterprise:

> Enterprise managers are strongly in favor of privatization to give them juridical guarantees of their independence from state control, particularly over the disposal of their profits. However, they are not willing to allow control to pass to outsiders. The form of privatization most attractive to the nomenklatura is one in which shareholding is diversified but a controlling interest remains in the hands of the labor collective. This is not because of any commitment to workers' self-management on the part of the apparatus, but because management has in the past been able to keep a firm grip on the organs of workers' representation, while the ownership of the enterprise by the labor collective provides the material base for a strategy of "social partnership" through which the management hopes to reproduce the subordination of the labor force in production, motivating the workers and reducing the labor turnover, while consolidating the political allegiance of the workers to the enterprise administration. Minority shareholdings equally have a specific part to play in linking particular interests to the fate of the enterprise. Shares in the hands of local and Republican government bodies retain connections with the state apparatus. The sale of shares to outsiders can consolidate links with customers and suppliers, as well as providing a source of funds. (Clarke 1992: 13)

Workers and other citizens outside of the managerial elite had much more cautious and ambivalent attitudes to privatization. In the survey cited above, the 89 percent level of support among managers for the government's privatization program declined to 60 percent among department heads and specialists, to 51 percent among skilled workers, to 43 percent among clerks and technicians, and to 38 percent among unskilled workers. Perceptions of social consequences of privatization were far from optimistic: while 43 percent of the nonmanagerial personnel agreed with the statement "privatization will make people's lives better," only 20 percent expected living standards of most people to increase "if Russia achieved a market economy." Eighty percent expected increased inequality; 82 percent, higher unemployment; 68 percent, a rise in crime; 57 percent, less close relations among people; and 41 percent, a decline in moral values (Nelson and Kuzes 1994b: 209, 211).

In August 1992, after the Yeltsin government announced a program of mass privatization through vouchers, a poll of Moscow residents revealed a generally positive attitude to the idea of a transfer of state assets to citizens. Muscovites, however, were unsure of how best to proceed. Dividing the assets equally among all citizens, as Yeltsin proposed, was supported by just 22 percent, with an additional 11 percent "leaning" toward support. Forty percent did not think the measure would have the desired effect, while 22 percent responded with a flat "no." As to the methods of privatizing a state enterprise, 53 percent favored "selling it to those who can buy it and will be able to effectively manage production," while 42 percent preferred "handing it over only to a work collective." As far as the terms of handing it over to a work collective, the largest number—48 percent—thought that each worker should receive free of charge his assessed share of the property and be able to buy more. Twenty-three percent preferred selling enterprises to work collectives; 21 percent, giving them to work collectives for free. Four out of five wanted to participate in the purchase of the enterprises they worked at (FBIS-USR-92-115 1992: 50–51).

Most Russians, looking for alternatives to the agonizing Soviet system, were giving capitalism conditional support: they associated private ownership in general with greater efficiency and they were wary of traditional egalitarianism and collectivism, but they also insisted that new owners be competent and they intended to become co-owners themselves. In other words, Russians clearly wanted a form of capitalism in which they all could be capitalists of one kind or another.

Evidence was overwhelming that very few Russians would be happy if state assets were to be taken over by the new rich. A poll conducted in July 1993 by the All-Russian Center for the Study of Public Opinion (VTsIOM), revealed highly negative attitudes of Russian citizens toward the new bourgeoisie. Asked to name reasons why people most often became rich, respondents gave the following answers:

45%	—resale, speculation, stealing, plunder, tricks
13%	—rich inheritance
10%	—graft
7%	—enterprise
7%	—economic instability
7%	—connections

In other words, observing the rise of the new Russian bourgeoisie, only a very few Russians saw a socially justifiable reason for its new wealth: "enterprise." Asked to name qualities characterizing Russian businessmen, respondents drew an appalling collective portrait:

58%	–greed
40%	–inclination to cheat
31%	–refusal to work honestly
23%	–sharp business behavior
22%	–unscrupulous use of means to achieve ends
18%	–low cultural level
16%	–adventurism
13%	–lack of professionalism, incompetence
12%	–initiative, persistence
11%	–hard work
9%	–rationalism
6%	–honesty, integrity
4%	–high professionalism

As we can see, negative assessments collected 198 percentage points, while positive ones collected just 42 (since "sharp business behavior"–*delovaya khvatka* in Russian–is a characteristic that may carry connotations of either admiration or opprobrium, we should consider it a neutral assessment).

One may wonder, of course, if this public image of the brand-new Russian capitalist was not an effect of ideological blinkers inherited from the decades of communism. But in the same poll, respondents were asked to characterize Western businessmen too, and the image of the Western capitalist that emerged from those answers–a model of hard work, efficiency, and honesty–was the exact opposite of the greedy, lazy, and unscrupulous Russian counterpart. Most Russians still believed in Western capitalism, which they had not experienced, but they did not like the Russian variety, which they were observing on a daily basis (*Izvestia*, August 7, 1993).

In 1993, Russian privatization assumed a distinct shape: the managers' insistence on insider privileges, the government's commitment to fast-track privatization, and the public's fears that state assets would be stolen by the rich and the powerful combined to produce a strong trend toward the takeover of enterprises by manager-led work collectives. By the summer of 1993, 70 to 80 percent of enterprises to be privatized had chosen Option 2 (Sutela 1994: 420). Government authorities were assessing the value of the firms' assets at very low levels. The limits on insider share of the stock were regularly breached, whenever the choice was selling stock to employees and managers or not finding any buyer at all.

Having forced the government to offer privatization terms acceptable to them, the managers were leaving the state sector like a sinking ship with one goal uppermost on their minds—survival. Together with their workers, they were becoming majority stockholders in their newly privatized companies, but the awesome tasks of restructuring these companies required what the managers had in very short supply: knowledge and experience with regard to running companies in a market setting, government policies which would help effect the necessary microeconomic changes, and, of course, real capital.

The one alternative model of enterprise most of them had in mind was classic capitalism. The boss, or bosses, would own the company and therefore have the power to run it efficiently and profitably. They naturally gravitated to that model and to its embodiment in the growing new breed of Russian private entrepreneurs. The emerging situation, in which managers were now in charge of formally private companies, but constrained in both ownership and management of those companies by the crowds of co-owners from the shop floor, who were even less prepared for the market realities than the managers, was bound to be perceived by many of them as transitory, an uncomfortable grey area between socialism and capitalism. The post-Soviet managerial class might have paternalistic traditions, kept alive by the managers' instinct of self-preservation, but to most of them, the notion of democratic management was a contradiction in terms.

A minority of Russian managers have resolutely tried to remodel their newly private companies along traditional Western lines. They abandoned old paternalistic practices, introduced higher wage differentials, fired poorly performing workers, sold off corporate social-welfare systems, and worked to concentrate ownership and control in their hands. Such strategies appear to have been only marginally successful and very problematic as to their sustainability (see Clarke et al. 1994: 205–208).

Most others would try to preserve what they could of the old ways. "Shock therapy" increased the value of corporate social-welfare systems to employees badly hit by rising prices and deteriorating state services, while the harsh external pressures worked to force enterprises to cut their traditional social functions. Between these conflicting pressures, many managers have avoided "rationalizing" enterprises at the risk of social conflict. Instead, they have fought for the continuation of state subsidies to keep their companies afloat in expectation of better times. In the meantime, they have tended to mightily increase their own incentives by raising their salaries and their stakes in the companies they run.

Only very few have tried to restructure their companies with the active participation of their co-owners, the employees. The government's hostile attitude to worker ownership, the authoritarian traditions among managers, and the absence of traditions of participatory governance in the wider society have emerged as barriers obstructing the one promising road that could be taken.

PRIVATIZATION: THE BALANCE SHEET

July 1, 1994, marked the end of the period of mass privatization launched in 1992. From that day on, the voucher was no longer valid as a means for buying stock, and shares could be obtained only for money (though grace periods were extended by the federal and some local authorities to those who had not been able to exchange their vouchers for stock before July 1).

Summing up the results of mass privatization, Vice Premier Anatoly Chubais announced that over two-thirds of Russia's industrial sector had been privatized: 74 percent of large and medium-sized enterprises (those employing two hundred people or more)—21,000 in all—and 70 percent of small enterprises (84,000) had become joint-stock companies. Of 148 million vouchers issued by the Russian state, 139 million (94 percent) were used to buy stock. Forty million Russians had become stockholders (*Radio Free Europe–Radio Liberty Daily Report*, July 1 and 8, 1994). The privatized companies were now owned in various combinations by employees, managers, outside investors from Russia and abroad, and to a limited extent the state, which retained ownership of some sectors of the economy which were not yet open for privatization and, temporarily, of portfolios of stock in some of the privatized companies. The highest levels of privatization were reached in food processing (78 percent), building materials (72 percent), services (72 percent), and trade (70 percent); the lowest, in construction (45 percent) (*Moscow News*, June 10–16, 1994).

Some in the Russian government proclaimed the arrival of capitalism on the grounds that the balance between state and private sectors in the Russian economy had shifted decisively in favor of the latter.

The figures announced in the summer of 1994 did look impressive. It had taken the Russian government just thirty months to dismantle the main base of the largest state-owned economy in world history and to enable a substantial segment of the population to acquire at least small-scale and formal private ownership of the means of production. Remarkably, the shift was achieved peacefully, through a bargaining process among key social groups involved.

Behind the impressive statistics, however, lay a reality which generated a lot of controversy, disappointment, and anger over privatization. The goals the government had proclaimed when it launched the program in 1992 have scarcely been met.

Progress toward the goal of creating a stratum of private owners was most visible in the emergence of 40 million shareholders—about twice the number in the United States and almost a third of Russia's adult population. More significantly, big chunks of stock in privatized enterprises were now owned by employees, as illustrated by a study by Joseph Blasi (1994c), a Rutgers University professor of management and labor relations who served as an adviser to the Russian government. Having surveyed two hundred large state-owned enterprises (with an average employment of three thousand) in forty regions of Russia which had been privatized, Blasi found that on the average, employees had acquired 66 percent of each enterprise, senior managers got 8 percent, 21 percent went to outsiders, while the Russian government retained 13 percent of the equity.

But this new private-owner status had not changed much in the socioeconomic conditions of most Russians. The average Russian continued to feel economically powerless—in fact, more so than before. While "shock therapy" undermined his savings and wages, his new "private capital" in the form of shares was miserable compensation for the very tangible losses.

As a small would-be investor interested in buying some profitable stock outside of his own work, the average Russian was encouraged by the government and mass media to entrust his money and vouchers to any of the numerous investment funds, newly created to service privatization; their number exceeded 650 by May 1994 (*Izvestia*, May 4, 1994). But the voucher's market price was two to three times lower than its nominal value, while the funds soon acquired a very negative reputation: a number of large funds were simply plundered by their managers who then disappeared, touching off enormous public scandals, and most of the rest were not able to pay any significant dividends.

As an employee of an enterprise to be privatized, the average Russian discovered that his options were quite limited, too. The more profitable the enterprise, the less likely it was that employees would be able to get a controlling share of the assets: as a rule, the best assets would find themselves in the hands of managers, corrupt officials, the new rich, and bosses of organized crime. As far as less promising companies were concerned, employees did have a chance to acquire controlling shares as their managers did. But in most cases, control of enterprises remained in the managers' hands. The Blasi study, the most detailed survey of privatized industries, showed that at most of the enterprises surveyed, the boards were made up entirely of senior managers, who wanted to see their share of the stock increased on the average to 40 percent and employees' share reduced on the average to 24 percent. Trade union power had largely vanished. Blasi concluded: "If anyone has too much power in these companies, it will be the managers, not the workers" (Blasi 1994c: A23; see also Blasi 1994b: 13).

One of the worst aspects of Russian privatization, seriously undermining its credibility, was the wave of new corruption generated by the massive ownership transfer. The London *Economist*, editorializing about dangers facing the nascent Russian market economy, stressed "the belief that property is theft. In Russia, it often is. Many of the country's new rich have made their money either by stealing state property and calling it 'spontaneous privatisation,' or by bribing an official to give them a license to corner some market. This has blackened the reputations of the honest along with the dishonest" (*Economist*, July 9, 1994: 4).

Russian media have published numerous reports on the involvement of organized crime in privatization. The way the process was structured, and the notable weakness of the new Russian state, manifested in the absence of both a stable legal order and an efficient administrative apparatus, combined to open opportunities for the mob. Since graft, intimidation, and violence could be effectively used to snatch attractive pieces of property, it was those best prepared to use those tools who got a unique advantage in the privatization process.

Public opinion polls indicated predominantly critical assessments of privatization's results. For instance, a spring 1994 survey of 3,500 respondents in thirty regions of Russia, commissioned by the Paul Lazarsfeld International Foundation, produced the following results. Forty-three percent of respondents had exchanged their vouchers for shares, two-thirds of them using investment funds. Only 21 percent were satisfied with their investment. Forty-seven percent associated privatization of the company they worked at with a heightened risk of losing their jobs; 51 percent, with the prospect of more intensive work. While about one-third of respondents expected that privatization of their enterprises would lead to product quality improvements and higher wages, only 16 to 18 percent thought employees would be able to have more influence on the administration of privatized companies (*Izvestia*, July 2, 1994).

The influential and usually pro-government Moscow daily *Izvestia* summed up its analysis of the situation at KRAZ, a recently privatized huge aluminum company in Krasnoyarsk:

> Yes, in the absence of private ownership we would have still been divided into the master, some smaller masters, and the remaining mass of lumpen and serfs. But how soon will we become free, having received our right to own land and factories? Tomorrow, in a generation, or in three or four generations? . . . We continue to be divided into supervisors and the supervised, if a plant manager or chief accountant can be paid tens of times more than school teachers. Nothing has changed if another plant manager builds a luxury villa for himself in full sight of his workers, who are exhausted from forced leisure and poverty. . . . What social partnership are we talking about? We are still masters and serfs. (*Izvestia*, December 10, 1993)

A worker from the city of Kovrov in the Vladimir *oblast* wrote a letter to the same newspaper, asserting that his views reflected the dominant mood in the industrial sector:

No one gives a damn. My comrades and I were active participants in the changes, supporting democracy and reforms. . . . But then privatization started, and what happened? The privatized enterprises have actually become the personal property of the bosses. They are ruling the roost as they want. . . . I am a high-skilled fitter, but my pay is miserable—65 to 80 thousand a month [the equivalent of $34 to $42 at the time], even though I have to work eleven hours a day, often including Saturdays. They consider me a skilled worker and say the company needs me, but as soon as I ask for a raise, I hear one thing: "If you don't like it, go away!" The plant's director and his elite get millions and spend vacations with their families only in the Canary Islands. But the money is just not there for the workers! The new masters of property behave as if they had bought it all with their own money. The workers have no rights and are treated like scum. . . . This privatization allows the bosses to plunder resources and assets freely and openly, with no thought of the production and the producers. Of course, this property fell into their hands from the sky for nothing! . . . We do not want to be slaves. Some of us are so mad that they are ready to go and destroy the new bourgeoisie. This is what is breeding a new social explosion—workers have nothing to lose again! (*Izvestia*, April 20, 1994)

Another goal of the privatization program, increased efficiency of production, remained even more elusive than the creation of a large class of new owners. In one of the very few positive assessments of the results of privatization, Joseph Blasi (1994c) reported "considerable evidence" of increased efficiency at state companies which had gone private: two-thirds of the sales of privatized companies were to the private sector, employee rolls were cut by 20 percent, every fifth enterprise was talking with foreign investors about attracting capital, and more than half of the companies surveyed had changed their product lines according to consumer demands. On the other hand, Blasi found the privatized companies starved for capital, operating at significantly reduced levels, and unable to find buyers for their products.

Blasi's account reflected potential increases of efficiency at best; besides, the credibility of his findings was somewhat undercut by the fact that he relied overwhelmingly on interviews with the management of privatized companies, which is obviously a group interested in putting things in the best light possible, especially with an American analyst.

Most other estimates of the efficiency of privatized enterprises, including those coming from the government's supporters, pointed to serious problems (Sutela 1994: 426–428). In a study published in June 1994, the influential Moscow-based Reforma International Foundation, headed by former Gorbachev economic adviser Stanislav Shatalin, charged that the method of mass privatization through vouchers was bound to create inefficiency. Shatalin dismissed the government's claim that the appearance of tens of millions of small shareholders in Russia was a great achievement. Very few of those people were real, responsible owners, he said. First, they had no say in the management of companies whose shares they now owned. Second, as absentee owners, they had no interest in production and cared only for high dividends. Third, their income from shares was in most cases minimal. The Shatalin report charged: "Privatization was guided primarily by political interests of an extremely narrow circle of people, and its results were used by rather small segments of the population. The realization of those interests often ran contrary to the real needs of the national economy and the majority of the population" (*Izvestia*, June 30, 1994).

Mikhail Khodorkovsky, chairman of the board of one of Russia's largest private banks, Menatep, was disappointed to see no sign that Russian private companies were any more productive than state-owned ones: "There is no visible correlation between ownership and efficiency" (*Manchester Guardian Weekly*, August 29, 1993). The Shatalin report similarly concluded that "there is no clear correlation between efficiency and form of property" (*Los Angeles Times*, July 10, 1994). *New York Times* economic observer Peter Passell commented that "privatization . . . seems to be working in the sense that industrial property is being transferred to private hands. But it has yet to make much difference in industrial performance" (*New York Times*, November 11, 1993).

Certainly, it was totally unrealistic to expect overnight changes, especially during a severe economic depression. The slump in production put a blight on all industries. Even consumer goods producers, like the textile industry, which was a pioneer in destatization, starting out as early as 1988, were in very bad shape. Enterprises which were expected to respond most quickly and efficiently to the new market incentives, both because of the nature of their business and because of the transformation they had gone through, were in most cases sinking just as fast as heavy industry, which was still dependent on state subsidies. Even showcase employee-owned firms like Saratov Aviation and Krasny Proletary were in the red.

Of course, the weightiest reasons for the Russian depression were macroeconomic, and they were so weighty that no enterprise, public or private, could be expected to perform well. The whole economic environment became hostile to producers. The government, which Soviet enterprises had traditionally relied upon both as a source of subsidies and a reliable customer, was withdrawing from those roles: instead, it was now slapping them with confiscatory taxes (sometimes exceeding 100 percent of enterprises' profits), bankruptcy proceedings, and other new regulations dictated by "shock therapy." Demolition of the USSR had blown apart the webs of productive and commercial ties between enterprises located in different republics. Hyperinflation reduced overall demand in the economy.

Yet the government's privatization strategy did contribute, at least in the short term, to the decline of Russia's economy. Any restructuring as massive as that was bound to make matters more complicated for producers. Although it heightened the inevitable transition pains in Russia, the government's policy did not even attempt to address the issue of efficiency, even though increased efficiency of production had been proclaimed as one of privatization's major goals.

The privatization program goal of raising funds for the social safety net was not even mentioned in discussions of the program's results. Having opted for speed over income from the sales, the government all but gave up on that goal long ago. All it was able to collect from the sales of state property was about $1 billion (*Los Angeles Times*, July 10, 1994). It was difficult to establish connections between privatization and financial stabilization, another of the program's stated goals. In addition, the goal of attracting foreign investment remained way out of reach: by the summer of 1994, direct foreign investment in Russia amounted to just $2.7 billion, about as much as in Estonia (*Journal of Commerce*, July 5, 1994).

All of those assessments could only be preliminary: too little time had passed since the program's start. What was more significant, the end of mass privatization and the debates around the policies for the next phase helped highlight the main problems the Russian society faced as it was trying to develop a new ownership system.

Characteristically, the neoliberal "shock therapists" were the first to sound a retreat from mass privatization. One of the best-known of them, former Russian finance minister Boris Fyodorov, readily admitted that the mass of new Russian shareholders could hardly qualify as real owners. He wrote in his weekly column:

> The first stage of our privatization had to be ideological because of the scale of the state sector and the need to reform the economy fast. In most cases, the transfer of shares to blue- and white-collar workers and to voucher owners did not and could not lead to changes. If shares are in the hands of people who have neither the knowledge nor the means for investment, it is stupid to expect growth in efficiency. (*Izvestia*, July 1, 1994)

According to Fyodorov, 40 million shareholders was too large a number for Russia. If the United States, with a population twice as large, had only half as many shareholders, then "the optimal number" for Russia should be 10 to 15 million. Thus, to create an efficient economy, Russia now needed to achieve concentration of shares in fewer hands (*Izvestia,* July 1, 1994). That approach was quite consonant with the preferences of the top managers of privatized enterprises. Thus, what was viewed as a key political condition for the success of privatization—giving as many people as possible stakes in the new private ownership system—was now denounced as an obstacle to making the Russian economy productive.

The second stage of Russian privatization, the terms of which were set by President Yeltsin's decree of July 22, 1994, was expressly aimed at reversing the process of mass dispersion of ownership rights which characterized the first stage. As one of the drafters of the new policy put it, its aim was "to make sure that ownership rights acquired during the initial distribution of property are transferred to really responsible owners"—meaning, of course, large private investors at home and abroad (*Finansovye izvestia,* October 4, 1994). This time the main objects of privatization were packages of state-owned shares in privatized enterprises, land used by those enterprises, and other real estate. Having cut off potential mass outside investors through the abolition of vouchers, the government moved against work collectives too. In the original version of the program, unveiled in early July, workers were to be offered a choice: up to 25 percent of nonvoting stock for free or up to 10 percent of voting stock at a 30 percent discount. It was a return to the original Chubais plan of December 1991 in a worsened form; at that time, workers could get both the 25 percent and the 10 percent and not have to choose one or the other. Just as in the spring of 1992, the government had to retreat from so impolitic a posture. The July 22 decree retained the option of worker buyout of a majority of voting stock. But, having kept that option formally available, the government made it meaningless by launching a steep upward revaluation of state assets, thus guaranteeing, as Chubais put it, that "most work collectives will not find the means to buy out 51% of shares at the new prices" (*Finansovye izvestia,* October 4, 1994).

Meanwhile, the rising disappointment over privatization was creating fertile ground for demands for reimposition of state ownership and control. Of course, the real beneficiaries of such a turnaround would primarily be reactionary groups in the managerial class, which would get a partial restoration of the stability of their positions in the economy though at the expense of losing the freedoms they got in recent years.

Since the fall of 1993, a strong authoritarian trend has been developing in Russian politics. The government, the opposition, and all major political forces are competing in appeals to the rising public demand for law and order. The relatively libertarian phase of the Russian democratic revolution, characterized mainly by the destruction of old Soviet institutions, has given way to a phase dominated by the idea of building a new Russian state. The managerial class is reasserting its influence, trying to become the dominant force in that state to keep and increase the economic power it was able to get in the process of privatization.

Two main strategies are open to post-Soviet managers. There is an authoritarian strategy, with which they would attempt to increase their power at workers' expense through an alliance with a strong government which would help managers fend off challenges from below. For Russia, it would be a familiar option, for a similar alliance existed in the country before the 1917 revolution. It is not hard to visualize a situation in which such a top-heavy corporatist regime could produce high social tensions, a stagnant economy, and ugly politics.

Under the other, democratic strategy, managers would not risk alienating the workforce and breeding new revolts, but would rather opt for durable and effective social partnership in the workplace. Whatever the intentions of the policy makers, a new reality has emerged from mass privatization of the Russian industry: formally at least, managers and workers have equal rights as co-owners of the means of production. Instead of trying to destroy that equality in the name of "efficiency," it is necessary to fill it with real content, helping workers become effective co-owners, which is impossible without giving them a significant say in the management of enterprises.

The Russian government should adopt a strong policy aimed at nurturing the sprouts of a new economy which have become embedded in the Russian soil in the past few years. Rather than stall the emergence of a new form of ownership, so well suited to the Russian historical conditions, the government should adopt a set of policies designed to facilitate this process. It should help newly privatized companies obtain credit. It should amend existing laws and draft new legislation to make it easier, not harder, for employees to assume ownership. It should launch educational and technical assistance programs to give newly privatized companies the tools to master the market environment and seek Western assistance for that purpose.

There is a huge potential base for a real democratization of the Russian economy and the introduction of powerful ownership incentives into Russia's economic life. If half-formed worker ownership, which came to Russia mostly by default, first as a largely cosmetic palliative and later as an unwelcome detour from the road to "real" capitalism, is cast aside as yet another failed experiment, Russia will turn away from the one option which contains both democratic and efficient solutions to its post-Communist crisis.

Much like the Bolsheviks in the 1920s who hated small family farms but were forced by the logic of political survival to give the peasantry considerable freedoms, neoliberal reformers had to accept worker ownership, which they considered distasteful but which was imposed on the Russian economy by Russia's real conditions. When the Bolsheviks moved in 1928 to abolish the New Economic Policy in the name of "real" socialism, they touched off a chain of tragic events which resulted in staggering human and material losses felt to this day. One would like to think that seventy years later, Russia's democratically elected leaders have more common sense than their Communist predecessors.

But the crucial factor which will determine the further evolution of the Russian ownership system is the degree to which Russian citizens are prepared to use the political and economic rights they have won. If they organize and teach themselves to use those rights, beginning with the most important arena, their workplaces, they have a chance to become real masters of their country.

4 From State Property to Employee Ownership: The BUTEK Experiment

Valery N. Varvarov

◆ THE only large-scale experiment with privatization and employee ownership prior to the mass privatization in the Russian Federation that began in 1992–93 was the Entrepreneurial Association BUTEK. BUTEK was formed in August 1989 and given special governmental sanction in January 1990. Within eighteen months, BUTEK grew to encompass more than four hundred companies, including sixty-six state enterprises which had successfully privatized.

BUTEK was a working experiment, developing in practice ideas which otherwise existed only in theory in the Soviet Union of 1990. This gave it some of the characteristics of trying to build a new airplane in dozens of different locations simultaneously without having any blueprints. It also meant that the BUTEK experience provides a wealth of concrete, empirical evidence about the role of employee ownership in the emerging Russian economy.

BUTEK was created in the context of a debate about the experience of the Soviet Union in the 1920s and its relevance to economic reform. During the New Economic Policy (NEP), the appearance of an ownership class among the people was the most important factor in economic growth. The transition of state enterprises to self-accounting ones—permitting commercial activities and trade freedom—during the NEP made it possible to increase employees' economic motivation and contributed to the rapid growth of output and labor productivity. Further, the transition from state to leasing enterprises in this period[1] increased the number of profitable enterprises. However, these positive changes created conflicts between the growing entrepreneurial market sector of the economy and the central planning system. In the 1920s this conflict caused the shrinkage and eventual dismantling of the NEP. A similar conflict caused the failure of the economic reform undertaken four decades later in 1965. (See Bob Clawson's discussion of the Kosygin reforms of 1965 in Chapter 2.)

Perestroika initiated a new era of political and economic life beginning in 1985. Reexamination of the NEP experience helped to restore forgotten forms of economic activity, such as reviving the idea of leased enterprises, and it paved the road for new ones. The leasing enterprises' success led to the passage of the Soviet Union's Law on Leasing in December 1989. Article 10 of this law provided for an eventual employee purchase of the assets that they were leasing when that would be permitted. The funds for the buyout could be generated from any available funds at the leased enterprise. After the buyout, according to the employees' decision, the enterprise could be reorganized into a collective enterprise, a cooperative, a joint-stock company, or any other form that operated on the basis of employee ownership.

BUTEK went beyond leasing as it existed in 1989–90 to create a mechanism for full private ownership of enterprises by employees. While BUTEK never lived up to the aspirations of its founders, who hoped that thousands of enterprises would join the Association and, in the words of Mikhail Alexandrovich Bocharov, "explode the planned economy from the inside," it deserves our close attention as the primary source of empirical experience with both privatization and employee ownership before mass privatization became the policy of the Russian Federation.

THE FOUNDATION OF THE BUTEK ASSOCIATION

BUTEK's origin can be traced to the initiator of leasing, the director of the Butovsky concern, Mikhail Alexandrovich Bocharov. Butovsky, which produced construction materials, was leased by its employees with the help of leasing's pioneer, Valery M. Rutgaizer, in 1988 as the first leased enterprise in the Moscow region. While the combine was previously unprofitable, under leasing the enterprise started to earn a profit. It increased salaries for employees, and it enriched its social programs. Based on Bocharov's initiative, several enterprises formed the Entrepreneurial Association BUTEK[2] in August 1989. Bocharov became people's deputy of the USSR and a member of the Supreme Soviet of the USSR in 1989; in 1990 he also became people's deputy of the Russian Federation. He used his legislative positions to push for economic reform.

BUTEK was established as a voluntary, nonministerial, multi-industry association of firms and enterprises based on employee ownership; in the event of BUTEK's dissolution, its property would have been distributed among its member enterprises. The Association was a legal entity with independent bank accounts and its own seal. The executive body of the Association operated on a non-profit basis in compliance with the pro forma statements approved by BUTEK's board of directors.[3] It carried out joint operational activities for its members, voluntarily centralizing such functions as scientific, technological, industrial, and social development. It also centralized certain investment, financial, foreign trade, and other activities.

The Association's primary goal was to develop further cooperation among enterprises on the basis of mutually negotiated contracts within the framework of BUTEK. To reach this goal, BUTEK sought to create the principles and mechanisms for the collective ownership at the enterprise level; to determine the conditions for enterprises to emerge from under the subordination of branch and government departments; to develop funds for state property buyouts; and to finance and develop a new infrastructure (including a commercial bank, auditing center, insurance company, trading house, and a consulting and learning center) to support BUTEK firms.

BUTEK was designed as a centralized—but nongovernmental—umbrella under which gradual change from the state-owned command economy to a collectively owned market economy could take place. In exchange for the fee of 1 percent of cost-accounting income that joining BUTEK entailed, BUTEK enterprises received the right to make that transition; advice on the appointment of management; and consulting on business development, creating networks among enterprises, and access to the international market. Its founders saw BUTEK as a kind of tunnel that would channel ownership from state to private hands.

The Association initially consisted of twenty-five enterprises, including Butovsky, from different branches of the economy and located in different regions of the country which chose to affiliate with BUTEK. These firms varied in ownership status and included state-owned, cooperative, leased, and other forms of enterprises and organizations. The prerequisite for a state-owned enterprise to join BUTEK, however, was a formal decision by the employees to purchase the enterprise; the sources of funds for the purchase had to be specified as well. The final decision to allow an enterprise to join the Association was made by the BUTEK board of directors. BUTEK member enterprises preserved their rights as legal entities despite membership in the Association and could withdraw from the Association upon a decision of the collective meeting of the employees.

Each BUTEK member enterprise had the right to determine independently the direction of its operational activities; to submit competitive bids for direct state orders; to locate its own wholesale suppliers; to establish direct links with the centralized supply of the material resources within the framework of the state order system; and to establish prices for its goods and services within the general framework of the state order system.

BUTEK helped to facilitate privatization. When the employees purchased the enterprise from the state, its shares could be distributed among the employees, transforming collective property into employee ownership. BUTEK's idea of employee ownership was adapted from the rich experience in the United States and some other countries where the efficiency of employee ownership had been proven. The enterprises in the USSR that were employee owned had to operate in the quasi-market-oriented environment created uniquely for them by the government's tax system, new forms of external economic activity, and a credit-financial system.

In October 1989, in order to work out the principles for a transition from state property to collectively owned enterprises with nongovernmental status, the State Commission for Economic Reform advised carrying out the BUTEK experiment before the Supreme Soviet adopted and the government implemented laws on property, taxes, leaseholding, and the other normative documents for developing economic reform. The commission emphasized the need for determining the principles of collective property during the purchase of the means of production from the state. It also stressed the necessity of defining the constraints for an enterprise functioning with collective property, such as employees' attitudes toward ownership and their rights and responsibilities when they leave the company or when the firm closes.

The commission's recommendation became the basis for the resolution of the USSR Council of Ministers "About the Economic Experiment in the BUTEK Association" (No. 77, January 25, 1990). This resolution and its accompanying provisions established the parameters for BUTEK's operation as an experiment in privatization. The intent of the experiment, in the words of the resolution, was "to develop a mechanism to move from state-owned enterprises to a collective form of property . . . within the system of socialist production relations."

State enterprises and organizations could join BUTEK after their assets were purchased from the state by the employees as collective property.[4] This permitted enterprises to escape their subordination to the branch and state administrative bodies and allowed them to act within the implementation regulations that were ratified by the same proposition of the government.

The resolution created a special tax system and tax privileges for BUTEK members. In a move that was very important in the economic situation in 1990, it also provided for greater flexibility in hard-currency transactions before the issuance of the general legislative acts. It granted the commercial bank (Kredobank) established by the BUTEK Association the right to accumulate hard currency funds and to undertake transactions with them with the guarantee of the Association and within the limits established by the State Bank of the USSR. In practice, these privileges applied only during 1990.

When the government resolution was published, new applications to enter the BUTEK Association started to arrive from state enterprises, cooperatives, leased enterprises, and new businesses. In the beginning of 1989, a confectionery factory in the town of Ribinsk became the first state enterprise to carry out an employee buyout of state property; it had 550 employees. By the end of July 1990, 202 enterprises had joined BUTEK. Most of them were cooperatives and other newly organized forms of business based on the principles of employee ownership that sought the protection of the BUTEK umbrella and its tax advantages. However, thirty state enterprises whose employees were ready to purchase their companies had also joined the Association.[5]

In all, by the end of December 1990, 425 new members had joined BUTEK. The annual sales of these firms totaled more than 2.8 billion rubles; they employed approximately seventy thousand people. Of this group, 136 were state enterprises; 57 of these had already privatized their companies. Unfortunately, while the idea of employee ownership attracted people, the absence of government support (addressed below) led to employee ownership on a less significant scale than had been hoped.

The process of developing employee ownership at the enterprises that joined BUTEK was based on collective ownership within what were called "people's enterprises." The concept of people's enterprise covered a variety of legal forms which shared certain common characteristics: (1) they were not state owned, (2) they followed BUTEK regulations, and (3) their ownership was to be subdivided among their employees. In theory, their property was supposed to be "collectively divided," but what this meant in practice was unclear to everyone, in part because what private ownership meant was unclear. The main feature of collective property during the initial stage was the purchase of the enterprise's assets from the state through a non-joint-stock form of ownership. The transaction could utilize a variety of financing sources (bank debts, the income from operations, or employees' personal funds). Later, as the enterprise operated, additional collective property was developed through new construction, expansion, reconstruction, and technical reequipment of production facilities; the creation of intellectual property; and the acquisition of new fixed assets, securities, and other assets through the expenditure of personal, collective, and/or borrowed funds.

BUTEK provided its member enterprises with a variety of services to support the successful development of employee ownership. These included providing training seminars for managers and board members, adapting the lessons of world experience with employee ownership to Russian circumstances, and developing a variety of printed materials and manuals.

In 1990, the BUTEK Association organized several two-day seminars to examine initiating and developing employee ownership. Approximately three hundred managers and members of the boards of directors of BUTEK firms took part in them. Seminars for BUTEK managers and personnel continued during 1991–92 with American employee ownership experts in an effort to learn from the American experience and adapt it to the Russian environment.[6] The American emphasis on long-run goals—contrary to Russian short-run measures—was persuasive in changing ingrained attitudes, although Russian conservatism in attitudes makes that a long process. Different forms of social-psychological training, computer and foreign language education, marketing seminars, and foreign partnership classes were also held.

The conversion of state enterprises to employee-owned ones required the development of informational and advisory materials. They were developed on the basis of the BUTEK Statute, the implementation regulations in the resolution "About the Economic Experiment in the BUTEK Association," and the Statute of the Standard Enterprise. The regulations for joining and leaving BUTEK, advisory materials on the mechanism of development and distribution of the property to the account of each employee, the contract system of employment, and other materials were prepared.

In retrospect, it is striking how vague were our ideas about employee ownership that were recorded in those initial BUTEK materials. A representative survey of thirty enterprises in 1991 revealed that the BUTEK members were looking for new materials and that a great number of those that had been prepared had already lost their immediacy. The transition of the Soviet economy to a market economy and the very energetic activity of the USSR Parliament, as well as the Russian Parliament, intervened in the economic and social life of the country and certainly contributed to the rapid obsolescence of published materials.

BUTEK'S PRIVATIZATION IN PRACTICE

In April 1991, the BUTEK Association conducted a survey of the sixty-six former state enterprises which by that point in time had been bought by their employees within the BUTEK framework. The survey addressed how state property had been purchased, whether and how ownership was subsequently distributed, what the empirical process and problems had been, and how the enterprises were organized including hiring, dividends, accounting practices, and relation to the state budget.[7]

Underlying the survey was our interest in determining how the totally new concept of privatization was actually working in practice.

Why Join BUTEK?

For the thirty BUTEK enterprises responding to the survey, the primary incentive to join the Association was to get economic independence and to escape subordination to a ministry or other state structures. The privileges of the BUTEK tax system and the possibility to determine independently the most profitable structure of income distribution were also attractive. The latter feature permitted management to encourage employees' interest in current and future operational results by salary increases and by the improvement of social benefits. This allowed BUTEK members to avoid the outflow of qualified labor that characterized state enterprises in the period.

The member enterprises also hoped for help from the Association in providing materials and technical support; in organizing foreign trade; and in acquiring methodology and information about personnel training and about the new forms of property development.

Redistributing State Property among Employees

There was no single technique of property distribution which might have been acceptable to all BUTEK enterprises, and the employees and managers understood this. Each enterprise had to go its own way to develop its process, taking into account its own complexity and problems. This required time and an efficient sharing of experience.

The collective property of the enterprise was derived from five sources. The first was the purchase of enterprise assets, funded by the enterprise's profits from operational activities, loans, and employees' personal funds. Second, outdated fixed assets were handed over free of charge by the state or by public organizations to the members of the Association. Third, new construction, expansion, reconstruction, and technological reequipment of the production facilities became the property of the work collective. Fourth, additional fixed assets, securities, and other property acquired through the enterprise's financial sources were part of the collective property. The fifth source was the creation of intellectual property (know-how).

The amount to be paid by the work collective was the residual asset value of the state property as determined by a commission headed by a representative from the local financial authorities. Based on this estimate, the local financial authorities issued a special ownership document to the work collective.

Developing a mechanism for property distribution was not easy. Some enterprises (for instance, the Moscow Wood Processing Equipment Plant and the Krasny Stroitel factory) initially took a "sit tight" position on property distribution because of the uncertainty of the BUTEK experiment and the limited time the tax privileges were valid. Tax issues complicated the financial position of the enterprises, especially those which had borrowed for the purchase, and that too had an effect on the principles for property distribution.

The division of collective ownership was carried out by distribution of the value of a part of collective property to the individual employees' accounts. There were two questions generated by this distribution: (1) what part of the collective property will be distributed? and (2) what should the criteria be for distributing property to individual employees?

Property that was to remain collective could not be allocated to individuals; it remained the property of the firm's employees collectively. It was prohibited to distribute individually the part of the property that was purchased with the enterprise's development fund, the production expansion fund, the research and development (R & D) fund, or depreciation deductions, or the part of the property that was handed over without charge to the enterprise's employees by the state or social organizations. However, both the purchase price and future retained earnings could be allocated to individual accounts. When the property was purchased with borrowed money, only the value of the part of the debt which had been repaid was distributed to individual accounts.

Depending on the individual firm, the criteria for distribution to individual employees could include salary, length of service, or individual contribution. In retrospect, it seems to have been more an ad hoc–almost haphazard–process than a systematic one. Often the approaches to distributing the initial value (the value of state property which had been purchased) and the value created in the process of operating the employee-owned enterprise were different. In addition, there were differences in the property conversion process between newly created enterprises and those that already functioned with some kind of collective property within BUTEK. The procedure for property distribution and the exact number of shares belonging to each worker (the share fund) were approved by the general meeting (conference) of the employees. Subsequently the ownership rights of each employee were usually legalized either through the order of the general director or the written decision of the general employees' meeting.[8]

By the end of 1990, almost 40 percent of all BUTEK enterprises which had bought their assets from the state had distributed the value of the property purchased to individual employee accounts. The practice of property distribution and the analyses of the employee general meeting documents showed that about half of them considered it fair to set account values in proportion to the salaries received. A quarter of them took into account mixed criteria including salary, length of service, and employees' personal investment. In the rare cases where enterprises were bought entirely with employee contributions, property was distributed among the employees individually according to their personal contributions. Retirees who had worked for leased enterprises were also eligible to receive their shares of that enterprise's property when the enterprise was privatized.

BUTEK firms generally also provided an additional ownership share for management. More than 60 percent of the BUTEK enterprises surveyed issued additional shares to the senior managers according to their contribution to and length of service at the enterprise.

If a worker decided to leave a BUTEK company, he was paid in cash for his personal share in the enterprise property, and he had no claim against the collective portion. The compensation procedure was also established by the general meeting (conference) of the employees. All types of an employee's individual income (including the annual dividends [payments through the share funds], the hard-currency deposits on the personal accounts, and the compensations paid for the property share) were subject to taxation under the special progressive scale when the total income exceeded a fixed monthly amount.

Practical Problems of Ownership

Ownership implies control and financial risks and rewards. BUTEK firms struggled with both these issues. They also had to deal with how to hire and fire employee-owners and managers.

In answering the question of how to allocate control rights among their new owners, 80 percent of the BUTEK enterprises that had not paid off the initial loan to purchase the property established the principle of voting at the employees' general meeting on the basis of "one employee, one vote." On the other hand, the enterprises that had repaid their debt established the principle of "one 'share,'[9] one vote." Management was far less concerned with the practicalities of democratic voting systems than with escaping from ministerial control, and often made pretensions of democracy without it having much reality. Changes in management in BUTEK enterprises were initially superficial: the old managers and Communist leadership stayed in place. But over time, that changed and in some cases managers who found themselves at loggerheads with employees ended up being replaced.

BUTEK enterprises solved the practical problems of paying dividends in several ways. Some of them decided not to pay dividends while the enterprise was in the process of formation and had borrowed money for the purchase of assets from the state. Others chose a dividend policy based on fixed rates from the future income flow. A third group of enterprises considered payment of dividends reasonable only when the enterprise operated efficiently and when it could pay dividends from the actual excess over the planned income.

In general, dividends were paid only after meeting debt-service requirements. The amount of dividends and frequency of payment were established by the decision of the general employees' meeting. Thus, twenty of the thirty enterprises which responded to the survey paid dividends according to the annual results; three enterprises paid dividends based on semiannual results; three enterprises paid dividends each quarter; only one enterprise proposed to pay dividends monthly; and three paid no dividends. The main reason for not paying the dividends in 1991 was the restriction on the salaries fund and the consumption fund. Some enterprises that used the enterprise profits and employees' personal funds for the buyout were not planning to pay dividends in the near future. They invested them in fixed assets instead (for example, the board of directors of Moscow Amusements invested in amusement parks). About half of the enterprises planned to pay dividends only after paying back the debts.

The transition to employee ownership demonstrated the necessity of developing new forms of work relations. Part of that change was to hire management and administrative personnel, and often workers as well, on a contractual basis. Half the BUTEK enterprises in the survey signed contracts with all personnel. Forty percent of enterprises signed contracts with the managers, the engineering and technical workers, and the office workers. In one enterprise in ten, only the general director was hired on contract.

Usually, contracts with the director and senior management were signed for five years, and only in some cases were they signed for a shorter period (the minimum period was one year). The contracts with workers were signed generally for three to five years, but there were examples of contracts for one year as well. The main difficulties that limited the period of a contract were associated with defining responsibilities, duties, and work requirements. However, from a contractual standpoint, being an owner did not mean any additional rights or advantages in case an employee was in danger of being fired. (When leased enterprises were purchased, layoffs very seldom took place, but when state enterprises were bought out, layoffs frequently occurred, and unemployment started to be a problem.)

An employee at an employee-owned enterprise is both an owner and an employee simultaneously. His rights as an owner do not protect him as an employee. In the BUTEK experiment, employee rights were protected by Soviet and Russian labor law, and this law was obviously outdated.

Besides establishing a guaranteed minimum salary, maximum hours, and minimum retirement pension, labor law needs to protect an employee in the contract system of employment as well. Similarly, the trade union's role and objectives needed to be restated in BUTEK enterprises. Some eliminated trade unions. In others labor unions remained partially as a vehicle for protecting the employees' interests against the management's. Moreover, due to a variety of reasons there will always be a group of employees who are not owners. This group needs protection by an institution that represents their interests. "Modern" legislative protection of employees' interests and the wide range of social problems arising from economic reform obviously leave a significant function for trade union activities at employee-owned enterprises. The BUTEK experience already has demonstrated that.

Administrative and Financial Problems in Buyouts

Only a limited number of state enterprises—sixty-six—were purchased as collective employee property in BUTEK. Despite the fact that the resolution of the Council of Ministers "About the Economic Experiment in the BUTEK Association" was adopted in January 1990, the first state enterprises were bought only in July and August 1990. Why?

This is explained by several factors. First, the Finance Ministry of the USSR did not establish the requirements, procedures, and regulations for purchasing state property until July 1990, occasioning a delay of five months in starting the process. Even so, some legal questions remained unclear.

For instance, the regulation for debiting the retained earnings and working capital was vague. It was unclear what value should be assigned to working capital for purchase: should its value be imputed by a formula or calculated as an actual value? Local financial authorities took advantage of this lack of clarity when setting the enterprise's price for purchase, and this often made an employee purchase more difficult and sometimes impossible.

Moreover, there were difficulties in dividing the purchase price paid among the state and the local budgets. The bottleneck in the purchase procedure was the relationship between an enterprise and different state authorities. The lack of clarity in determining each entity's rights and authority was a problem. In addition, there was no legal requirement for the enterprise being purchased to ask for authorization at higher levels, but there was a list of enterprises that were excluded from possible purchase because of the Law on Leasing. Consequently, the local authorities sometimes abused the law, finding ways to limit the purchase of state enterprises or even to make it very complex. That was repeatedly confirmed by the BUTEK experience.

The reason for making employee buyouts difficult was not only the bureaucratic fear of losing power, but also the absence of concrete economic benefits. The proceeds from the purchase were received by the state or local budgets. Moreover, an employee purchase of a leased enterprise was even more unprofitable for the higher organization that had leased the enterprise to its work collective: the higher organization lost the payments that it had previously received from renting the assets of the enterprise to the employees.[10] Therefore, the rights of leased enterprises and state enterprises were unequal during a buyout. The latter, unlike the former, could be bought without the involvement of higher authorities.

The relations between the enterprise and the local authorities were equivocally developed in the buyout process. Generally, the local administrative authorities supported the purchase of state enterprises and their conversion to the collective form of property when they dealt with enterprises of "nonlocal" subordination. But most BUTEK enterprises were owned by local governmental units, not by the Soviet Union; and with the decline of central authority, local authorities thought they could ignore Union regulations.

In particular, BUTEK enterprises had problems with the local financial authorities, who often did not care for BUTEK's tax system and demanded additional taxes; for instance, they taxed the incremental value of the labor compensation fund, the company's funds set aside for paying salaries and wages. (Unsympathetic local authorities could thereby limit wage increases.) Both the imperfection of the legislative acts on enterprise buyouts (among them, the normative acts that dealt with BUTEK as well) and the disregard of the government resolutions on the experiment at the Association were "brakes" that restricted the buyout process.

Another serious problem was the source of financing.[11] According to the regulations, the enterprise could solicit employees' personal funds or use bank debts for the purchase in case the enterprise did not have enough of its own funds to accomplish the buyout. Bank credits were acquired from some state banks (Jilsotsbank, Agroprombank, and Promstroybank) for that purpose, with the BUTEK Association guaranteeing the loans.

Commercial borrowing was rarely used. Only two firms obtained credits from commercial or cooperative banks because of the high interest rates they charged. (The commercial bank Kredobank which was created by the members of the BUTEK Association was not much help because the interest rates at this bank were no lower than those in other commercial banks; BUTEK's bank engaged in its own commercial activities instead.) Three enterprises used loans from other firms, social organizations, or cooperatives; usually, these creditors were interested in the operation of that enterprise. Two enterprises acquired assets exclusively at the expense of the employees' personal funds.

Worker Participation and Management

Worker participation in management was not a new idea at all for the former socialistic state enterprises. In the command economy, activating the employees was the backbone of success. However, experience showed that usually this activation was limited to the employees' own work or, even in the best case, did not go outside the production department. To speak about taking into account a worker's interests in solving the main problems of enterprise development (such as electing leaders, determining the principles of solving ownership problems, or discussing alternative uses for personal savings funds in enterprise financing) was idealism—or conscious illusion.

The new concepts of full freedom from the traditional dictates of ministries or industrial branch administrative authorities and of employee-owners having a role in the enterprise management stimulated the workers' activities. Too frequently, however, this freedom was treated as an unlimited right either to oppose the management in solving problems or to complicate the solution of problems. That might have been because of lack of competence or simple inexperience. In any case, the external form of production democracy was not enforced by the strict internal delineation of the rights and responsibilities of worker-owners.

The fundamental change of ownership relations and employees' motivations caused the appearance of a new structure of management in the BUTEK enterprises. The highest authority at most enterprises became the annual general employees' meeting. It elected the board of directors to act in the period between the annual meetings.

While democratic in theory, this system was not always democratic in practice. On most boards, the general director chaired the board, managers dominated the proceedings, and adequate employee representation was simply not guaranteed. Sometimes that negatively influenced the results of an enterprise's operations. It could also lead to conflicts between employees and managers. (For example, the Moscow enterprise Mosorgtekhnika faced such a situation in 1991, a year after it had carried out its buyout that led the board to replace the management.) There were no "external members" on the board of directors ("external members" means representatives from banks, suppliers, customers, lawyers, experts in employee ownership, or others not employed by the enterprise) in BUTEK firms. Such external members might have promoted more objectivity at the board meetings.

At the initial stage, many enterprises faced the problem of coordinating the rights of the board of directors as the "legislative institution" with those of the managers. It seemed to be the hardest problem, and in some cases it was insoluble. Employees' skepticism toward ownership was based on mismanagement by the board of directors and executives. Yet the employees' annual meeting had the right to select both board and management. Each enterprise and its employees had to work through that contradiction to find forms and methods to resolve it.

At the same time, the managers often continued their old behavior (i.e., to act only on orders). The regulations needed for the new environment were absent. Under these circumstances, when management tried to base its decisions on advanced managerial methods, the result was often mismanagement and generally decreased work efficiency even in comparison with the previous level.

No matter what the company structure, during the first years of the development of employee ownership, the role of the top manager was crucial. In most cases—50 to 60 percent of the companies—the general director was simultaneously president of the board of directors and chief executive officer. The ability of the leader to combine these two functions successfully was determined by his attitude toward democratic leadership. The accessibility of the manager, his willingness to listen to the employees' suggestions, and his ability to let them feel that they had been heard were all factors that created a positive and healthy work environment.

These problems underscored the necessity to develop a culture of ownership and encouraged recognizing the potential efficiency that employee ownership offered. That included simultaneously activating shop-floor employees' interests in the enterprise's ultimate financial results and enforcing their responsibility for production and decisions. That was not a substitute, however, for the professional management function; well-trained managers must still be responsible for the operations and results and must have the appropriate rights to accomplish these tasks.

Over time, the psychological climate inside the BUTEK work collectives and the relations between managers and employees started to change. Primarily that was due to the greater availability of economic and financial information to the employees. Similarly, the management structure developed toward more rational systems, emphasizing managerial structures that dealt with the total quality, distribution, marketing, and finance. Overall, a reduction in the number of managers and an increase of their informational and technical equipment level (e.g., the use of personal computers) were observed. Personnel administration, retraining, and educational departments grew in importance.

Government Support

The BUTEK experience indicated that other financial support mechanisms should have been created to facilitate purchases of state enterprises. Government loan guarantees, privileged state credits, or tax privileges for commercial banks which made loans for employee purchase of state enterprises would have been useful. Tax privileges for enterprises in repaying debt would also have been helpful, such as excluding principal payments for the purchase of state property from the enterprise's taxable income.

The accumulated experience of the system of Employee Stock Ownership Plans (ESOPs) in the United States suggested that the purchase of the state enterprises by employees would be financially beneficial to the state through the improved economic performance of firms. Moreover, in the Russian case, the state budget received part of the proceeds of the sale in addition to the taxes paid. Nevertheless, the state did not encourage the buyouts by providing either tax benefits or lower interest rates.

Once BUTEK firms got over the purchasing hurdle, however, the tax law for the Association members in 1990 did provide significant stimulation for certain uses of enterprise funds (Figure 4.1). The principle of separate taxation based on end use of the enterprise's earned income stated that the tax rates for the employees' personal consumption fund and for the production development fund had to be different. The tax rates on the R & D, social, and production development funds were therefore considerably lower than the rate on the consumption fund (in the BUTEK experiment they were 8 percent and 17 percent, respectively). Furthermore, an enterprise could apply for additional privileges when it paid its corporate taxes. If the enterprise produced or processed agricultural products an 80 percent tax discount could be applied, and if the enterprise produced consumer goods and public services a 50 percent tax discount could be applied. The members of the Association paid 40 percent of their tax payments to the state budget and 60 percent to the budget of the city or the region. Net profits remained at the enterprise and could be used for dividends.

Hard-currency earnings were subject to separate tax rules. Ten percent of all hard-currency inflows from export operations were payable to the state budget; 5 percent of hard-currency inflows were payable to the Executive Committee of the municipal or regional Soviet of People's Deputies. BUTEK members had to spend at least 70 percent of the remaining hard-currency profits on further production and social development, and this sum formed part of the indivisible employee collective property. The rest of the hard-currency profit (up to 30 percent) could be distributed among the employees, deposited in the employees' personal hard-currency accounts, or used under the Law on Noncash Operations to buy imported goods for the employees or to pay their tourist expenses abroad.

Overall, this tax system provided some real benefits to BUTEK enterprises in comparison to the conventional tax system, provided the enter-

Figure 4.1
The Tax System for BUTEK Enterprises in 1990

Sales

Less: Cost of materials and similar expenses
Payment of interest on debt

Taxable income

Less: Taxes—which varied with use of funds

| Portion of gross income spent on capital investment, production development, and social budget | Remaining part of the income (including wages and salaries) |

Tax rate: 8% —— 17%

tax payments

40% to state   60% to local
budget   budget

Equals: Cost-accounting income

Thereof a fee of 1% was paid to finance
the BUTEK Association

Tax breaks on BUTEK enterprises' income

Production and processing of agricultural products	80%
Production of consumer goods and services	50%

Income in hard currency

To the state budget	To the local budget	To the BUTEK Association
10%	5%	1%

prise did not allocate more than 62 percent of gross income to the consumption fund. Moreover, the principle of higher taxation on spending for wages than for capital improvements made the long-term investment of earned income more attractive to employees. The collective ownership institution strengthened this incentive because all owners could determine the division between consumed and accumulated parts of income. The owners could distribute wages into the share funds, and that increased the total share of income accumulation. That is why, if the mechanism of collective ownership had operated in full strength, the tax system used in the BUTEK experiment might have had a significant impact.

EVALUATING THE BUTEK EXPERIENCE WITH EMPLOYEE OWNERSHIP

Although BUTEK continues to exist and provides some services on a commercial basis, its days as an economic experiment ended in 1991. Its privatization privileges expired at the end of 1990; the review and possible extension that were to have occurred were lost in the struggle between the Russian Federation and the USSR. The crash program of mass privatization through voucher sales has sped past BUTEK's program of gradual employee purchase of enterprises. BUTEK enterprises have been required to change their legal status to conform with current laws. Still, the BUTEK experience is instructive.

The BUTEK experience argues strongly that 100 percent employee ownership is efficient in the Russian context. BUTEK operations led to profit growth, rapid diversification, emphasis on quality and customers' needs, improvement of employees' material conditions, their social protection, and considerable changes in their attitudes toward work. The experience disproved the main arguments of opponents that Russian employee-owners have no ability and are not interested in efficient, profitable operation and that they are interested only in "eating up" (consuming) their capital. Spot checks of some BUTEK enterprises showed that they did not increase their spending on personal consumption; indeed they decreased it in comparison to the consumption fund formed before the transition to collective ownership.

Thus in retrospect, the results of employee ownership at the BUTEK enterprises must generally be evaluated positively. The scale, variety of production, and range of branches of the economy where the effectiveness of private ownership was proved all contribute to this positive evaluation. The base of BUTEK's success was governmental support of privatization, as well as the use of world (especially American) experience, adapted to the Russian (earlier to the Soviet) conditions. BUTEK drew on the experience of some leading programs which have supported employee ownership in the United States, and they contributed foreign experts' practical assistance in the analysis and development of the recommendations for Russian enterprises converted to employee ownership. The existence of a special department in BUTEK's administration which concentrated on the development of employee ownership through scientific-methodological and informational support was also helpful.

At the same time, BUTEK's experience in the new market conditions showed that the development of a new culture of ownership is a prolonged process that requires constant efforts, attention, and support. Moreover, a lot of problems were revealed. Solving them will foster a more in-depth development of employee ownership. It will help us also to solve the problems connected to the creation of an economic environment that will promote this ownership form. The following points might be mentioned as a program of action:

1. Creation of a legislative and normative basis to support employee ownership. Experience demonstrates that this can be achieved through developing and adopting interrelated legislative acts and making changes in the existing ones.

2. Organizational support for the program. The collaboration of all structural entities that support the idea of employee ownership is helpful. Creating joint scientific, methodological, and consulting centers and coordinating joint operations are required. Difference in methodology and "friendly competition" among centers must not prevent joint efforts from reaching joint objectives. Financial support is also extremely important. The interested parties should support joint projects.

3. Methodological support for employee ownership. This includes development of the privatization concept; consideration and analysis of the foreign and Russian experience with privatization through employee ownership; methodological and practical help for privatized enterprises (economic and legislative consulting, management and personnel retraining, etc.); and publicity for employee ownership (an informative advertisement of the different employee ownership forms through the mass media, revealing the problems that arise during the privatization and after it; the criticism of those who have misrepresented the essence of the employee ownership idea; the creation of a parliamentary lobby; and the like).

4. Preparation of training materials and recommendations. The list of materials needed today includes those on developing business plans; the modern systems of finance and accounting; the organization of marketing research; the regulation of income distribution to the consumption funds and the rules of accumulation on main accounts (e.g., taxes, investment, salary, dividends); the recommendations of property shares (stock) distribution and reimbursement of employees for their shares of ownership in case they leave the enterprise; the educational programs and retraining of different personnel categories; and the role and functions of labor unions at the enterprises.

When the governmental support for BUTEK reflected in the Council of Ministers' resolution of January 1990 was suspended in 1991, the future development of employee ownership in the newly privatized enterprises became problematic. Subsequently, most BUTEK enterprises that had borrowed money for acquiring fixed assets had a difficult time getting the BUTEK tax privileges under the general tax system. That limited their success in operations. The high tax rate on their profits and the taxing of profits spent on repaying debts created barriers to finding funds for capital improvements; those practices also limited the ability of the enterprises to establish appropriate salary levels for employees.

Yet the BUTEK enterprises all survived, albeit some did so only with difficulty. Quite a few were highly successful, not least because their managers were energetic and had a taste for innovation. Many were liberals, educated during the thaw in the 1970s. BUTEK gave them the freedom to experiment.

Paradoxically, the BUTEK experiment had no discernible impact on the subsequent privatization debate, despite the intentions of the State Committee for Economic Reform. (Indeed, Bocharov's active political stance created a negative reaction among members of Parliament. He had predicted that thousands of enterprises would join BUTEK; instead they were numbered in scores.) Instead, subsequent privatization laws ignored BUTEK's experience and started from scratch. Most fundamentally, while BUTEK's privatization transferred property from the state to employees against compensation, subsequent privatization has been premised on the free distribution of privatization vouchers.

As the debates in Parliament on the state program of privatization for 1992 indicated, some of the deputies and the new leaders of Parliament attached limited importance to employee ownership. Hence, the state support needed for developing employee ownership was more restricted than in the framework of the ESOP program in the United States. The State Property Committee, which was to carry out privatization, demonstrated considerable hostility toward employee ownership in this period. The establishment of the auction pricing system, the absence of privileged credits and tax breaks, the restricted ability to use "vouchers," and the consequences of the liberalization of prices led in practice to a virtual cessation of privatization through employee ownership between March 1991 and the latter part of 1992.

The only possible route for further development of employee ownership in this period was in leased enterprises where the lease contract provided clear requirements for the purchase of ownership. Only these enterprises could accomplish the buyout of the enterprise's property without an auction or competitive examination and could establish closed joint-stock companies. The problems of granting privileged credits or installment payments, however, were not even mentioned.

Today, when Russia is carrying out the hard search for ways of transition to a market economy, the BUTEK experience suggests that employee ownership has huge potential. It can serve as the historical chance for the "postcentralized" Russian economy. The combination of "democratic" privatization and the "voucher" mechanism can contribute to the success of privatization. Employee ownership has the demonstrated ability to reorient the economy toward the market in an effective way, to develop an employee psychology of ownership, to increase the efficiency of enterprises and the economy as a whole, and to encourage social stability and democratic development.

NOTES

1. There were around four thousand leased enterprises at the end of 1922.

2. The abbreviation BUTEK combines the name of the firm initiating the lease movement (Butovsky combine) and the Russian acronym of the slogan of the Association—*Budushchee tovarnoi ekonomiki*, rendered in English as "the future of the market economy."

3. Later, in July 1990, an amendment to the BUTEK Statute permitted the Association's management to undertake commercial activities. From the viewpoint of this author, who participated in preparing the Council of Ministers' original resolution, the amendment created a possible conflict of interest if the managers became involved in activities other than creating employee property. This problem led to creating the nonprofit Privatization and Enterprise Reform program within the framework of Russia's Economic Reform Foundation to support the development of employee-owned firms. This program was designed to widen the network of enterprises beyond those in BUTEK and to create opportunities to receive consulting and technical support from foreign experts and managers.

4. The term *collective property* means private property that is under the joint management of employees. It is important to stress that this form of ownership was unacceptable for critics from both the right and the left in the Soviet debate of the time. The right wing attacked this type of ownership as private ownership of the means of production; during 1989–90, that wing met a strong rebuff from the so-called "social regulated market" group. The left saw it as a new form of communism; left critics speculatively claimed that "the new 'industrial kolkhozes' are obviously inefficient" and reminded their opponents of the Yugoslavian experience. However, they never mentioned the fact that there had never been any form of private property in *kolkhozes* (collective farms).

5. There were a total of thirty buyouts of state enterprises through October 1990, fifty-seven through the end of 1990, and sixty-six through April 1991. Hereafter, because of the termination of key privileges (e.g., purchase at residual value and tax breaks), entrance to BUTEK was suspended. However, the process of conversion to employee ownership continued to develop outside BUTEK. At the end of 1991, the number of enterprises converted to employee ownership in Russia was close to two hundred. The authorization in practically every case was made on the level of the USSR government (e.g., for Saratov Aviation) or, later, of the Russian Federation. If the enterprise was in municipal ownership, the authorization of the buyout was made on the appropriate level. Moreover, employee ownership was also achieved by the transformation of cooperatives

into joint-stock companies (such as Moscow Ventilator or MOVEN, the Kazan Electro-mechanical Plant, and others).

6. The methods demonstrated by the American specialists for personnel training seemed to be very efficient to the Russian audience. They were based on the principles of self-education and exchange of mutual experience.

7. Thirty of the sixty-six responded to the mail questionnaire; those responding seem to be representative of the entire group. For a more extensive account of the results, see Varvarov 1991.

8. About 8 to 10 percent of the employees in BUTEK enterprises did not become owners. The reasons included an insufficient period of service at the enterprise and an unwillingness to contribute to the buyout with personal funds when it was required for the purchase.

9. The BUTEK firms were not actually operating with shares at this time but rather with accounts to which the value of property (based on book value, as established by a 1984 appraisal) purchased on which debt had been repaid and retained earnings sub-sequent to purchase were allocated.

10. Usually there were heavy penalties for canceling a lease contract. The lessor could sue the leasee to claim all the rental payments for the remaining useful life of the assets in a lump sum or in installments over the life of the agreement. However, leased enterprises purchased by employees within BUTEK were exempt from these penalties.

11. By the beginning of 1991, fifty-seven former state enterprises in BUTEK had bought assets with a total value of 120 million rubles. They employed twenty-seven thousand, and their annual production exceeded 1.4 billion rubles. Both enterprise funds and bank debts were used to finance the buyouts. More than 20 percent of the enterprises were bought exclusively with enterprise funds, and 34 percent of the enterprises used debts (usually the term of the loan was between six months and three years at 7 to 20 percent annual interest) for at least part of the purchase. The share of enterprise funds used during the purchase varied between 40 and 70 percent of the total cost of the property.

PART TWO

CASE STUDIES IN RUSSIAN EMPLOYEE OWNERSHIP

5 Introduction: Employee Ownership in Practice

John Logue

All theory, dear friend, is grey.
And the golden tree of life is green.

–Johann Wolfgang von Goethe, *Faust*

◆ THE best case for employee ownership in the process of privatization in Russia is the simplest: it works. The experiments of the Gorbachev years with various forms of microeconomic reform–cooperatives, leasing, BUTEK, collective ownership by the personnel of the enterprise–have created a significant base of experience with economic innovation at the enterprise level. As a consequence, it is possible to examine working models of Russian employee ownership.

We asked American and Russian colleagues to look at how employee ownership as a strategy of privatization was being implemented in practice in Russian firms. We asked them to examine the empirical reality of Russian employee ownership in firms that now had some years' experience. How had these firms been privatized? How was employee ownership structured? What did the new owners think? What was the impact on management? And how had the firms performed?

The case studies that follow examine six firms that were fast off the starting blocks in the process of economic reform. All of them committed themselves to fundamental change during Mikhail Gorbachev's reforms of 1987–90. They had already broken away from the pack of lethargic state firms before the Soviet Union collapsed in 1991 and the Russian government made privatization the slogan of the day. Their development illustrates the complexities of the process of microeconomic reform under the rapidly changing Soviet and Russian legislative and political circumstances. Spread across the landscape of the Russian manufacturing economy, they are as varied as the strategies of those who sought economic change when economic change was risky.

The first two firms–MOVEN (Moscow Ventilator) and Kazansky Elektromekhanichesky Zavod (KEMZ)–embarked on the road to privatization as cooperatives in 1988 and 1989, respectively. (The ministry that controlled MOVEN, however, regarded MOVEN as a leasehold enterprise owned by the state rather than a cooperative owned by the workers collectively and being purchased with state credit until the full purchase price was paid in mid-1989, and the Tatarstan state property committee required that employees purchase KEMZ a second time in 1992–93.) Unlike most cooperatives, which were set up from scratch in the service sector (e.g., restaurants and repair shops), both MOVEN and KEMZ were state-owned manufacturing enterprises. Both were also in terrible shape. MOVEN, which fabricated industrial fans, was bound for certain bankruptcy in the view of Alexander Mironov, who had just become its general director. KEMZ, a producer of truck-mounted cranes, was in an even worse position. It was shut down for two months in 1987 as an object lesson–the victim of a national campaign to improve product quality; employees succeeded in purchasing it from the state on January 1, 1989, only after its bank had petitioned for its liquidation.

By contrast, Veshky and Stroipolymer are typical of the group of light manufacturing firms which were starved for capital under the state economic plan and which sought independence from the command economy initially by having their employees lease the enterprise. Both embarked on leasing before the legislation permitting it was promulgated; in fact, Stroipolymer, which produces polymer construction products such as linoleum, was the second firm in the Russian Republic to be leased when it signed its agreement in 1988. Like other leased firms, Veshky (a manufacturer of furniture and kitchen installations, leased in 1989) and Stroipolymer essentially leased the fixed assets (plant, property, and equipment) of the enterprise from the Soviet state. These fixed assets continued to belong to the state, but both profits and retained earnings (after lease payments) belonged to the work collective, that is, to the personnel of the enterprise. As a consequence, new buildings constructed and equipment acquired during the leasehold period belonged directly to the enterprise's employees, while the old equipment continued to belong to the state. Many, but not all, leased enterprises had a right, written into their lease contracts, to buy the state-owned assets when that became legally possible.[1] Stroipolymer and

Veshky both flourished as leased companies and moved to purchase the assets they had leased when that became possible.

As Valery Varvarov described in Chapter 4, the first large-scale Soviet experiment with complete privatization occurred through BUTEK. Among the firms examined here, Stroipolymer's employees utilized this model to purchase their enterprise, and the firm was one of the first to be fully privatized through BUTEK, in August 1990. Selling to an apparently insatiable market for construction materials, Stroipolymer used its independence to expand its product line, invest in new equipment and buildings, and meet the housing and social needs of the community.

All of these four enterprises were, by Soviet standards, small, and none were defense related. At the time of privatization, each employed three hundred to six hundred. Larger firms were rarely permitted to lease assets, much less to reorganize themselves as cooperatives. The same conditions applied to the BUTEK experiment, although there was some greater flexibility there; the largest firms which purchased their assets through the BUTEK "people's enterprise" structure were two paper mills which employed about two thousand each. There were, however, some major experiments with larger firms that were specifically permitted by exceptional legislation.

Saratov Aviation is possibly the most prominent of these. A major defense firm employing about seventeen thousand, Saratov Aviation specialized in fighter aircraft; it built almost a quarter of the World War II Soviet fighter planes. In recent years, it added naval cruise missiles to advanced fighter production. It was one of the first defense firms to move away from defense production at the end of the 1980s. A special decree of the USSR Council of Ministers permitted its privatization as a "workers' collective" in January 1991 through a purchase of the fixed assets by the employees. Thus it is a study in economic conversion as well as in employee ownership. In its dual transition from defense to civilian production and from state to employee ownership, Saratov Aviation has been assisted by Stanford University and by the Foundation for Enterprise Development, and our case study has been written by a member of this American team.

The final case is that of Krasny Proletary, a major Moscow machine tool builder which supplied defense plants and which was, at one time, the world's largest producer of lathes. Krasny Proletary, which employs about 4,300, remained a state-owned firm until April 1993, when it was privatized under Option 2 of the Russian Federation's privatization law, which provides for majority employee ownership. While Krasny Proletary is typical in a legal sense of the current process of privatization of state-owned enterprises, it was among the first Russian enterprises to attempt thorough managerial reform in the Soviet period. Beginning in 1990, Krasny Proletary undertook a systematic restructuring of its management and operations, drawing heavily upon Western experience and advice. The case study of Krasny Proletary includes an account of the process of management reform by the American consultants instrumental in implementing it, general director Yuri Kirillov's reflections on that process, and a description of the process of privatization itself. While Krasny Proletary is certainly atypical of Russian firms in its early commitment to management reform, the constraints of its privatization process are typical of state enterprises privatizing under the Russian Federation rules.

The case studies that follow, therefore, are those of enterprises on the cutting edge of the privatization process, and they are not particularly typical of the privatization of Russian state-owned enterprises carried out under the 1992 and 1993 privatization legislation, although Krasny Proletary has been privatized under these laws. These are studies of firms which welcomed the idea of privatization and which moved to privatize while the very notion was politically premature. They have ended up in the forefront of Russian microeconomic reform only because the political system followed them.

Consequently, the commonalities in their empirical experience are not imposed by the prescriptions of legislation or the regulations of the Goskomimuschestvo (State Property Committee, or GKI). Nor do they reflect the neoliberal theories currently in vogue among Western governmental and international organization assistance teams. They reflect instead homegrown efforts to grapple with the very real, practical daily problems of reforming the Russian firm: in ownership, in management, and in meeting the demands of a market economy.

In short, their experience is informative precisely because it has developed independently out of Russian practice under Russian conditions. For those who see economic reform as an empirical process, instead of just legislative prescriptions and governmental edicts, and for those who have to live with the results, their experience is educational.

NOTE

1. Estimates of the number of leased enterprises are much disputed, and it is unclear what proportion of them had a right to buy in their lease contracts. A middle-range estimate is that about two thousand sizable state enterprises were leased and that the majority of them had a contractual right to purchase the assets of the enterprise. Leased firms exercising this right to buy constituted a significant portion of the enterprises privatized in 1992. In cases of leased firms without a contractual right to buy, the 1992 privatization law appears to permit their work collectives to negotiate the purchase of the long-term lease of the assets.

6 It's Time for Us, It's Time for You: The MOVEN Story

Oleg Tikhonov

◆ THE Moscow Ventilator Factory (MOVEN) has become sort of a household name in Russia, though not because of its industrial fans. Its notoriety stems from its being one of the first companies to run commercials on Russian television. MOVEN's advertisement featured pretty girls dancing and singing, "It's time for us, it's time for you." It did not advertise any products, just the brand name. It was simple, but fresh and upbeat; people liked and remembered it.

At first glance, however, it doesn't appear that there is much that is either fresh or upbeat about MOVEN, although it was one of the first Soviet factories to become a private, employee-owned company. Located in Perovo in the industrial eastern part of Moscow, the firm looks like many other industrial firms: dull grey and yellow buildings constructed twenty-five or thirty years ago, some of them looking quite shabby. The plant's equipment does not differ much from that found elsewhere. But upon closer inspection, one can immediately notice a few things that make this plant a little different. There are many trees around the facility, and in May everything is in blossom. The place is unusually clean for a Soviet factory, and there are a few brand-new Volvos and Fords with company license plates in the small factory parking lot. It is little things like these and big things, like employee ownership, that make MOVEN and its workers stand out against the bleak background of the Russian economic depression.

THE ROAD TO JOINT-STOCK OWNERSHIP

Why did the workers at Moscow Ventilator decide to convert to employee ownership? The answer, according to Alexander Mironov, the firm's general director, was simple: "We had no other choice." In December 1987 when Mironov became general director, the company was on the verge of collapse despite being one of the Soviet Union's largest producers of industrial ventilators. "We were in debt; we had poor work discipline, low wages, and inferior skills," said Mironov. "At that moment we realized that if we continued to be state owned, we would go bankrupt. We understood that we could rely only upon ourselves. And we had only one alternative to state ownership at that time: cooperatives."

In 1987 the first cooperatives that were allowed to move away from total government control became more competitive. This was partially because they motivated their workers better and because the Law on Cooperatives, adopted in 1988, was very favorable to them. The law permitted cooperatives to set their own prices, choose their own customers, and keep a reasonable part of their profits.

Given these advantages, MOVEN's management decided to turn the state factory into a production cooperative. They managed to persuade the ministry which controlled the plant (the Ministry of Road Construction Equipment Manufacturing) to liquidate the factory as a state enterprise and to create a cooperative which would buy the assets of the enterprise over ten years. The assets were priced at their residual value of 6.5 million rubles.

In 1988 the employees established a cooperative and signed an agreement with the ministry on the conditions of the buyout. However, though the employees of MOVEN considered the act as a purchase on credit financed by the selling ministry, the Ministry of Finance regarded the enterprise as a leaseholding entity. It taxed the new cooperative so severely that MOVEN had to sell some current assets to pay its taxes.

That was MOVEN's first serious trial. In March 1989, after careful consideration, MOVEN's top management decided to buy out the factory over two months instead of ten years to avoid the ministry's heavy taxation rates.[1] To finance this purchase, MOVEN asked several of its most respected customers for loans and offered to pay them back in additional amounts of product instead of interest. Those familiar with the day-to-day uncertainties of the Soviet economy will understand how appealing such a proposal was. Several enterprises responded. For example, the big electrical equipment manufacturing company Svetlana from Leningrad gave a 3-million-ruble loan for ten years without interest and received more of MOVEN's production as compensation.

The second trial was trying to develop a sense of ownership among MOVEN's employees. Management tried to accomplish this by linking payment to membership in the cooperative. Employees were asked to pay a stock buyout contribution of three hundred rubles (which was roughly equal to the monthly wage at that time) and a membership fee of fifty rubles to become members of the cooperative.

Despite the relatively small sum, it was critically important, Mironov argued, to establish a connection between one's own wealth and the company's future capital. He believed that everyone who would like to be an owner ought to take at least a small risk. So a distinction was created between the employee-owners and the hired workers in the cooperative. The overwhelming majority agreed to become members of the cooperative, while about forty people decided to remain as hired workers. But despite the fact that more than three hundred people had voted to set up the cooperative, only eighty-seven initially paid their contribution and fee. Clearly, nobody wanted to risk his money.[2]

The lack of employee support convinced management of the necessity of creating some incentives for ownership. Since the financial situation of the company had stabilized, management initiated dividends at 20 percent per quarter to those who had paid the three hundred-ruble stock buyout contribution. With such significant rewards, three hundred workers quickly made their contributions.

Understanding individual ownership within the cooperative structure was a difficult concept. Employees, however, were educated gradually. For example, all employee contributions were equal initially. This was established because management was concerned that an unequal distribution—for example, if it was based on the amount an employee could contribute out of his pocket—might cause conflict among the employees. Those who could not make monetary contributions would resent those who could and accuse them of getting more profits than they deserved. But after three months under this arrangement, at the general meeting of cooperative members, the management proposed that those who wished could reinvest their dividends to increase their stock ownership. All members had a choice whether to spend their dividends or to reinvest them. The differentiation in ownership that followed was considered fair because everybody was given an equal starting point.

After fourteen months as a cooperative with collective ownership, MOVEN moved further to establish individual property rights. The enterprise paid all its current debts and legally ceased to be state property, but the cooperative structure still presented problems. The cooperative was the property of all employees; in effect, it was still nobody's property because individual ownership rights did not exist in the initial cooperative form. All employees were in theory the collective owners of the enterprise.

But in fact what they "owned" mostly was the long-term debt. To address this issue, the management proposed to the workers that the cooperative be converted into a closely held joint-stock company. As part of the transaction, workers who were willing to assume part of the long-term debt would be rewarded with the corresponding number of shares of company stock.

The attitude of the employees toward property ownership changed very slowly. Mikhail Proshin, an informal, shop-floor leader, says that the most difficult stage was the transformation from a state enterprise where nobody was responsible for anything to the cooperative where you had to share the responsibility and risk your own money. In the cooperative, people were risking their wages, which were no longer guaranteed. Mikhail Polyakov, a technician employed at the factory for twenty-five years, similarly felt that it was difficult for him to adjust to the cooperative setting; he guessed that it was easier for the younger workers. Compared to the transition from state to cooperative ownership, says Proshin, "the transition from the cooperative to employee ownership was easy."

In creating a joint-stock company, the authorized total value of the stock was set at 6.5 million rubles–the purchase price of the assets–and 6,500 shares were authorized with a nominal value of 1,000 rubles a share. Each share had one vote. The maximum number of shares any employee could buy in the initial subscription was limited to 50, worth 50,000 rubles. Everyone who agreed to pay 200 rubles in cash had the right to obtain an interest-free 800-ruble loan for a period of ten years; shares for 4.5 million rubles were purchased under these terms for 900,000 in cash and 3.6 million in loans. Those who could not afford to pay any cash at the moment were offered another option: a 5,000-ruble, three-year, 15 percent interest loan. That loan actually allowed the borrower to acquire up to 25,000 rubles' worth of shares. Employees borrowed 400,000 rubles under this latter provision, which enabled them to borrow an additional 1.6 million and thus to subscribe for the remaining 2 million rubles' worth of shares.

In 1991, outside stockholders appeared on the scene as well, including suppliers from whom MOVEN sought on-time delivery. They, too, have a right to vote, but together they cannot own more than 10 percent of the stock.

COMPANY STRUCTURE

The structure of the joint-stock company is designed as a stockholder democracy (see Figure 6.1). The stockholders vote by secret ballot to elect a company president and members of the stockholder council. There are sixteen members of the council; they are not paid for their council work. This council oversees the activity of the president and the management

Figure 6.1
MOVEN's Company Structure

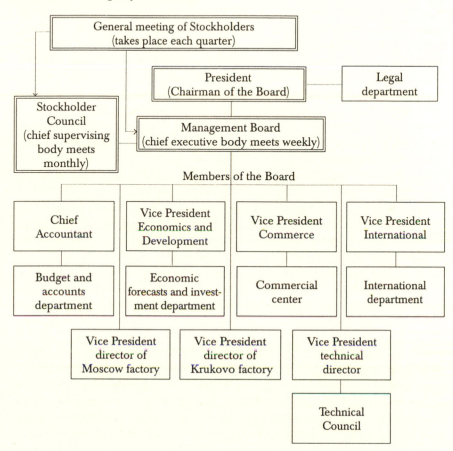

board. Without the council's consent this board has no right to make major investments or to sell stock to an outsider. The management must submit a quarterly financial statement to the stockholder council for its review.

The president (who is also the chairman of the management board) is elected by all stockholders at the general meeting. He then nominates candidates for the management board who have to be approved by the council. Board members do not have to be MOVEN stockholders. The president's term of office is determined by his contract, which delimits his rights and responsibilities; his term cannot exceed five years. When his term expires, it means automatic expiration of the terms of all board members. Board members can be reelected for a new term, if they are nominated by the new president. No one can simultaneously serve on the stockholder council and the management board.

The president and the management board have the responsibility for day-to-day operations. In fact, they are the top management of the firm. The board is the company's chief executive body and it represents the company in relations with third parties and government authorities. Everything which is not specified by law or the company's charter to be the sole prerogative of the general meeting and the stockholder council is the responsibility of the board. The board introduces proposals concerning (1) creation, reorganization, and liquidation of subsidiaries, (2) approval of organizational procedures and the company's structure and bylaws, (3) acquisition of stock issued by the company, and (4) changes of the authorized stock. All of these proposals are subject to approval by the stockholder council or general meeting.

The president has the right (which was granted to him by a general meeting of stockholders) to permit top managers to take part in windfall profits. Specifically, if the yearly dividends for all personnel exceed 25 percent of stock value on average, then 15 percent of the sum after dividends and taxes are paid (i.e., the windfall profit) is distributed among several top managers.[3]

Board members are allowed to engage in business activities outside the company but must report all their personal holdings of other companies' assets in excess of 10 percent of the other firm's authorized stock.

PRIVATIZATION GETS RESULTS

As far as transformation of ownership is concerned, MOVEN looks like a successful case. But what about its business performance? Available statistics indicate that after becoming a cooperative, the enterprise raised its prices very sharply. According to MOVEN officials, profits before taxes rose almost six times between 1988 and 1990 (from 2.5 million rubles to 13 million rubles) while the volume of production only doubled. Though this gap can be attributed to some extent to the absolutely unreliable Soviet accounting system, there has indeed been a great price hike. Thus MOVEN's actual production results are less impressive than a first glance suggests.

Despite the improved workforce performance, quality has only inched upward so far. The initial market situation stimulated increased production, but did not improve quality because the company's products were still in great demand at their existing quality level. This started to change after the government freed prices in 1992, and overall demand began to shrink. As some customers have fallen behind in payments, MOVEN has had to slow down production. That allowed it to tighten quality controls somewhat. Ironically, the company could not afford to do that previously.

At the same time, the factory cut the payroll by about 5 percent after becoming employee owned. Total employment was cut to 480 people, down from a little more than 500. MOVEN managers argue that only habitual absentees, drunkards, and lazy people were fired. They stated that they had to employ such people before because the wages were very low and they could not attract better workers. Now the situation changed; in 1989–90, wages grew by 2.5 times (*Ogonyok,* April 1991: 18), and employee turnover plummeted. Not only did the wages become competitive, but the workers now had an opportunity to become owners, and they valued this opportunity.

As a state-owned factory, for example, MOVEN repeatedly tried to raise production volume to 2,500 ventilators a month and failed. For a year now as an employee-owned company it has been producing more than 3,000 ventilators per month. Since the factory has not yet introduced major technical innovations, the increase in production is for the most part a result of higher labor productivity due to the changed attitudes of the workers.

"For me the main result [of privatization] is that our employees now regard this company as their own business," Mironov explains. "Every time I come to the stockholders' meeting, which takes place every three months, I see a room full of people. They are concerned, attentive. They ask thoughtful questions. These people are genuinely interested in the fate of their company. I always compare it with the situation when the factory was state owned. We tried to lure people to the meetings by selling beer on the premises and arranging shows after the meetings. But nothing could attract them. That's the most vivid evidence of the changes we achieved: the changed attitude of workers."

What is obvious to the managers seems to be right for the workers, too. Arkady Getmanov, a welder, is a member of the stockholder council. He also believes that the main change at the factory is the new attitude of workers. Interviewed in the plant, Getmanov was quick to cite obvious evidence of the change: "The current shift is supposed to stop working at 4 P.M. Now it's twenty minutes to five, but everybody is still working. Nobody forces them and they will not get extra pay, but they have an urgent order from a customer. They weren't able to complete the job in time, so they decided to stay and work until it's finished."

In general, MOVEN employees are supportive of the transition. Another employee in the shop, Anatoly Usov, left the Metropolitan (the Moscow municipal subway company), where he had been a repair shop supervisor, to come to MOVEN. He says that wages are higher at MOVEN, and the style of management is different. "The approach of managers is more human and reasonable than at other places. They value professionalism," which Usov considers a real advantage. Victor Kuseev, who had worked at MOVEN thirteen years ago and subsequently took another job, recently returned. The reason, as he put it, is that at MOVEN people are given a chance to use fully their capabilities and talents. Another reason is wages. "At state-owned enterprises, wages and salaries are much lower, while here you get what you actually earn."

The company has been able to attract qualified managers as well. The company's vice president in charge of international activities used to work in the Soviet foreign trade ministry, where he was responsible for the country's entire foreign trade in electrical engines. As a consequence of his connections, MOVEN is now selling parts and components abroad for hard currency, something which the firm never did before, and several other Russian enterprises are also selling their products abroad through MOVEN. MOVEN earns a commission on the overseas sales it generates for other companies.

The company's finance director, Alexander Deripasov, who holds a degree in economics, had previously left MOVEN to take a job at the State Planning Committee (Gosplan). Attracted by the idea of employee ownership, he returned to MOVEN and brought with him a wealth of experience. His experience and connections to other Russian companies, especially suppliers, have helped MOVEN. MOVEN has even managed to hire a former professor, Russia's leading specialist in ventilator design and technology.

"Perhaps our main achievement," says Deripasov, "is that we have managed to develop a team of people in top management who share common values and beliefs. These people feel that they can realize their potential in this company, because we are independent and because we don't report to any state structure. Besides, one can become a real owner here: we can earn capital."

Others also see the advantages of ownership. "I was a shop supervisor at the factory when it was changed from a cooperative into a joint-stock company," says Alexei Miluchikhin. "I supported the idea. I told the shop-floor workers that if the general director and the shop supervisor were risking their money, the workers might give it a try too. I could not force them, of course. But those who did not follow me at that time came to regret it three months later."

Ownership has also led to improvements with customers and suppliers. "Relations with the customers improved significantly, though they had their doubts at the beginning," Miluchikhin stated. "The suppliers are keeping their word, because they were given some shares. The main condition is that the dividends are paid them only if they supply in time." Of course, now MOVEN works with its customers and suppliers directly, without commands from the ministry.

MOVEN's gradual transition to market principles stood it in good stead during the economic turbulence of 1992–93. While other companies borrowed heavily to avert collapse, MOVEN had completely repaid its debts by the spring of 1993, increased its authorized stock to 400 million rubles, and, in the second quarter of 1993 alone, paid a 250 percent dividend on the nominal value of the stock outstanding.[4] Of course, evaluating these figures requires taking into account the country's inflation rate, which averaged 25 percent a month in the first six months of 1993, and the annual interest rate on short-term commercial loans, which hit 180 percent in the same period.

While MOVEN has well-established markets for its products and has developed several new models which seem to be competitive in the world market, with the help of its Swedish and British partners, the company continues to face significant problems. Mironov argues that there is an urgent need for continuous improvement, which means continual new investment. Other influential people, some of them members of the stockholder council or of the management board, argue that under conditions of skyrocketing prices the company must divert all its profits into dividends in order to help its employees keep pace with inflation.

ELEMENTS OF SUCCESS

Among the factors that led to MOVEN's success, the strong and intelligent leadership of the company's president, Alexander Mironov, played a major role. Many managers with backgrounds similar to that of Mironov[5] firmly believed in the command style of management which dominated the Soviet economy for more than seventy years. Mironov was different. He is one of the best representatives of a growing number of industry people who understand that this country simply will not be able to revitalize its economy unless it realizes the creative potential of millions of its workers. And to realize this potential you have to make workers into owners as well. That is the main lesson from MOVEN.

But this is not the whole picture. Yes, the attitude of the workers has improved greatly, the discipline is better, and workforce turnover has been reduced. The enterprise has expanded its volume of production significantly. But it is also an indisputable fact that the visible commercial success of the majority of new, non-state-owned enterprises (co-ops, leased, and employee-owned firms) after 1988 must be attributed in large part to their freedom to set their own prices. In the highly monopolistic environment of the Soviet economy, where real competition was practically nonexistent, freedom from state control meant only one thing: skyrocketing prices. Even though these new enterprises are much more flexible and better suited for a market environment, they still have to prove their ability to operate effectively in new conditions.

MOVEN seems to be one company which has what it takes to move in this direction.

One of MOVEN's top managers argues the point in a more strategic way. He believes that the biggest problem in the future is to make the factory people-oriented instead of production- or plan-oriented. There must be good relations among workers on the floor and among suppliers, producers, and customers, and workplace conditions must be improved. He gives an example: there used to be one big locker room for all employees. That was cost effective, but the people from different shops had to walk down the street in winter without warm clothes. So they set up separate locker rooms at each shop and later decided to build saunas at each shop to make workplace conditions more comfortable.

It is small steps, like these, taken in the right direction that can make a big difference at MOVEN in the long run.

NOTES

1. Since it was a leveraged cooperative, 90 percent of MOVEN's profits were subject to taxes. Paying off the ministry's loan reduced the tax rate to about 50 percent of profits.

2. Actually the risk was not that great since it did not involve pensions or other social benefits. Because new cooperative enterprises continued to pay the same amount of social insurance taxes and contributions as state-owned enterprises, their workers were still covered by the social insurance system.

3. An example may help clarify how windfall profits are distributed. Assume there are ten shareholders and the stock value is $10 per share. If, on average, stockholders receive $3 in dividends during the year, the windfall profit will be distributed. If the yearly profit is $200, then $30 will be paid in dividends, and—for the sake of this example—$70 will be paid in taxes. That leaves $100 available for the windfall profit. Top management will divide up 15 percent of this amount ($15).

4. Presentation by Mironov at the Privatization and Experience with the Development of Worker Stock Ownership conference, Moscow, July 7, 1993.

5. MOVEN president Mironov's career is typical of that of many Russian managers of his generation. He started work as a shop-floor worker at a large industrial enterprise. While working he attended evening classes at Bauman Technical College, where he got a degree in engineering, and he subsequently took a degree in management from the Moscow Institute of Management. Then he was employed at a local Communist Party committee in the Perovo district of Moscow for seven years. He left there for a senior job at the Ministry of Energy, but he did not like it and quit after eight months. In December 1987 he became general director of Moscow Ventilator.

7 A Smell of Fresh Paint: Kazansky Elektromekhanichesky Zavod

John Logue and Olga Maiboroda

◆ LOCATED at the bend of the Volga River approximately six hundred miles due east of Moscow, the ancient city of Kazan is the capital of the former Soviet Tatar autonomous republic, now the republic of Tatarstan. The city presents a rich mixture of exotic cultures; Muslim mosques and Christian churches, the Russian language and the Turkic Tatar, rub shoulders on almost every street of the old town. The newer sections of the city display the drab, faceless apartment blocks and massive factory walls characteristic of post-Stalin industrial reality.

Every Russian schoolchild of proper age still associates the city's modern history with its connection to V. I. Lenin. His home when he was a student is a local shrine; his books, bed, chess set, the rooms of his brothers and sisters, and the family's solidly bourgeois possessions are all on display. In the summer, elderly women sit and gossip on the benches in the park that is the front yard of Lenin's home. An unheroic statue of Lenin relaxing on a bench with a pile of books beside him graces the park in Kazan's kremlin. The University of Kazan was his alma mater, where his version of proletarian ownership of the means of production germinated. That ideological commitment, given much lip service but realized only in slogans under Communist power, has found local expression in the emerging free-market system at the employee-owned enterprise Kazansky Elektromekhanichesky Zavod.[1]

THE RISE AND FALL OF A STATE ENTERPRISE

Kazansky Elektromekhanichesky Zavod (Kazan Electro-Mechanical Plant, or KEMZ) was founded in 1949 through the merger of several small agricultural implement repair shops in Kazan; some of its current shop buildings were originally used to stable horses when it served local collective farms. In the 1950s and 1960s, a period of relative liberalization, the plant prospered with heavy new investment and the development of a new product line: truck-mounted heavy-duty cranes. The plant was one of three producers of these cranes in the USSR. Profitability peaked in the mid-1960s when the plant produced roughly six hundred cranes per year and employed 1,200.

In the late 1960s, when ministerial controls were tightened and wages were capped, KEMZ began to hemorrhage skilled labor to nearby military plants which paid higher wages; KEMZ's profits went back into the state budget rather than into reinvestment. While the plant continued to produce cranes with roughly average levels of profitability, it fell behind plan norms. This initially caused little problem because of the laxity in enforcing the plan, but beginning in 1982, when Yuri V. Andropov took office as general secretary, enforcement of plan quotas was tightened, bonuses were eliminated for plants not meeting quotas, and KEMZ's decline accelerated. Its compensation levels fell to the point where it was simply unable to recruit skilled labor. Despite its low labor costs (and partly as a consequence of the resulting staffing), in 1983 production costs began to exceed prices received under the plan.

In 1987, during the quality campaign pushed by Gorbachev, the local external quality control committee, which KEMZ managers argued had no knowledge of crane design or quality, found the company's papers in disorder; KEMZ's two design engineers (the company was limited to two by the plan) had their hands full designing cranes and were behind on the paper trail. Despite the committee's negative findings, KEMZ's cranes are said to have been of decent quality and in demand. Still, the quality committee shut the plant for two months as an object lesson. At this nadir, the general director resigned.

Vadim Georgivich Vrachev, who was elected to take his place, was an unlikely choice. He had little experience at KEMZ, having just been hired as an electrician in 1986. He had previously helped build the huge Kamaz truck complex, celebrated the rolling of the first truck off the line there in 1975, and worked his way up from foreman to assistant head of engineering. But when he sought to move back to Kazan to take care of his mother and mother-in-law, Kamaz refused to release him; he won his freedom from what he terms "industrial serfdom" only after he took Kamaz to court and after the party regional committee intervened on his behalf. Back in

Kazan, he was hired at a troubled typewriter plant in 1984 only to be fired in 1985 after a disagreement with his boss. He then sought to go back to school to study philosophy and, he hoped, embark on an academic career. (He had lectured for years in the party's political education program on scientific atheism and world religions.) The University of Kazan turned him down for a correspondence degree because of his lack of academic credentials; he was a factory worker, they complained, and they had more than enough *real* students. The economics department at the Pedagogical Institute agreed to admit him if he took a degree at the local Marxism-Leninism institute and managed to pass the entrance exams. Vrachev took his degree and passed his philosophy entrance exam in late 1986. He still keeps his well-thumbed Hegel–"my teacher"–by his bedside.

Looking for a job within walking distance of his apartment which he could combine with his studies, Vrachev responded to KEMZ's advertisement for a skilled electrician. After examining his work record, KEMZ's general director tried to persuade him to sign on as department head instead, but since the pay was 250 rubles a month as an electrician versus 160 as a manager, Vrachev insisted on the former. Ultimately he left the interview with both jobs–and with an agreement for time off to finish his entrance exams if his department improved its performance.

As it turned out, events relegated his academic career to the back burner. With the general director's resignation, an election was held to select his successor. The inside candidate was KEMZ's chief engineer. Vrachev was called in by the district party secretary and asked to run as well. He tried to beg off, but the district secretary was adamant. "We can't have uncontested elections any more. We need one more candidate. You're a good Communist. It's your obligation to run. But don't think you'll get elected." In that brief window of free, contested elections of plant managers, Vrachev beat the chief engineer, "and I had to lay philosophy aside."

When Vrachev was elected in March 1987, the plant was formally shut. It was a plant in deep crisis economically. Employment was down to 325 employees, and annual production to about two hundred cranes and about twenty aerial lift trucks for doing telephone and power line repair, or roughly a fourth and a third of earlier levels, respectively. Much of the equipment was worn out. Moreover, morale was horrendous. Practically every story told about the problems of Soviet industrial production seems to fit the facts at KEMZ. The plant was best known locally not as Kazansky Elektromekhanichesky Zavod or by its acronym KEMZ but by its nickname: the Drunken Plant. Vrachev had his work cut out for him.

Vrachev reopened the plant despite its formal closure and turned to the options available under the Soviet law of the time. He sought, first, to get the enterprise reclassified as an "experienced enterprise" in order to raise wages, pay bonuses, and compete for skilled labor,[2] and then, to win some freedom to maneuver, he tried to convert KEMZ from a state-owned enterprise to a cooperative under the new 1987 legal provisions.[3] The work collective endorsed the cooperative initiative in the late spring of 1988. Both efforts, however, were initially rejected by the authorities, and the company's decline continued. Without capital to reinvest, equipment continued to deteriorate, and accounts payable continued to rise, reaching 2 million rubles in 1988 on sales of 3.4 million.

Ironically, what broke the logjam was the national campaign to shut down hopelessly money-losing firms. As part of this campaign, KEMZ's creditor bank petitioned for KEMZ's full payment of debt or its liquidation. Under these circumstances, Vrachev was finally successful in persuading the ministry administering KEMZ to permit the enterprise to become a cooperative.

KEMZ UNDER COOPERATIVE OWNERSHIP

On January 1, 1989, KEMZ was converted into a cooperative under the provisions of the 1988 USSR Law on Cooperatives, about seven months after the initiative began. The ministry "gave" the cooperative the firm's assets (which had a residual value of 1.75 million rubles) in return for KEMZ assuming the outstanding 2-million-ruble debt. While 280 of the firm's 327 employees had attended the work collective meeting that made the final decision to establish the cooperative by a unanimous vote, and while 170 signed up to join, only 67 actually joined initially by paying the 300-ruble membership fee (which approximated two months' average pay at the plant).[4] The primary reason for their recalcitrance was fear of losing pension rights. (The cooperative legislation was not clear on this issue.) The others remained as hired labor with clear pension rights.

KEMZ started as a cooperative almost literally without cash and without a ministry to guarantee its credit. On the surface, the situation looked worse than it had previously, but KEMZ now had the signal advantage of independence to innovate. It finessed its cash shortage by the simple stratagem of not paying salaries for the first two months; it is a testimony to Vrachev's leadership skills—and to the fact that the average age of KEMZ's employees was fifty-two—that this desperate measure worked.

The plant's survival was also threatened, to use Vrachev's diplomatic language, by "employees' indifference to the plant and to their work," which, he argues, resulted from paying them all the same no matter how hard they worked[5] and from the lack of any internal cost accounting. To deal with these problems, Vrachev undertook a radical democratization, reorganization, and decentralization of the plant.

Vrachev subdivided the plant into mini-enterprises which were in effect leased by their employees and which were treated as quasi-independent, self-governing shops. The members of the cooperative in each shop elected their representative to the board of directors and nominated the shop manager; as KEMZ's general director, Vrachev retained the right to reject nominee managers whom he considered unfit. Each shop kept its own internal accounts. The internal cost accounting system was based on the simple principle that "everything which comes into the shop is purchased, and everything that leaves the shop is sold." Internal prices were based on historical levels of input of labor, raw materials, and energy; fines were levied for the delivery of low-quality products. The units were permitted to retain any savings over historical levels for distribution among the work group, increasing wage differentials on the basis of differential productivity among departments. Workers, in Vrachev's words, "began to earn their salaries, instead of just receiving them"; they started to "look into their own pockets, not into someone else's." This proved to be key to the turnaround.

While the teams initially sought to improve returns simply by liberating materials from each other, it rapidly became apparent that the slack in the old system was far greater than even Vrachev believed. Significant economies were achieved as raw-material use declined dramatically; Vrachev had anticipated that existing raw materials and work in progress could sustain two months of production, but in fact the new self-management and incentive system so slashed waste and hoarding that it sustained eight months of production. As a consequence, the teams had to confront the puzzling issue of how to divide the savings; after lengthy discussion and considerable trial and error, each group has ended up with a different system, though Vrachev imposed a common cap on supervisory wages at 2.5 times the average wage in the group.

Despite the shaky start, in its first year as a cooperative, KEMZ met its delivery schedule, while it increased production 20 percent and sales 70 percent (see Table 7.1). Moreover, KEMZ repaid the 2-million-ruble debt by September 1989,[6] reestablished its credit worthiness, reinvested heavily in much-needed new plant and equipment, and more than doubled wages to levels competitive with those at neighboring military plants. The modest profit remaining was distributed among co-op members on the basis of time worked (not salary). By the end of the year, 254 of the firm's 275 remaining employees had joined the co-op.[7]

KEMZ's success continued in 1990 and 1991. In 1991, sales (in constant rubles) were 2.7 times those of 1988, salaries were up 2.25 times, production had more than doubled, and profits were up by a factor of 40; employment had increased only by a third. Both sales and production had risen every year since 1988; the product line had increased; and the plant had reinvested heavily in new construction and new equipment. There had only been modest improvement, however, in the technological sophistication of its products, because the company was more concerned with providing ease of repair than with increasing technological complexity.

Table 7.1
KEMZ's Performance, 1983–1993

	1983	1984	1985	1986	1987	1988	1989	1990	1991	1992 Projected	1992 Actual	1993 Projected
					In 1982 prices						In current prices	
Value of production (in thousands of rubles)	4,547	4,153	4,059	4,182	3,054	3,379	5,748	7,120	9,055	19,231	227,443	1,700,000
Profit (in thousands of rubles)	457	30	1	97	37	63	1,073	1,055	2,461	4,923	71,349	417,000
Cost of goods sold and selling, general, and administrative expenses as a proportion of value of production	.878	1.00	1.21	.93	.92	.95	.72	.80	.79	n/a	.69	.75
Total employment	344	384	379	374	356	344	350	385	446	500	530	600
Number who are hourly workers	262	261	261	258	248	231	225	223	310	320	344	430
Profit per employee (in rubles)	1,328	80	2	260	100	180	3,200	2,740	5,520	9,850	135,000	695,000
Average monthly compensation (in rubles)	181	181	184	181	173	187	401	401	421	538	5,890	54,000
Truck-mounted cranes	277	249	234	265	211	166	186	302	330	400	343	414
Aerial lift trucks	76	72	64	62	23	16	32	64	93	120	106	144
Consumer goods (in thousands of rubles)	—	—	—	—	—	—	—	—	n/a	n/a	1,983	20,000

Sales in 1992 were projected to double in constant rubles on the basis of a 25 percent increase in output and a 3 percent increase in production employment. Achieving those projections in the judgment of management, however, depended on the availability of raw materials and the continued ability of customers to settle their bills.

NAVIGATING TROUBLED WATERS

Instead, 1992 began with the government's policy of "shock therapy." Price "liberalization" sent inflation spiraling heavenward. The credit crunch in the spring and summer caused demand for capital equipment to plummet. The political collapse of the Soviet Union, growing civil strife in several of the successor republics, and centrifugal forces within the Russian Federation itself disrupted the established economic ties. What was left of state orders outside the defense complex and plan deliveries disappeared. Throughout the economy, production fell.

As a consequence, KEMZ's projections proved embarrassingly optimistic. However, even in this distinctly hostile environment, KEMZ achieved considerable success. The firm managed to increase unit production about 6 percent with an 11 percent growth in the number of production employees. Its aggressive pricing combined with rapid inflation pushed sales in current rubles up by a factor of 25 and costs down from 79 percent to 69 percent of sales. In the context of an overall 30 percent drop in industrial production in Russia during 1992, KEMZ belongs to the handful of capital goods manufacturers that increased production.

Profits rose by a factor of 29, to 71 million current rubles. That was fortunate, since the Tatarstan Republic property committee chose to regard the previous transfer of ownership of the facility as falling outside the scope of the 1992 privatization act[8]; KEMZ employees were obliged to purchase the assets of the firm for an additional 17.2 million rubles in 1992–93.[9] Given inflation and reinvestment, this remained a bargain: in July 1993, the company's assets were valued at 250 million rubles (in January 1, 1993, prices), including the plant and its related kindergarten, holiday camp, and youth facility.

Following changes in the law, KEMZ was legally reorganized as a *tovarishchestvo*, a partnership with limited liability, and it perfected the use of an internal account system to track employee ownership which has some similarities to that of the Mondragon cooperatives in Spain (or the Industrial Cooperative Association in the United States); KEMZ, however, developed it independently of foreign models. Of 530 employees in July 1992, 412 were full members and 60 were candidate members subject to approval at the next annual meeting. The remaining 58 seemed to be primarily very new employees. In July 1993, between 450 and 460 of the plant's 600 workers were members.[10]

Each employee has an account within the firm which holds his or her membership contribution (which was pegged at two months' pay, e.g., 8,000 rubles in July 1992, and 50,000 rubles in July 1993, to adjust for inflation) and his or her share of the acquisition price of the company's fixed assets. The value of fixed assets acquired each year is allocated annually among current working members on the basis—initially—of hours worked; following Vrachev's exposure in 1992 to the principles of American Employee Stock Ownership Plans (ESOPs), KEMZ adopted an allocation formula that includes hours worked, pay, and seniority. Thus new members are automatically included in the ownership structure without diluting the old members' account values. Each member receives an annual statement of his or her account; the employees we talked to all knew their account values. Members can cash out their accounts when they leave. With the beginning of rapid inflation in 1992, KEMZ started indexing account values to compensate for inflation by revaluing assets to reflect current prices. As of January 1, 1993, employees who had joined the cooperative in 1989 had accounts valued at 550,000 rubles; those accounts were estimated to be worth 2.75 million current rubles in July 1993. Since workers have seen their account values grow, Vrachev believes, "they are willing to make certain sacrifices for the enterprise to survive."[11]

Working capital, by contrast, remains the indivisible collective property of the employees. A consequence of a decision by the general meeting of owners, this principle is enshrined in the statute of the company. It is, says Vrachev, "our insurance fund." In the event that the firm were to be liquidated, any remaining working capital would be divided among the members.

With the acceleration of inflation in 1992–93, KEMZ speeded payments of dividends and profit sharing. As of July 1993, dividends were paid monthly, as was a profit-sharing bonus which mixed an equal distribution (40 percent), a salary-based distribution (40 percent), and a seniority-based distribution (20 percent).

The KEMZ method of allocating the value of capital improvements to individual accounts seems an effective counter to the presumed tendency of employees to prefer to consume the profits. Workers we spoke to were as investment oriented as management.

INTERNAL DEMOCRACY

KEMZ's highest governing body is the general meeting of all employee shareholders.[12] The general meeting elects the president of the company and the other seventeen members of the company's council for a two-year term, and members are subject to recall by the general meeting (see Figure 7.1). The council in turn hires the general director and the other five members of the management board. Currently Vrachev is both president of the board (elected

Figure 7.1
Governance Structure of KEMZ

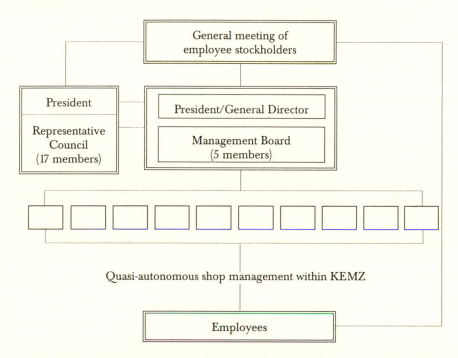

by the general meeting) and general director (appointed by the council). The seventeen members of the council include three (of six) top managers, five other supervisors, and nine production workers.

The council, which serves many of the functions of an American board of directors, meets three or four times a month to discuss both strategic and operational issues. It is the decision-making body for strategic questions like capital investments, division of profits, and approval of financial plans. The management board—which is, in effect, simply the management team—handles daily operational issues and prepares questions for the council. These top managers, including Vrachev, have individual contracts with the council.

The council session we attended in July 1992 covered travel reimbursement (a hot issue which was ultimately tabled), purchase and storage of paint, setting foremen's wages (by contract or by shop profits were the alternatives), and raising the enterprise's child allowances. The tone of the session was informal with a good bit of levity. Vrachev presided but did not dominate. Indeed, on the divisive issue of travel costs, Vrachev did not vote (the vote was 6 to 1 to 6 for three different alternatives with 2 abstentions; a majority of at least 9 votes was required for passage).

Vrachev himself maintains that KEMZ's organizational principle combines "the democratic participation of each member of the cooperative with a strictly authoritarian scheme of managing production itself." The functions of each administrative level correspond strictly to the instructions approved by the plant director. This "democratic authoritarianism" permitted quick and decisive action, quite unlike the chaos that existed in the plant previously.

A CULTURE OF OWNERSHIP?

As the first state plant to privatize in Tatarstan—and one of the first in the Russian Federation—KEMZ has struggled with the problems of changing the culture in the workplace. This is no easy task. "A state-owned enterprise is like a railroad track. There's only one way to go. Now we have to learn how to choose" is the way one manager summed up the dilemma. "I've gone from stability to the will of the work collective," commented a bemused draftsman who had previously worked in a defense plant.

Interviews in July 1992 with about twenty employees in four of KEMZ's shops (top managers were not in attendance) and group discussions in 1993 demonstrated substantial understanding of both KEMZ's ownership structure and internal governance among those who had been with the company since 1989. Recently hired employees, however, were much less clear about ownership. One recent hire interviewed in 1992, for example, had no idea how to become a member of the cooperative, and in our 1993 focus group an outspoken, recently hired assembler commented, "Initially I didn't pay much attention to employee ownership. I still don't see many changes. I put in my eight hours a day, but I don't feel any sense of ownership."[13] All seemed to understand the wage and bonus situation.

Despite Vrachev's proclaimed "democratic authoritarianism," work groups and individuals have substantial latitude for choice. For example, some of the work groups have developed effective systems to elicit and implement suggestions for production improvements; one idea (which avoided adding a second shift on a machine used to cut geared rings for crane bases) had been implemented within two weeks of being proposed by the operator. This machinist, Piotr Nikolaivich, had started at KEMZ ten months previously and had formerly worked in a military plant. He was stunned by the speed with which his suggestion had been implemented; when we interviewed him, he was already running trial pieces with the new methods to check quality. "Things just move a lot faster here," he told us. "When I used to make suggestions for production improvements [in the defense plant where he previously worked], I really ended up losing because we cut the labor content [of production]. Now I benefit through ownership. If we produce more, we make more money. Once we meet our plan within the company, we can use the rest of our time to produce extra for orders from inside [i.e., other profit centers] or outside." Why had he come to work at KEMZ? "At my old state plant there was often no work and no money. Here there's plenty of work—and the more we produce, the more money we make."

The dimensions of a radically different industrial culture become clear in our discussions with other shop-floor employees. To Valentina, the senior employee in the 1993 focus group (with twenty-three years of work in the plant), the difference was workers' attitudes: "Before 1989, we worked separately, earning for ourselves. Now we get paid in relation to our input, and we try to help each other. We have a much higher sense of responsibility." Added Irina, who had fifteen years of seniority at KEMZ, "Previously we were all paid the same, irrespective of how you worked. Now we really have to use all our capabilities." Newer workers were generally positive in comparing KEMZ with their previous places of employment. "There's more independence here, more freedom," commented one white-collar worker with only four months at KEMZ. "Anyone can make his own future here regardless of a party card," supplemented another new hire who had put in five years in a defense plant where that had not been the case. "We have our shortcomings, certainly," was the judicious appraisal of one manual worker who joined KEMZ three years ago, "but we have more information, more access to management than I've ever seen before. Still, we need more participation."

In-depth shop interviews revealed much about the process of change. Consider the comments of machine operator Edic M., who, after two years of army service, began to work at KEMZ while it was still a state-owned enterprise. Subsequently, structural changes at KEMZ dramatically transformed employees' attitudes to their work. "It all started when the new general director and his management team brought the workforce together to explain their concept of worker ownership," he said. The open, candid nature of those discussions made Edic and other employees feel respected by the management in direct contrast to practice in state-owned enterprises.

Edic argued that he and his coworkers could make their plant successful by working as an employee-owner team given effective responsibility. In his mind this stood in stark contrast to practice in his father's defense plant, where employees felt that they were cogs in the machinery they operated. In fact, the profound changes in Edic's job had convinced his father to leave his state-owned factory and join the KEMZ workforce.

Edic felt that one of the most important features of the new scheme was management's willingness to support employee participation in the industrial process. "I would never hesitate to suggest changes in operations; they will always be taken seriously." Interestingly, Edic's primary motivation at the time of the interview in July 1992 was not increased income, although he was certainly not opposed to that; it was, rather, job satisfaction based on KEMZ's system of participation.

Still, such attitudes were not universal. In 1992, there was substantial frustration in the assembly shop with the unbelievable crowding. Employees explained to us at length that they knew who their elected representatives were and had complained. And, yes, their man on the board of directors had reported back to them. But no, there were no results. The shop was still hopelessly crowded and, in consequence, dangerous. The assemblers, who were playing dominoes at lunch, went on to complain about problems in supply. "If we *really* were owners," one commented, "we would do something about it."

LEADERSHIP FOR CHANGE

The success of KEMZ cannot be attributed only to new organizational structures that have been instituted. It is also largely due to the superb leadership instincts of KEMZ's general director. "As Vrachev's formal power has diminished," commented one manager to us in 1993, "respect for him has grown."

In contrast to general directors of state-owned enterprises, Vrachev does not create barriers between himself and KEMZ's ordinary employees. His office is organized in a way that makes him physically accessible. During KEMZ's turnaround, no secretaries or other intermediaries were located between him and the workforce, and part of his office was used as display space for lamps, the company's new consumer product. With the completion of the new office building, the physical layout is more traditional, but Vrachev shows a positively nonmanagerial enthusiasm for having his office converted into a training room. His open style of management has helped to build trust and cooperation throughout the factory, and it has rubbed off on other managers, although some clearly remain uncomfortable with using it themselves.

In employee meetings, the culture he has fostered allows everyone to voice opinions freely, without fear of management disapproval. Vrachev's ability to achieve consensus derives from his personal experience as a shop-floor worker as well as his commitment to employee involvement. This assures credibility and acceptance and generally results in enthusiastic support for implementing decisions. Vrachev's intuitive understanding of both micro- and macroeconomics guarantees an educated personal baseline for industrial decisions.

Vrachev is a synthesis of old and new. Representative of the new generation of Russian managers, he has developed extensive personal computer skills from word processing to complex financial spreadsheets.

The computer sits next to him in his office and is an integral tool in his daily administration. His concepts of management reform are antithetical to the old order. Yet at the same time, there is much that is traditional about him. He walks to work and lives in a two-room apartment which betrays its hurried construction under Khrushchev; the upright piano of his daughter, an accomplished pianist, is squeezed into her parents' bedroom. His library is heavy on Soviet classics of economics and politics, and he has added old works that are again available—a 1990 edition of Trotsky's *History of the Russian Revolution* sits among half a dozen official histories of the Communist Party of the Soviet Union. Sandwiched into the bookshelf on top of a set of Marx and Engels is a volume of Dale Carnegie. When he moved his office in 1993 to KEMZ's newly completed office building, the portrait of Lenin moved as well.

While effective personal leadership style may not be a teachable skill, examples like those provided by Vrachev suggest that, as American experience shows, organizational structures alone are not sufficient. Management's personal commitment to and understanding of the essence of employee ownership are crucial to success.

THE SMELL OF CHANGE

Though an italicized hammer and sickle still points the way to KEMZ and Lenin still holds the place of honor behind Vrachev's desk in his new office, the predominant sense at KEMZ is one of change.

Vrachev's window overlooks a courtyard ringed by Kazansky Elektromekhanichesky's buildings, where steel, bricks, and girders for a new building and still-crated equipment compete for space with finished cranes awaiting inspection. The construction crew's activities add to the confusion and crowding. KEMZ's construction program had, by 1992, brought cutting steel to length and welding in out of the rain and snow for the first time; previously all that work had been done outside. By the summer of 1993, the crowding which had evoked such bitter comment the previous year among assemblers had been alleviated. Even before new buildings are finished, they are often in use. In July 1992, about 20 percent of the KEMZ workforce crowded into the largest room in the new office building then under construction for a discussion of employee ownership with their American guests for two hours on unpaid time. A smell of fresh paint pervaded the room.

Despite KEMZ's success during its first years as an independent worker-owned firm, the challenges of the future seem as daunting as those of the immediate past.

The firm faces a full range of business challenges. It is struggling with the collapse of supply in the post-Soviet era: in the fall of 1993, for example,

Zil was unable to deliver trucks to KEMZ for mounting cranes because of the lack of tires which Omsk Rubber could not deliver to Zil because oil, which otherwise had gone to produce rubber, was being exported for hard currency by the increasingly independent petroleum complex. Furthermore, defense plants continued to have first claim to the tires available. To add insult to injury, a fire in the Kamaz engine plant added truck motors to the list of items in shortage.

The supply difficulties were less of a problem than they might have been, however, because KEMZ's customers were caught in the general credit crunch. KEMZ has responded by relying increasingly on repair work. In 1990, shortly after becoming a cooperative, it established a new department to guarantee service on its cranes to customers, following Western models. Repair business has been contributing about 5 percent of KEMZ's income annually since then, but will unquestionably play a larger role in its survival strategy. The firm has also launched a line of lamps to try to reach the consumer products market.

When the economy recovers, KEMZ will face tough competition: its main competitor produces five thousand cranes annually, a dozen times more than KEMZ's four hundred.

KEMZ also faces a major challenge in creating a sense of ownership among newly hired personnel. While the workers who participated in privatizing KEMZ have a strong sense that they have benefited from their initiative, the same is not true for many of the new employees. The company's turnover of about thirty-five employees a month is concentrated in this group—especially among welders who quit to take work during the summer in private construction. For new employees, "inflation has made the situation very difficult. Everything depends on salary." KEMZ's salaries have dropped back relative to those in neighboring defense plants (which were still subsidized in July 1993) as KEMZ has focused on capital improvements. While this built the accounts of owners, new employees tend not to become owners, and hence don't share in the benefits. To alleviate this problem, the company has undertaken an ownership education program patterned on that of some American employee-owned firms, and management is considering making a one-time contribution of a one-thousand-ruble share to give all employees some stock after three months' work to qualify.

Management, too, remains a challenge. "We used to debate the topic of 'any kitchenmaid can run the state,' " says Vrachev. "But despite all of our slogans, the *real* motto of the past was 'any initiative is punishable.' When we had a centralized system, we didn't have to concern ourselves with regulations. They were set. Now we have to make our own. Previously every department had absolute clarity on what it was to do; now we have to figure out how to form horizontal ties between departments." Further decentralization remains on the agenda.

It is a sign of the times that the economics department at Lenin's alma mater, the University of Kazan, has fliers up for its new courses: "The basis of management and marketing" and "The basis of transition to a market economy."

NOTES

1. This case study draws on V. G. Vrachev's analysis of KEMZ's transition from state to worker ownership in Vrachev 1992 and Vrachev 1993; on our interviews with Vrachev in July 1992, November 1992, and July 1993; and on our visits to KEMZ in July 1992 and July 1993.

2. In 1988 the average monthly salary was 187 rubles at KEMZ and 270 rubles at neighboring defense plants.

3. Vrachev's analysis of the plant led him to conclude that leasing under the then current terms would not improve its financial situation. Cooperatives, under the 1988 Law on Cooperatives, had lower taxes on profits, gave management greater latitude to choose what to produce, and, crucially for KEMZ, enabled the enterprise to set prices on the basis of real costs, not to follow the price established by the state plan.

4. Vrachev had proposed a one-thousand-ruble membership fee to raise money to buy three pieces of new equipment. The lower fee was a compromise to get support and members.

5. After KEMZ became a cooperative, management fired some of the worst workers, replaced them with new hires at higher salaries, and imposed fines for infractions of labor discipline. The understanding among employees that the management had a choice to fire and hire strengthened work discipline.

6. Part of the reason for this success was that KEMZ was still able to buy raw materials at state prices through the plan. Since it was able to squeeze eight months of production out of its initial raw materials and work in process through its internal lease system, the company was able to sell part of its raw-material allocations under the plan to pay down debt.

7. In 1990, new legislation froze wages at 1989 levels, causing discontent about the fact that KEMZ had reinvested so heavily in 1989 rather than raising wages further. Cooperative members ultimately benefited from the distribution of the artificially inflated profits that resulted, but KEMZ's hired labor lost ground and was tremendously discontented.

8. The Tatarstan Republic adopted a 1991 Yeltsin decree requiring re-registration of firms which had privatized prior to the 1992 privatization law. KEMZ's re-registration process began in February 1992 and was completed by December 1992. While some firms were re-registered without charge, KEMZ was assessed a second purchase price; "when the state saw our profit, it sought a means to get it" is Vrachev's explanation. "Every president begins his administration by repealing the acts of his predecessors. It's the tradition. The general secretary dies, and the new general secretary begins a new era. It happened with Stalin. It happened with Khrushchev. It's just the same with Yeltsin."

9. The price was calculated by taking the 1989 depreciated asset value of 1.3 million rubles, adjusting it for inflation to 16 million, and adding in the 1989 working capital without an adjustment for inflation. KEMZ sought to pay entirely in vouchers, but was ultimately required to pay 12 million in cash. Payment to the Tatarstan state property committee was completed in May 1993.

10. KEMZ's management investigated converting the legal structure of the enterprise to a joint-stock company but found the law too inflexible.

11. Account shares repurchased from retiring workers are distributed equally among current workers who are members, and the firm will eventually sell some shares to outsiders to cover the costs of repurchasing accounts. Workers can also buy shares from each other. KEMZ's charter permits foreign ownership of up to 20 percent of the company, but the firm has no foreign partners as yet.

12. Initially, the structures of managing at KEMZ were formed in accordance with the Law on Cooperatives and laid down in the cooperative's bylaws. The highest authority was the general meeting of the members of the cooperative, which would choose the board of directors and its chairman, confirm the financial strategy of the plant, decide on the use of the profits, and so on.

13. The dichotomy between owners and new hires complicates management. In a July 1993 focus group, one manager—who had been hired only two months previously from an aircraft plant—noted that of the thirty people in his department, only three or four were owners. They were highly motivated, he thought, but the others were not, and there was a lot of turnover among them.

8 Privatization at Stroipolymer

Victor B. Supyan

◆ BEFORE my first visit to Stroipolymer, I had heard some controversial opinions about this enterprise and its general director, Boris N. Makharinov.[1] Some saw Stroipolymer as a model of how to represent the interests of Russian workers in the privatization process. Others, however, were more skeptical about whose interests were being served and insisted that Stroipolymer was on the road to becoming a traditional capitalist enterprise with all its problems and contradictions. Since Stroipolymer has been one of the pioneers of privatization, the answers to these questions are especially interesting.

Founded in 1920 as a brickworks, Stroipolymer now manufactures laminated construction products including linoleum, wallpaper, vinyl wall coverings, sealants, glue, and handrails. The plant, located in Khlupino, about fifty kilometers outside Moscow in the Odinzovo district, employs about five hundred; another two hundred are employed by Polys, a transportation and service firm spun off by Stroipolymer.

The privatization and technological reconstruction at Stroipolymer has been a great economic success. There has been a significant increase in productivity and production, an increase in employment by almost one hundred employees during 1991, and an improvement in wages and salaries. Most of the employees are satisfied with their wages and social situation. There is practically no absenteeism and no drinking at the workplace anymore. There are few social conflicts at the enterprise, and what is especially important is that there are positive changes in the workers' attitude toward their work.

In my estimation, however, Stroipolymer's experience of privatization is not a pure employee ownership approach. It is rather a mixture of different approaches in privatization, management, incentives, and so on. Stroipolymer is in transition from state ownership to private ownership, but thus far it remains unclear what the final form of private ownership will be. Despite the spreading of ownership inside the company and perhaps, in time, outside it as well, Makharinov believes that real control of ownership and management should be consigned to a limited number of hands. Makharinov himself often argues provocatively that employee ownership is just a transitional stage on the road to conventional capitalist ownership.

Putting aside the final outcome, there is no doubt currently that the employees of Stroipolymer are interested in all these changes that have happened and welcome them.

THE ROAD TO PRIVATIZATION

Stroipolymer was one of the first enterprises in Russia to begin privatization, and the process has been neither straightforward nor simple. Throughout the process, the work collective has been determined to chart the best way of achieving increased effectiveness and motivation of workers. In 1988, the plant became the second enterprise in the USSR (after the Butovo construction plants) to be leased by employees.

Becoming a leased enterprise demanded a new business strategy. Makharinov and his colleagues polled employees and organized a seminar away from the plant near the city of Svenigorod to brainstorm ways of working in the coming market economy. The group of forty participants, representing management and workers and facilitated by the sociologist V. Dudchenko, discussed the future form of ownership, technological and organizational modernization, methods of management, courses of social development, and other challenging issues. The seminar broke into five working groups of eight people each to elaborate different aspects of and approaches to the economic and social development of Stroipolymer. These analyses demonstrated that privatization was needed and that technological modernization and social investments were vital. Participants estimated that the enterprise needed about 70 million rubles to realize this program of economic and social reconstruction, including 40 million for capital improvements and 30 million to meet social needs.

Since the profit of the enterprise was then only about 3 million rubles annually, Makharinov's initial reaction was to describe this wish list as "raving madness." But seminar members responded to Makharinov's challenge by brainstorming ideas for improvements in company performance, including recycling and new products, that ultimately promised significant increases in profits. "The seminar demonstrated how many good ideas employees had," commented Makharinov, looking back. "It showed also that an improvement in economic results could only be gotten through involving every employee in ownership."

Although Makharinov's slogan that "all Stroipolymer employees have to become millionaires" seemed utopian, after the seminar many participants proclaimed their belief that together they could create better working and living conditions. A subsequent plant meeting communicated some of the excitement of seminar participants to other employees.

As a leased enterprise, Stroipolymer had very good results. The average wage increased from 220 rubles a month in April 1988 to 360 in February 1990. The firm built sixty apartments and a clinic for employees. The profit for 1989 was 3 million rubles. From this sum, 1.5 million rubles were spent on the lease payment, 1 million were used for the public budget, and 500,000 remained for the enterprise. While it did well, the restrictions of leasing were quite visible. The leasing agreement gave Stroipolymer employees independence and freedom in production and sales, but it did not guarantee ownership by the employees, nor was there a provision for an employee purchase in the lease contract.

An initial effort to buy the plant proved abortive, despite Makharinov's pledge of increased productivity and higher tax revenues to local and regional authorities. The first secretary of the Moscow regional committee rejected the proposal as "idiotic" and "antisocialistic." However, the ministerial decree which permitted the establishment of the BUTEK Association of enterprises opened a formal avenue for privatization. In the summer of 1990, after Stroipolymer had become a BUTEK member, management initiated another employee buyout effort, and the work collective approved it.

In August 1990 employees bought the plant for 20 million rubles. From Stroipolymer's residual value (initial value minus depreciation), 5.7 million was deducted from the purchase price for capital improvements made while the lease was in effect; 1 million was paid in cash; and 13.3 million was borrowed from the state bank with an eight-year term and an initial interest rate of 5.5 percent.

Before the buyout, much analytical work was done and many questions were answered. Who had a right to be an owner? What would be the criteria for determining this? How much should each individual own? All these problems were discussed at a meeting of all employees. It was decided that ownership would be limited to those who had at least two years' seniority and a good evaluation of their job performance. For those who met the threshold criteria, shares would be allocated according to seniority and wages.[2]

Some 295 employees (of the 600 then employed) met these criteria and received shares ranging from 60,000 to 160,000 rubles in value; the average allocation was 75,000 rubles. The general director's allocation was initially set at 220,000 rubles, but at the workers' suggestion, the amount was increased to 550,000 rubles. To justify allocating shares on which the loan had not yet been repaid, each worker either paid in cash or signed an individual contract agreeing to repayment by pledging the future dividends from these same shares. It was suggested that future shares be traded publicly. Initially, retirees had to sell their shares back to Stroipolymer at face value. In such cases, those shares were then resold among the employees of Stroipolymer. (This principle is similar to that of the American Employee Stock Ownership Plan [ESOP] model.) In 1992, Stroipolymer's employee-owners received the right to keep their shares after retirement or layoff and leave the shares to their heirs.

CHANGING THE STRUCTURE OF THE ENTERPRISE

From the initial buyout in August 1990 to the summer of 1992, there were many changes in the organizational and managerial structure of the company and in its ownership form. After the August 1990 buyout, Stroipolymer initially had the legal status of a "people's enterprise" like other BUTEK members. Subsequently, in February 1991, it registered as a shareholding society. Inside this society twenty-two small enterprises were set up in 1991. These have full financial independence, including their own accounts in banks and their own seals.[3] At the time of my visit in May 1992, there were five more small enterprises in the process of being established; by July 1993, there were a total of thirty of them. While not totally independent, these enterprises are permitted to determine their own plans for production, obtain their own seals, deal directly with suppliers, hire labor, set wages, and establish their own prices. Their status is similar to that of profit centers in Western corporations.[4]

The initial decision about establishing these small enterprises was made at the conference of shareholders in the fall of 1991 when only 52 percent of shareholders supported Makharinov's idea. Successful decentralization, however, won support. At the shareholders' meeting in 1992, by contrast, the experiment of restructuring Stroipolymer was approved by an overwhelming majority of about 90 percent of employees.

Establishment of these enterprises was conditioned by the necessity of so-called psychological privatization (which is described below) and by technological circumstances and goals. In spite of these enterprises' autonomy, the general guidance of the whole stockholding company is conducted by its top management and primarily by Makharinov.

Although dividends on shares have not yet been distributed to employee-owners because they are earmarked to repay loans employees took to purchase their shares, 15 percent of the enterprise's profit is distributed to all employees of Stroipolymer, whether shareholders or not. Of that, workers receive 10 percent and management 5 percent.[5] Another 20 percent of profit is formally committed as dividends and used for the loan repayment. Another 5 percent of profit is used for managerial improvements in the company (training managerial staff and providing other incentives for management, which constitutes 20 percent of all employees). The remaining 60 percent goes to development, capital improvements, and social goals.

While workers have not benefited immediately from share ownership—the dividends are repaying the loan—they have benefited handsomely in other ways. The price of each share increased substantially; from a 500-ruble initial nominal value, shares rose to be worth 1,500 rubles each by May 1992. This means that the average employee, with 75,000 rubles in shares, actually owns 225,000 rubles. So far, there has been no inflation indexation of the shares.

Wages also rose significantly. The average wage rose from about 220 rubles a month in April 1988 to 360 rubles a month in February 1990, 700 rubles in July 1991, 5,500 rubles in March 1992, and 10,000 rubles in July 1992. By May 1993 wages had reached 80,000 rubles per month. Of course, most of the rise of wages in 1992–93 reflects Russia's high inflation, but the gain in wages at Stroipolymer was higher than the industry's average and much higher than that in the economy in general.[6]

PSYCHOLOGICAL PRIVATIZATION

Psychological training and adaptation is an extremely important element of the privatization process and the improvement of workers' job performance. Makharinov calls this "psychological privatization." Everybody in the plant needs to have a feeling of ownership of the enterprise, says Makharinov, not just the company's president and his closest associates. "The main thing is to set people's energy free."

But in a society where private ownership has been virtually unknown for almost seventy years, how can this goal be reached? Makharinov's belief is that distributing property among employees is not enough. Stroipolymer has developed three principles which, together with private property, can direct people's energy in the right direction and which can overcome, as Makharinov says, "Brownian movement" in a collective. (This expression comes from physics and means irregular movement of molecules and atoms.)

1. Do away with command management and decentralize to get departments and workers to take responsibility for their own work. The intent is to give them a lot of freedom but at the same time full economic responsibility.

2. Develop shop-floor participation in decision making, which gives employees a possibility of discussing and recommending how to solve strategic questions.

3. Establish a strict relationship between wages and other income and the final results of work in individual divisions, which every worker can see and evaluate. People usually feel uncomfortable when they do not know why their wages increased or decreased.

These principles were originally used by a group of eight employees involved in producing polymer stabilizers who now run their department as a separate subsidiary. They had produced thirteen tons of stabilizers the previous year; as an independent subsidiary, however, they rapidly reached a level of eighteen tons a month. Makharinov thinks that until now many employees were not ready psychologically to be the owners: "They are accustomed to living in a cage. They need to learn to live at large."

Since employees leased the plant in 1988, Stroipolymer has sought to promote a culture of ownership by teaching people to be responsible for their work. This effort has met with some success. Now many workers have begun to understand that their current incomes, the capital accumulated in shares, and future dividends all depend on their work performance. For example, Anatoly Aleshnikov, a worker with thirty years' seniority and ninety thousand rubles in shares, emphasized that many of his colleagues, after becoming owners, have tried to be more active by suggesting new technical and organizational improvements: "Previously we were on fixed wages. Now when we get greater production, we benefit directly. So now we try to implement good ideas."

Makharinov and his management team have tried to teach people how to work in the new conditions and how to be owners. For that, Stroipolymer does not have a formal system of training and retraining the workers; there are no systematic lectures or seminars inside the company on privatization. But because of personal contact between Makharinov and almost every person in the plant on a regular basis, the understanding of privatization is growing. "The main thing," judges Makharinov, "is not to explain but to create necessary conditions." He tries to follow this approach, in part by discussing each impending important decision with both top management and shop-floor workers. Besides that, Stroipolymer readily shares its experience in privatization and transition to new methods of work with other enterprises throughout the country. Stroipolymer's specialists already have conducted several seminars for different organizations on this matter, creating yet another line of business for the company.

MANAGING STROIPOLYMER

The management of the shareholding society Stroipolymer is organized traditionally. The highest ruling body of the company is a meeting of shareholders, which elects the board of directors (see Figure 8.1). The shareholders' meeting has a right to make principal decisions about changes in the charter of the company, about distribution of profit, and about the organizational structure of the company; it also approves the report of the shareholding society's administration. The board of directors is made up of seven persons, all from Stroipolymer. One member represents the manual workers.

The chairman of the board of directors is also the president of the company. He appoints the presidents of all twenty-two profit centers which are the members of the shareholding company. These presidents form the council of chief executive officers, which is actually the main executive body at Stroipolymer under the guidance of Makharinov. The presidents sign contracts with each other and with the chairman of the board of directors.

Stroipolymer has implemented a contract system of employment. The median age of employees in the company is about 42 to 43 years. Although in the 1980s the average labor turnover at Stroipolymer exceeded one-third of the workforce per year, by 1990–1992 it decreased to 2 to 3 percent

Figure 8.1
Structure of Management of Stroipolymer

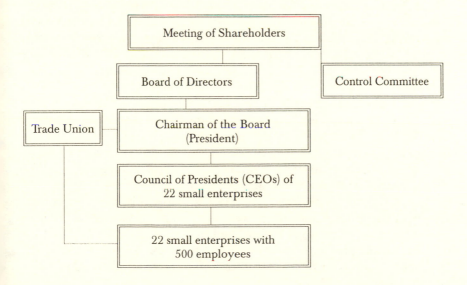

annually. The composition of the labor force at Stroipolymer is 80 percent manual workers and 20 percent managerial staff. All of them sign three-year contracts. Makharinov signs a five-year contract with the board of directors.

In the beginning, many workers mistrusted the contract system of employment. But because the labor agreement includes some possibilities of significant incentives (up to 80 percent of wages) for being ready to hold several occupations and obligations, for keeping property safe, for working without wasting time, and for achieving similar standards, the workers' attitude changed.

The chairman of the board of the shareholding society has far-reaching authority. He makes decisions about many strategic questions concerning the company's development (except those covered by the shareholders' meeting) and has a right to spend up to 500 million rubles without shareholder approval.

Stroipolymer's system of management combines two types of leadership: a paternalistic style of management represented by Makharinov and significant delegation of authority on specific questions to autonomous units, as discussed above. In the case of Stroipolymer, such a combination seems to be reasonable. It has historical roots: Makharinov is not just the company's president, but he is also the informal leader of the work collective.

Makharinov's career up to the privatization of Stroipolymer was not atypical of Russian managers of his generation, although he advanced more rapidly than the average. Born in the Ukraine in 1939, Makharinov left school after seven years to go to work before serving four years in the navy. After the navy, Makharinov worked at a steel mill while attending an evening high school. In 1965, he entered the prestigious Moscow Bauman Technical College. Every summer while at this school, Makharinov participated in student labor camps as leader of students.

Makharinov came to Stroipolymer in 1971 after graduation from the Moscow Bauman Technical College, and he became its director in 1973. Very soon the enterprise became profitable after many years of losing money. At the same time he paid much attention to social problems and to improving employee living standards. In 1988, Makharinov initiated leasing and, subsequently, the buyout of the enterprise's assets.

The general director's leadership in the privatization process is typical for many Russian enterprises, and the changes in managerial practices reflect Makharinov's leadership as well. As discussed above, the significant decentralization of authority within the firm was initiated by Makharinov despite initial opposition to change in the work collective. Similarly, Makharinov initiated the creation of a new firm, Polys, to give Stroipolymer greater flexibility.

Polys was created in September 1991 by all shareholders of Stroipolymer (295 individuals) with an initial share capital of fifty thousand rubles. Its legal status is that of a closed shareholding society.. Polys was established to create a mobile commercial structure to handle supply, marketing, transport, and technical assistance for Stroipolymer and other firms. It also increased Stroipolymer's flexibility and avoided the cap on profits that limited the parent company. The assets of Polys amounted in 1992 to several dozen million rubles. Every month Polys paid Stroipolymer several million rubles for using Stroipolymer's equipment, transportation, and other facilities. During these years Polys became an owner of its own equipment (computers, trucks, cars, etc.). Its profitability enabled Polys to grant Stroipolymer a loan to pay off its credit to the bank taken for the buyout. In 1992, Stroipolymer had already repaid Polys 10 million rubles.

ECONOMIC PERSPECTIVES AND SOCIAL PROBLEMS

Today Stroipolymer is doing very well. Production grew by about 20 percent per year during 1988–91, despite the overall decline in the Russian economy during this period. In 1991, profit hit 22 million rubles on production of 80 million rubles (in 1991 prices), a seven-fold increase that reflects both increases in the volume of production and in prices. It is expected that in 1992, production will reach 1.3 billion rubles and profit will reach 300 million rubles or more (1992 prices). The company plans massive technological reconstruction, and it needs several billion rubles (also in 1992 prices) for investments. When completed, this project will more than double existing production capacity, add additional product lines, develop business cooperation with foreign companies, and establish joint ventures. (Stroipolymer now has one joint-venture company called Ontamo with a Canadian firm. It is involved in lumber production and utilization of Stroipolymer's waste material.)

At the same time, the firm has experienced difficulties which are typical for today's situation in the Russian economy. Many customers cannot pay their obligations to Stroipolymer. These sums already exceeded 200 million rubles in 1992. Because of this, Stroipolymer has its own debt of 30 million rubles. Moreover, as a result of the general crisis in the Russian economy, in the summer of 1992 only 30 percent of the productive capacity of the enterprise was utilized.

Much attention continues to be paid to social questions at Stroipolymer. Almost all of the apartment houses in Khlupino village belong to the company. In 1991, the enterprise constructed a new apartment building with sixty apartments for its workers; two more similar apartment buildings are now under construction. The company has also begun to build modern detached houses of Western style, equipped with all amenities; the first eight are expected to be completed in 1993. The company's intention was not to distribute these new apartments and houses free of charge, but to sell them to Stroipolymer workers for an initial down payment and a long-term, low-interest loan guaranteed by their Stroipolymer shares. Regrettably, inflation has pushed the price of the individual houses to a level of at least 60 to 80 million rubles each (in May 1993 prices) and has made long-term, low-interest loans a thing of the past, virtually precluding their sale to employees. They will probably be sold to outsiders.

Besides paid social services, Stroipolymer has a system of free social help. For example, all employees of the enterprise receive free meals during the working day. The shareholding society provides big subsidies for its kindergarten and for workers' vacations. Following a Stroipolymer proposal, the Foundation of Social Protection for the population of the Odinzovo district was established. The cofounders of this foundation were the company Polys and the district administration; Stroipolymer contributed 360,000 rubles to the foundation. Under the foundation's sponsorship, four cafeterias provide free dinners to low-paid citizens twice a week. In 1992, Stroipolymer transferred 1.5 million rubles to the old people's home in the city of Svenigorod, not far from the enterprise. The board of directors also decided to add 200 rubles to the pension of each of the enterprise's pensioners, and it plans to continue raising pensions in the future.

The company's management, including Makharinov, is strongly against encouraging the dependence of healthy people on social transfer payments. They are ready to support people, but only those who actually need this help, such as pensioners, invalids, women with dependent children, and families with many children. It is important to emphasize that the consumption fund of the enterprise, which is spent for wages and salaries and for different additional payments including recreation, vacations, and other social goals, is the same both for the employee shareholders and for employees who do not own shares.

The function of social support and protection is also achieved by the trade union organization. Many questions of social administration, for example, firing workers, have to be coordinated with the trade union. But the individual contracts which employees sign with the management state that under some circumstances management can fire an employee without coordination with the trade union (such as serious problems with discipline, hard drinking, stealing, and the like). The trade union solves many social problems of workers and is involved in issues of job security and health security, among other things. There is no other labor organization at the company except the trade union. This is atypical of Russian enterprises, for recently many new labor organizations have arisen, such as councils of work collectives. Management's opinion at Stroipolymer is that there should be only one labor organization—the trade union—at the enterprise; competing channels of employee representation would be fraught with the potential for conflict and struggles for power and influence. In fact, such conflictive situations have already occurred in many enterprises in Russia.

RESULTS OF PRIVATIZATION

The main approach which Makharinov has tried to implement is to change the employee shareholders' consciousness. Ownership of private property means not only dividends. It also means greater responsibility: a willingness to take risks, to develop a culture of ownership, to encourage skills of management and entrepreneurship, and to promote knowledge of how to grow the enterprise.

Employees of Stroipolymer are sure that international experience of privatization (including American ESOPs) could be very useful. But at the same time, they think that it is necessary to proceed from their own conditions. Besides selling shares to their own workers in privatization, Stroipolymer's management eventually plans to involve external investors as outside owners. It is also very important for the enterprise's development to work in the conditions of a market environment. To be a successful owner is not simple for everybody. It is necessary to learn this skill and to learn it well.

NOTES

1. This chapter is based on interviews with general director Boris N. Makharinov in April 1992, May 1992, March 1993, May 1993, June 1994, and July 1994; and on data from the 1991, 1992, and 1993 Annual Reports of Stroipolymer.

2. About sixty soldiers, who worked at the enterprise at that time as construction workers under an agreement between Stroipolymer and the Ministry of Defense, did not participate in privatization as owners.

3. A separate seal and bank account are marks of the independent enterprise.

4. In July 1993 Makharinov told the participants in the conference on Privatization and Experience with the Development of Worker Stock Ownership (Moscow, July 7, 1993) that Stroipolymer's extreme decentralization has permitted the company to adapt to the new conditions; "if you can go bankrupt, you have to work harder and to think harder." The company is moving toward full independence for these component units, Makharinov said, but Stroipolymer will retain a controlling interest—perhaps 55 percent ownership—in each.

5. Of the 5 percent going to management, 2 percent goes to Makharinov, 1 percent to the deputy general director, and the remaining 2 percent to thirty-eight top managers.

6. The average wage in the Moscow area in May 1993 was thirty-thousand rubles, up from about three hundred rubles per month in July 1991.

9 Pioneer of Privatization: Veshky

Yakov Keremetsky

◆ THE Veshky company can be viewed as a unique phenomenon in the history of the transition from a state-directed economic system to a free-market economy. Perhaps earlier than any other enterprise in Russia, Veshky demonstrated how employees can change their company and their lives when their desire and determination to become free producers are sufficiently strong to break through the system's walls. In Russia, where the stifling reign of bureaucracy and its brutal control over the labor force seem to have extinguished the spirit of ownership and the motivation for working, awakening interest in the free economy is a very difficult process. The process of changing attitudes toward private property is connected, in the eyes of the employees, with the exploitation of the many and the enrichment of the few. There is a strong social antipathy to letting individuals appropriate the net worth of "public" ownership as private owners.

Seventy years of brainwashing by the propaganda of the totalitarian state have distorted society's consciousness. But people working at Veshky have succeeded in parting with the stereotyped perceptions faster than the population in general. Thanks to their management, they made the decision to become the arbiters of their own destiny. As fate has willed, they found themselves on the cutting edge of restructuring property relations in post-Communist Russia.

SECRETS OF PROSPERITY

The seven Veshky employee-owned enterprises are a forty-five-minute drive from the Kremlin. They are located in the Veshky township in the Mytishchi region, about thirty kilometers from Moscow.

Six years ago Veshky, like most state enterprises (with the exception of defense industries), was a stagnant manufacturer of kitchen furniture. Today it is a dynamic, diversified company making window frames, floor panels, shoes, shirts, packages, and even bread. It employs five hundred people. Its gross revenues in 1992 were more than 1 billion rubles, with profits growing by 40 to 50 percent per year.

What are the secrets of this prosperity?

The first "secret" is Valery Voronov, forty-eight years old, the general director of the Veshky company. Having worked in the old Soviet system of total state control, he has become a fierce proponent of economic freedom. He likes to say that if the political situation in Russia were to change again and the Communists should return to power and restore the totalitarian system, he would prefer to become a street sweeper than to go back to obeying the orders of the Communist Party regional secretaries. "I don't want to be a slave of the partocracy anymore. I want to be a free and independent entrepreneur for the rest of my life," Voronov remarks as he tells his story. It is important to remember that the growth of employee ownership in the various republics of the former USSR, and especially in Russia, was to a great extent due to the enthusiasm, energy, and enterprise of people like Valery Voronov.

In the early years of Gorbachev's perestroika, very few top managers were ready to take the risk of making themselves and their workers into free producers. Most were resigned to being the passive executors of orders from the ministerial bureaucracy. Knowing from personal experience the power of this bureaucracy and the strength of its resistance to half-hearted attempts at economic reform, most top managers preferred not to challenge the highly centralized, command-administrative system of management. They did not believe in the success of perestroika and they were right. Only the collapse of the Communist Party opened up real possibilities for the restoration and development of strong work incentives (Keremetsky and Logue 1991). People like Valery Voronov had to have courage to fight for economic freedom. They also had to have the capabilities and experience to overcome the highly unfavorable conditions for setting up private, employee-owned enterprises: the absence of laws to facilitate buyouts, the lack of access to bank credits, the corruption of bureaucracy, the total absence of a market infrastructure, and especially the lack of experience with establishing employee-owned enterprises.

Veshky was typical of the spontaneous initial stage of privatization in Russia. It was "privatization at one's own risk and on one's own responsibility." Like many other enterprises, Veshky began moving down the road to employee ownership by leasing the plant's assets from the state and obtaining a right to purchase the plant in the future. "We couldn't wait for the law on the privatization. We had no time to wait," remarks Voronov, explaining his choice of leasing.

Veshky's four hundred employees voted to lease the plant with its antiquated building in 1989. At that time, the value of the building was estimated at a half-million rubles. The company immediately undertook a program of heavy investment, and by the end of 1990, the value of the company's new buildings, new machinery, and new houses constructed for workers totaled 10 million rubles. This new equity belonged to the enterprise's personnel. Economic and psychological foundations had been prepared for the buyout.

In February 1991, employees bought the original assets from the state under the terms of the December 1989 leasing law. The regional government valued the company at only a half-million rubles. They used the standard Soviet method of assessment, deducting imputed employee payments from the assets' acquisition price at the time of leasing. That is usually called a purchase at residual value—a common practice in the absence of a market infrastructure. The buyout was approved by the trust Torgmash, of which Veshky was a part, and by the regional Soviet of People's Deputies, which owned the enterprise. To make the purchase possible, the management of Veshky raised the required half-million rubles from the employees.

To restrict inequality, limits were set on maximum and minimum ownership. The maximum share was 2,000 rubles and the minimum was 500 rubles. The fixed nominal price of a share was 250 rubles. Of the 400 personnel at Veshky, 350 bought shares and became owners of the plant; the number subsequently has grown to 400 as employment increased. Furthermore, fifty outsiders were allowed to become shareholders too. These people were from the companies connected with Veshky by common business interests, and Veshky turned to them because of its great need for investment capital. Voronov and his team know by experience that ownership is largely determined by who has access to capital credit. They also know that in modern post-Communist Russia, enterprises have practically no access to bank credit. Interest rates are more than 100 percent because of inflation and the absolute power of the corrupt Central Bank officials (and no less corrupt officials of weak commercial banks, who know nothing about competition, which makes any borrowing at all difficult). Moreover, there are no tax incentives to encourage employee ownership.[1]

Practically the only possibility to obtain investment capital is to find enterprises which have money to spend and attract them by making their managers shareholders. From the beginning of the buyout process, Veshky was very successful in finding such "donors." When Veshky converted into a joint-stock company in 1991, it sold 25 percent of the value of its capital investment during the lease period to such companies as Atomenergo, which is involved in the service and maintenance of atomic power stations, and Zenit, which is a commercial firm of the Defense Ministry. These companies invested more than 3 million rubles and began to work with Veshky on a number of projects. Veshky employees retained a controlling 75 percent interest as the main shareholder.

Today Veshky, like most Russian companies, is interested in setting up joint ventures with foreign firms. It has established joint ventures with an Italian firm to produce sports shoes, with a Finnish company to produce furniture, and with a German company to manufacture wood products.

"Why do we do it?" asks Voronov rhetorically of the joint venture with the Germans. "We do it because the two companies have a common business interest. We have the raw materials here in Russia, and we know that the West will buy our wood products. But the most important reason is that we need hard currency for investing in the production of many kinds of goods, including shoes and our bakery. We are not after hard currency for the sake of accumulating hard currency. Instead our goal is new technology."

Voronov is sure that foreign capital can be attracted by low labor costs. Wages at Veshky are double the average for Russian enterprises of the same profile, but yet they account for only 4 percent of the costs of sales.

Voronov and other Veshky senior managers usually show the sports shoe factory to visitors who come to find out the "secrets" of the firm's prosperity. Voronov proudly shares them. The factory was built with the help of the Italian company Simod. In its technological level, its organization of the production process, and its physical appearance, this factory resembles some of the best modern Western enterprises. The sports shoes are designed by the Italian partner, and 60 percent of the raw materials are supplied from Italy. Veshky is going to shift to cheaper local raw materials in the near future. The Italian partner's share is 25 percent of the authorized capital, and it receives 25 percent of the profits.

Like many other employee-owned enterprises in modern Russia, Veshky is not afraid of a larger foreign ownership share, even to the point of yielding control of a joint venture to a foreign partner. Voronov explains why: "We are not against 100 percent foreign ownership. Owning one of our enterprises, a foreign investor will have a bigger stake and be more attentive to our needs. If he doesn't have an economic interest, he will not work here. This 100 percent stake might occur through our leasing the enterprise to them or through the regional soviet leasing our partner the land. Today none of our enterprises is 100 percent foreign owned. We need a precedent; we need to see this process started so that others will be willing to invest 100 percent. Our partnerships can develop in all kinds of ways."

Most of all, Voronov is interested in Western know-how. His desire to overcome technological backwardness and begin to compete with foreign companies in the world market overrides all other business considerations. Simod, for example, received an initial fee of one million dollars for its shoe designs and for organizing the technological process, and it continues to receive 6 percent on sales annually.

In early 1992, Veshky was making three hundred thousand rubles in profits every day selling sports shoes at free-market prices. (Prices were changed in accord with the fluctuations in the rate of ruble-dollar exchange.) The factory manufactured 1,500 pairs of shoes a day. Veshky is one of those companies in Russia which understood long before others that a modern market could only be won with high-quality goods. That is the reason why Veshky's customers include such Western companies as McDonalds, Baskin-Robbins, and Coca-Cola. Veshky has signed a contract with Pepsi and other American corporations to build a packaging plant. According to the plans, fifty workers at the plant will be producing 250 million fast-food cups and plates per year.

"It's very easy to become a millionaire in this country now," laughs Voronov, describing the possibilities of making enormous profits in a market with unlimited prices and limited competition. But he knows that this situation cannot go on forever because privatization and the development of market relations are gathering strength. "The range of our interests is defined by the situation in this country," says Voronov, speaking about the strategy of diversifying production. Veshky tries to move production facilities to the sources of raw materials. It is therefore searching for partners in various regions of Russia, especially in Siberia, and buying enterprises located there.

Like all other general directors of Russian enterprises, Voronov thinks that the economic crisis in Russia was aggravated by the government's "shock therapy" policy launched in 1992. The liberalization of prices in the absence of any substantial private sector, the increasing volume of contradictory laws, the absence of laws stimulating employee ownership, and especially the exorbitant tax rates in the name of balancing the state budget have all combined to retard the development of a free-market economy and put Russian enterprises in the situation where their main concern is simple survival. Veshky is in a much better position than most state, cooperative, and private enterprises due to its rich experience in adapting to the changing economic situation and to the considerable skill of its management.[2]

ORGANIZATIONAL STRUCTURE

Veshky is a rather well-known company thanks to its advertising activities and the growing interest in it on the part of the mass media in Russia and abroad. Representatives from more than six hundred plants and factories have visited the prosperous company to learn its "secret." They have been impressed most of all by the decentralization of its organizational structure. Veshky is a Russian version of a holding company embracing seven different enterprises. All of them are profit centers. They are all legally independent. The holding company owns different amounts of stock in each of them and gets its profit according to its ownership share. Voronov is the director of five out of seven enterprises.

Veshky's controlling share and Voronov's leading position enable him to control the capital flow. Voronov makes the final decisions on how to spend money. In each of the enterprises there is a group of senior managers who are responsible for day-to-day decision making. They solve all the production and sales problems. The parent company intends to establish a sort of trading house, which will handle supplies and sales for all the enterprises. The holding company will work with it, as with other enterprises, on a contractual basis. Among Russian managers trying to cope with the overcentralization of decision making and the extreme bureaucratization of work in state companies, this type of decentralization in decision making is known as the "Veshky system."

The Veshky company is decentralized. But does that mean that it is democratically run? As a joint-stock company, Veshky has a Russian variant of the board of directors called the control council (see Figure 9.1). It consists of five members, all of them top managers from Veshky or from its main partners Exportles, Atomenergo, and Zenit. The members of the control council are not elected by the meeting of shareholders. Instead, all of them have proxies from the employees which give these top managers the right to represent the interests of the shareholders at the meetings of the control council. Valery Voronov, for example, has the authorization to represent the interests of four hundred employee co-owners. The top managers appoint each other to the control council. The voting power of the members of this body is based on the proportion of shares for which they hold proxies. As the main shareholder, Voronov has 75 percent of the votes; the rest together hold 25 percent of the votes.

The control council nominates the management board, which is the administration of the joint-stock employee-owned company. This managerial board consists of the general director, executive director, financial director, social policy director, personnel director, and chief accountant. Voronov occupies the posts of company president and general director. He develops and refines company policy and hires management. Voronov

Figure 9.1
Veshky's Organization

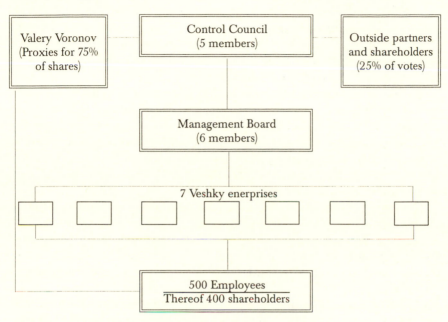

believes that successful professional management demands the concentration of administrative power in the hands of the leader. He is, as he constantly repeats, against "collectivist management": "I believe in employee ownership but I don't believe in collective management. Ten people can work at and manage an enterprise together without a director. But when it's one hundred people, this is questionable. I don't believe in this. I believe that so long as the conditions of work are good and people receive their dividends, the boss should have the authority. You may say that my decisions are authoritarian, but they do pay for themselves."

This is an increasingly widespread view among top Russian managers. Voronov says that he doesn't know any workers in his company who would want to participate in decision making concerning Veshky's financial and production policies. Interviews with the workers corroborated this view. Worker-owners have never challenged management's decisions since the buyout. They do not even suspect that the final authority rests with them as the owners of the enterprise. Workers are loyal to Voronov. "We trust Voronov. He is a good boss. Thanks to his leadership our life has improved greatly," says Vassily Sidorov, a production worker on one of the lines in the factory producing sports shoes. "We see him every day. He shakes hands with each of us. He knows everyone by his name. He is fair," adds packager Sergey Ivanov.

Sometimes Western experts visiting Veshky ask Voronov about the reasons his employees have for not wanting to be elected to the control council: do they feel they don't possess the knowledge necessary to be members of the council or do they simply not know what it is to be owners? Voronov's usual answer is that employees often behave as if they have forgotten that they are owners. He admits also that the proportion of employees who understand ownership is small.

The old trade union structure at Veshky disappeared in the transformation of the enterprise, and it has not been replaced by any new structure of worker self-representation. It is Voronov's view—shared widely among Russian top managers—that there is no role for a trade union to fulfill at employee-owned companies. After workers and managers became owners, the differences in their interests disappeared, and employees can rely on fair treatment from management.

There are no special training programs to educate workers about ownership. Since Voronov is sure that management has to lead the change, the educational role is given to managers. "If change is necessary," he insists, "management has to see it in time and take the lead." Voronov believes that the full dedication of top and senior managers to the idea of employee ownership is the sine qua non for its implementation. The most difficult problem in managing the Veshky enterprises, in Voronov's opinion, is finding managers who are able to work in an employee-owned company. Veshky makes high demands on the intellectual faculties of the managers. They must educate the workers about ownership and also be able to explain the political and economic situation in Russia. In 1992, for example, managers were trying to explain to the workers how the government's monetary and tax policies were damaging the profitability of the Veshky enterprises and how Voronov and his team were trying to find ways to soften the blows from above. The managers wanted to create a team spirit at the enterprise. Voronov has changed ten of his deputies and many other senior managers in the past six years because their values proved to be inconsistent with the character of work at Veshky. Some of those managers were corrupted by their previous work at state enterprises. "Now," says Voronov, "we have managers who understand their obligations."

Managers try to do their best to escape situations which would generate social conflicts. Even though there is no labor union at Veshky, Voronov assures visitors that the employees have the power to change the management of the company if they are not satisfied with its work. "Maybe I'm something of an idealist," remarks Voronov, "but it seems to me that we have established a real partnership between managers and workers. Veshky looks like a family. The workers know that they are treated fairly." Speaking with workers (usually in the presence of managers), I did not hear any complaints from them. They seemed to be in complete agreement with the management's assessment of what is good for them. They did not express any desire to share decision-making power with the managers. Voronov and his managers do not think that power sharing is at the heart of most issues of increasing profitability.

MOTIVATING EMPLOYEES

"We're proceeding from socialism and we're working with the human resources we have. We must take into account the psychology of people," says Voronov to explain his views concerning the problem of motivation. Employee psychology has been shaped by low standards of living in a society of shortages; as a consequence, Russian workers are mostly interested in getting good incomes and improving their material conditions. "Our workers," he continued, "have the psychology of hired people; they are eager to work less and to get more. They are happy when the conditions of work are good and they are getting their dividends." Before the buyout, there was much absenteeism among workers, and some of them would come to work drunk. Now all this is in the past. Voronov attributes the change in the workers' attitudes to the development of a culture of ownership. "The psychological problem is the most difficult one. Russian workers don't understand what ownership means," and the process of changing workers' consciousness is going very slowly. To help workers understand what ownership is and what responsibilities they assume when they become shareholders is therefore crucial.

It is important to see "the educational function" of holding shares to make employee ownership more than just a piece of paper. Veshky employees got their first lesson in ownership six months after buying the leased enterprise. Those who contributed 2,000 rubles to the buyout got 7,000 rubles (350 percent) in dividends. Their share in property in their individual accounts increased up to 53,000 rubles. According to Voronov, the people who contributed 500 rubles were a bit envious because they got less. Since that time the number of workers who wish to buy more shares has been increasing. The capital of Veshky is growing constantly, and the company issues new shares and sells them to those who do not have stock. The management of Veshky insists that the development of the culture of ownership is possible only if the employees pay for shares directly. "That which is not paid for is not valued" is a motto I heard very often.

But of the total workforce of five hundred, there are only four hundred shareholders. The ratio of shareholders to employees is not very low compared to that in many other employee-owned enterprises in Russia. The view that by nature not all employees are capable of being owners is widespread among top Russian managers. They divide workers into "good" and "bad" employees. To become "good," workers must earn a good evaluation of their job performance. If they get good evaluations, then they have a preference in buying shares. Most of the nonowners of Veshky are those who came to the enterprise only recently. They have to prove their worth to become owners.

Veshky's bylaws do not have adequate provisions for including new employees in the ranks of owners, such as the allocation formulas, vesting and distribution schedules, put options and the first rights of refusal that characterize American Employee Stock Ownership Plans (ESOPs). The reason is that Veshky shares are bought for cash. Furthermore, the shares are "inscribed" with a fixed value and are more like bonds than real common stock. These "shares" cannot be resold. The acquisition of such shares gives one a lifelong right to get dividends and to bequeath them to family members. The individual worker's shares do not appreciate when the business does well, although current dividends can be increased.

The management of Veshky admits that almost nothing has changed in production relations or labor-management relations since the employees became shareholders. Employees do not act like owners on a daily basis. As Voronov puts it, "Something changes, but these changes are not deep. This is our most important problem. A worker working at our enterprise is a worker and a co-owner at the same time; these cannot be separated. A worker must understand that the machine tool he's working with belongs to him, but at the same time he must understand that it is a means for making profits and that that is more important."

The natural contradiction between the positions of workers as owners and as hired labor hinders the development of the culture of ownership, especially during the initial stage of employee ownership. There is still ample evidence at Veshky that the workers are mainly interested in wage increases, rather than the company's financial success. For that reason the first issue that Veshky's management had to address was wages. Voronov is sure that it is impossible to even begin to develop the sense of ownership before the company provides its employees with adequate wages and benefits. "If I do not have a ruble in my pocket and am asked to invest in the prosperity of my company, I can only regard this suggestion as an insult. I will reject it. The way to persuade me to become an investor is to help me increase my income."

That is the reason why Veshky relies heavily on improvements in the systems of payment in its attempts to strengthen work incentives. The optimal system of payment must stimulate workers to cut production costs. Voronov believes that the company now has found such a system which stimulates workers to produce as much as they can and at the same time to save raw materials and make more effective use of resources. For instance, the company leases an automobile to a driver. It estimates the cost of his services and the lease he is to pay to the collective of employee-owners. His profit is the difference between the cost of services and his material expenditures on gas, oil, and spare parts for the car. Most Russian enterprises have constant transportation problems. Veshky has solved them. Its drivers are eager to do as much work as possible. This system has been in place at Veshky for more than five years, and transportation costs have been reduced by one-third.

In contrast to state enterprises, there is no fixed system of pay at the Veshky enterprises: one gets paid according to one's performance during the current month. Each employee's performance is assessed on the basis of positive and negative quotients. For instance, if a worker overfulfills his daily norm, he gets 0.8 points; if he fails to fulfill it, he loses 0.8 points. Failure to execute a foreman's order will cost him 0.5 points; production of defective goods, 0.2 points; using obscene language, 0.2 points; violating rules for equipment use, 0.5 points; and so on. Foremen and team leaders get punished for concealing violations of work discipline and for not taking disciplinary measures.

Fairness, Voronov and his team believe, is the most important factor motivating the workers to work better. Those workers with whom I had a chance to discuss the problems of their work agreed that they were treated fairly. When it is necessary to work a double shift or on a holiday, people usually agree. Nobody says, "How much do I get for it?" or "You don't have the right to make me work!" They believe that they'll be paid fairly for their work. The Veshky workers have a sense of dedication to the firm and they know that they are respected by the managerial staff.

The sense of dedication is strengthened greatly by the company's social policy. The most acute crisis in modern Russia is in housing. People stay on waiting lists for state apartments for twenty years or more. The collapse of Communism has aggravated the situation because the new state has no money and expects market forces to fill housing needs. The state has also tried to shift the burden of housing construction to enterprises. Veshky actually began building new apartments for its workers before it finished the construction of its first new plant. Workers gave the company's housing policy high marks. The apartments are either given for free or are sold at very low prices compared with what is available in the market.

Veshky workers do not pay for meals; they use special coupons at the company's dining room. This is yet another way to foster commitment to the company. "I may be an idealist but it looks like a family to me," says Voronov. Some workers also compare Veshky to a family.

But what about the future? The company is sailing into the uncharted waters of a real market economy. While it is better prepared for the journey than regular state firms, Veshky has yet to reach maturity as an employee-owned enterprise. The time may come when it will be difficult to tell the employees of the Veshky enterprises that they are the real owners without providing them with a role in managing the company.

NOTES

1. Incidentally, it is this unfavorable situation that makes Voronov think that the technique of financing that has led to the rapid expansion of ESOPs in the United States—allowing employees to acquire their stake not with their personal savings or wages but with loans to be repaid from the future earnings of the enterprise—is not going to work in Russia, at least not in the foreseeable future.

2. Voronov maintains that the Russian government has underestimated the importance of employee ownership as the most effective method of increasing workers' motivation to do good work in a country with entrenched collectivist traditions.

10 Combining Defense Conversion and Privatization: The Saratov Aviation Plant

David Binns

Those who risk nothing always lose.

—Alexander Yermishin
General director, Saratov Aviation Plant

◆ THE Saratov Aviation Plant (SAP), located in the city of Saratov on the Volga River in southern Russia, is at the forefront of efforts to promote economic reform in Russia today. One of the first major defense firms to convert to primarily civilian production, SAP was also one of the first large manufacturing firms to be privatized as a workers' collective in the experimental economic reforms initiated by the Soviet government in the early 1990s. The company has subsequently transformed itself into a closed joint-stock corporation owned entirely by the SAP employees. Perhaps most important, despite the difficult economic conditions of the early 1990s, SAP has managed to maintain production levels and increase productivity, has successfully increased sales of their civilian aircraft on the international market, and has been able to make significant capital investments to improve production and administration.

Though the circumstances faced by SAP are unique in several important respects from the conditions faced by other Russian enterprises undergoing privatization, the SAP experience is nevertheless relevant to other firms initiating the transition to a market-based economy. Given the large numbers of Russian companies likely to become significantly employee owned as a result of the Russian government's privatization guidelines,

SAP's efforts to make the transition to an employee-owned, joint-stock corporation based on Western models of corporate structures provides a useful insight into the challenges facing Russian firms today. The SAP story has already been featured several times on Russian television, and its experience has been widely publicized throughout Russia as a leading example of a company making a successful transition to a privatized, market economy.[1]

The Saratov Aviation Plant today specializes in commercial airplane manufacturing, but the company has a long and proud history of producing fighter aircraft for the Soviet military. It manufactured more than thirteen thousand YAK-1 and YAK-3 fighter planes, which constituted 23 percent of the fighter planes produced by the Soviet military during World War II. These planes became mainstays of the Russian army and were some of the most effective fighter planes in the war. Since then the plant has continued to develop military aviation products. It has developed more than fifteen basic types of aircraft and helicopters including, in recent years, the YAK-38, a vertical-takeoff, jet fighter plane. In addition to manned aircraft, the plant also produced naval cruise missiles.

Having been a prominent defense firm for most of its history, SAP enjoyed many of the benefits traditionally provided to Soviet enterprises. Consistent state subsidies to fulfill military orders allowed SAP to mobilize extensive manufacturing resources, and the company developed a very broad range of suppliers. As with most defense firms, its privileged position within the Soviet economic hierarchy enabled SAP to attract managers and engineers from the upper echelons of the Soviet labor force. Further, its position as a large manufacturing enterprise enabled it to provide relatively high wages, which attracted a skilled labor pool. As a prominent firm, SAP was also provided with extensive social facilities, including about 350 large apartment complexes for SAP workers, a workers' sanatorium, day-care and educational facilities, a cultural center, and extensive recreational facilities.

In 1988 approximately 55 percent of SAP's capacity was dedicated to military production. The accelerating economic difficulties faced by the Soviet Union in the late 1980s made it increasingly clear that military production could not be maintained at preexisting levels throughout the Soviet economy. When the first directives on military conversion were announced by Mikhail Gorbachev, SAP was one of the first major manufacturing companies to opt out of military production to pursue civilian manufacturing markets. The company moved aggressively to convert its production into nondefense work, and in 1992 only 6 percent of current revenues came from military contracts.

SAP's primary civilian product is the YAK-42, a 125-seat commercial airplane which is supplied to the Russian government and to several foreign clients. In addition to working on upgraded models of the YAK-42, SAP is also working on a deal which would enable it to resume production of the smaller, thirty-passenger YAK-40 airplane, which SAP's managers feel could be competitive in the European market as a corporate or short-range commuter plane. When financing is available they plan to produce the T-401, a small six-passenger airplane suitable for corporate uses or patrol purposes. The company is also involved in the initial stages of a project to produce a new type of advanced cargo plane.

SAP currently employs twelve thousand workers in the production of commercial airplanes and occupies about 4 million square feet of production space. Operations are divided into fifty-seven different production shops and units operating in fifteen separate physical plants. An additional five thousand employees are involved in agricultural production, the manufacture of commercial goods, and the provision of social services for SAP workers, including food services, housing, and health care.

SAP'S PRIVATIZATION PROCESS

SAP got an early start on the road to privatization by becoming one of the first large companies in the USSR to take advantage of the initial economic reforms introduced by Mikhail Gorbachev permitting the establishment of workers' collectives. Envisioned as a possible "third way" between socialism and capitalism, workers' collectives allowed for private ownership of corporations, but the ownership was shared collectively by the workers in the enterprise. A sort of microeconomic version of the socialist system of "ownership of everything by everyone," workers' collectives provided employees with no divisible, individual shareholdings. They were nevertheless seen as a tentative step in the direction of private property.

As such, they did represent an unprecedented legal opening to allow for privatizing state-owned enterprises, and the SAP management was quick to capitalize on the opportunity. In January 1991 the Council of Ministers of the USSR approved a proposal to transfer ownership of the enterprise to the SAP workers' collective for a negotiated price of 250 million rubles. Of this total, 135 million rubles (54 percent) was transferred to the workers' collective at no charge based on the depreciated value of the company's capital assets. The remaining 115 million rubles (46 percent) was bought on credit provided by the Soviet government. An initial payment of 1.5 million rubles was due at the end of 1991; the remaining debt had no fixed term and no interest rate.

After the privatization agreement was finalized, SAP immediately initiated a process of allocating individual shares (or, more accurately, internal share accounts) to each individual SAP employee according to a formula based on salary, seniority, and professional expertise. Each share was valued at one ruble, and each SAP employee was given a booklet to record individual share ownership. To raise the money needed to meet its initial debt payment, SAP also sold individual shares to employees. To encourage participation in the share purchase plan, the company matched each share purchased with additional shares contributed from the collective fund. In the initial sale employees were given three shares for every one they purchased. Subsequent sales provided two shares, and then one free share, for each purchased one. Through this process sufficient capital was raised to allow SAP to meet its initial debt payment. As a result, the SAP employees directly owned approximately 18 percent of all SAP shares by the end of 1991, with the remainder still held by the workers' collective. The collective shares were in principle owned by all SAP workers, though there was some disagreement as to the legal status of the unallocated shares and how individual share rights would work in a workers' collective.

At this point, sales of shares from the workers' collective were suspended and the SAP management began efforts to convert the company to a joint-stock corporation to conform with the overall privatization strategy introduced by the Russian Federation government, which had replaced the collapsing Soviet Union. As part of this effort, SAP general director Alexander Yermishin brought in a team of outside consultants to begin the process of revising SAP's corporate structure. The consultants worked closely with SAP's top managers to familiarize them with market-based corporate structures, management systems, financial controls, governance procedures, and employee ownership systems.

Before the transition from a workers' collective to a joint-stock company could be completed, however, subsequent legislative changes—made in the summer of 1992 to the Russian Law on Corporations—outlawed workers' collectives. This ruling forced SAP to temporarily adopt the legal structure of a "partnership with limited liability" (*tovarischestvo*). This legal structure was used simply as a transitional stage pending the company's final conversion to a closed joint-stock corporation in February 1993. Fortunately, SAP's relative economic success in 1992 earned the company sufficient income to allow it to repay the entire debt remaining from the initial privatization buyout. This debt payment was made to the Russian government, which had inherited the original SAP privatization loan from the Soviet government. The repayment of the debt and the company's receipt of a privatization decree formalized SAP's status as a fully privatized, employee-owned, closed joint-stock company.

The new regulations governing SAP's transition also required that SAP distribute all of the shares from the workers' collective to the individual employees prior to the adoption of the joint-stock corporate structure. SAP management determined that the most effective and equitable means to accomplish this distribution was to make the shares available for sale on an equal basis to all qualified SAP employees. Because the company had made the decision to become a closed joint-stock corporation, "eligible employees" were determined to be active employees on the company's payroll as of November 1992, the time when the decision to distribute the shares was made. While SAP management expressed a willingness to consider an eventual transition to an open joint-stock company which could include outside investors, its initial strategy was to preserve the firm's status as an entirely employee-owned company. Therefore, management was determined to restrict ownership opportunities to current SAP workers.

In order to address the concerns of SAP pensioners who felt they had a legitimate claim on the value of the privatized shares, SAP management decided to separate the company's housing and social services from manufacturing. Since pensioners were traditionally major users of the company's social services (including health services, the workers' sanatorium, and restaurant facilities), housing and social services were transferred to a new SAP subsidiary to be owned in part by the SAP pensioners. This firm started with the 70-million-ruble value of the housing as determined in the initial privatization buyout. In addition, 13.5 million rubles from SAP's 1992 profits were used to fund equity investments in the new social-services company on behalf of SAP retirees. One of the company's four collective farms was also separated into an independent company with ownership shared between SAP, the farm's employees, and a foreign investor. The other farms remained with the new social-services company.

The organizational separation of social services, housing, and farm collectives from the manufacturing facility reduced the value of the SAP airplane manufacturing facility to 180 million rubles, 18 percent of which had already been distributed to SAP employees, leaving approximately 130 million shares remaining to be distributed. These shares were divided by the total number of eligible SAP employees, and each employee was given the right to purchase the per capita shares available to him or her (approximately eight thousand shares). As with the initial sales from the workers' collective, shares were valued at one ruble apiece for purposes of the sale. Employees were allowed to finance the purchase of their shares by taking a payroll deduction from future paychecks. Unsold shares remaining after the first offering to the employees were made available on a second round, but at a price of two rubles per share with a purchase limit of three thousand rubles per person. Unsold shares after the second round were made available for sale on a final round at a price of three rubles per share, subject to a maximum individual purchase of two thousand shares.

The sale of shares and any changes to SAP corporate structures, bylaws, and policies were subject to approval by the company's general assembly.

Representatives of all SAP workers voted on a one-person, one-vote basis, as was traditionally the case with workers' collectives. However, once the transition to a joint-stock corporation was complete and all the shares had been distributed to employees, SAP changed its governance procedures to provide for voting on a one-vote-per-share basis.

MANAGING A PRIVATIZED COMPANY

In early 1992, just at the time when the first major economic reforms were introduced by the Russian government, SAP general director Alexander Yermishin invited a team organized by Stanford University's Center for International Security and Arms Control to work with the SAP managers on developing strategies and plans for the company's transition to a joint-stock corporation. The Stanford team spent several weeks in Saratov in January 1992, after which top SAP managers visited the United States. Consultations between Stanford and SAP continued throughout 1992 as the company moved forward with its transition effort.

SAP managers engaged in discussions with the Stanford team about a broad range of issues including the legal and financial structure of corporations in a market economy; the distribution of equity ownership; management systems and manufacturing plans; the role of the board of directors; the dynamics of stock systems; legal and accounting requirements; internal financial controls; compensation systems and human resource management; employee communications; and employee ownership strategies and techniques. SAP managers used these discussions as a basis for initiating a new set of corporate bylaws, stock structures, and corporate policies for the new joint-stock corporation.

In determining how to restructure the company, one of the biggest problems facing SAP early in the transition process was relations with several newly independent divisions. As part of the initial economic reforms established by the Soviet government in the late 1980s, many large enterprises granted legal independence to some of their smaller divisions in order to allow them to engage in the production of consumer goods. In SAP's case, as with some other Russian enterprises, some of these small enterprises had become more profitable than other SAP divisions that had remained within the formal SAP corporate structure. Their newly won independence and their relative success in selling their private production made these managers reluctant to return to a recentralized corporate structure; they were able to make higher salaries than the other SAP employees because of their own success in bringing in outside contracts and sharing the profits with their employees. Yet their independence was creating internal supply and coordination problems when they fulfilled outside contracts (for a higher profit) at the expense of an internal order from SAP.

The problem was complicated by competing interests, diversified (and often unreliable) accounting procedures (including separate bank accounts for some of the independent divisions), and uncertainties about appropriate management structures which together caused a great deal of difficulty and mutual recrimination. For those reasons, the SAP experience typifies that of many other Russian companies that have granted greater autonomy to small enterprises to allow them to pursue independent work.

The SAP managers wanted to bring the independent companies back under the SAP structure and adopt the legal status of a joint-stock corporation complete with a charter and bylaws. They also hoped to introduce centralized financial accounting procedures and develop a compensation system based on a combination of cash and stock bonuses tied to the individual performance of each division. That last point was critical, since the independent companies were loath to give up their hard-won financial and management autonomy. The independence of the small enterprises proved to be a difficult sticking point in the negotiations over the transition to the joint-stock corporate structure.

The initial ownership of the workers' collective was based on 180 million shares (after the divestiture of the social-services division), each worth a static value of one ruble; thus it was necessary to develop a strategy for transition to a joint-stock company in which stock could have a variable value based on SAP's performance. The concept of shares of stock which could change in value according to economic conditions proved to be very difficult to communicate to SAP managers and employees. Their lack of experience with capital markets and the difficulty of developing a market-based price for their stock obliged SAP to base initial transactions on the static one-ruble-per-share value. This was true even toward the end of 1992 when the remaining shares from the workers' collective were sold to the SAP employees. (Despite the fact that some small enterprises were legally independent, their employees nevertheless participated in the stock ownership system of SAP.)

By this time, however, SAP managers had already begun to develop their own internal system of trading for the shares. Prices for the shares owned by employees are on a bid-and-ask basis, with prices posted in a room available to any employee interested in buying more stock. Departing employees have three months to sell their shares on the internal market. If the shares are unsold after that time, the company can either repurchase them at par value or allow the employee to hold onto them. Given the financial strain that would be required to repurchase all such shares, SAP hopes that departing employees will temporarily defer the sale of their shares. The company expects to eventually become an open joint-stock company, perhaps in several more years, both to attract outside capital and to create greater liquidity for shareholders wishing to sell their shares. For the meantime, however, SAP hopes to maintain ownership within the employee group.

Company management has also embarked on a major corporate communications campaign to explain the changes in its ownership structure to its employees. These efforts include extensive articles in the company newspaper, radio call-in shows with general director Alexander Yermishin fielding the questions, and a series of meetings by the SAP general assembly where worker representatives vote on proposed changes to the SAP corporate structure. While SAP employees appear to be supportive of the company's pathfinding efforts to adapt to market conditions (a long waiting list of people interested in working at SAP is another recognition of the company's success), convincing employees to accept the risks and rewards of private ownership and educating them about basic dynamics of a market economy will be a long, slow process. In an effort to encourage employees to better understand and appreciate the value of their ownership, SAP also plans to issue stock certificates to replace the notebooks in which were recorded the original, individually owned shares from the workers' collective.

As with most large Russian enterprises, a central element of employee involvement at SAP is the general assembly. The general assembly comprises approximately five hundred SAP employees who each represent approximately thirty of their coworkers and is responsible for voting on key corporate governance issues, including the election of the management council. Decisions are made on a one-person, one-vote basis. During the transition from a workers' collective to a joint-stock corporation, the general assembly maintained this voting procedure. But once all the shares were distributed to the employees, plans called for changing from a one-person, one-vote basis to a one-share, one-vote procedure. The company will presumably implement some form of proxy voting to accommodate this change, while retaining the representative structure of the general assembly to maintain traditional channels of communications and corporate governance.

In terms of organizing the company's production and marketing, SAP faces many of the same daunting challenges facing every Russian company during the difficult transition from a centrally planned to a market economy. SAP can no longer simply plan to produce a predetermined number of planes, but has to time production to meet client orders. Therefore, the company's system of production had to be modified for better coordination. Top SAP managers have made great efforts to implement management systems more in line with those in market-based practice. Key challenges in these areas included securing reliable suppliers; obtaining a fair economic valuation of SAP stock, so that proper investment decisions could be made; separating SAP's social services (health care, education, farms, recreational facilities) from aircraft production and making them self-supporting so as not to affect aircraft production costs; and improving production efficiency through the implementation of modern production technology based on Computer-Assisted-Design/Computer-Aided-Manufacturing (CAD/CAM) methods.

Similarly, the company has had to depend increasingly on its own sales efforts. No longer able to depend entirely on a centralized government authority for promoting international sales of its aircraft, SAP has moved aggressively to initiate contacts with other countries interested in purchasing affordable and reliable air transportation. A number of foreign governments have expressed interest in the YAK-42, SAP's principal product. A top priority for the company is to attain international standards for aircraft quality control to enable the company to penetrate additional international markets.

With more than 1,600 suppliers, many of which face trying economic conditions, SAP also had to establish dependable market-based relationships. The company has implemented an incentive system whereby suppliers are paid premium prices for on-time deliveries. While this has not completely solved its supplier problems, management feels that SAP is in a preferred position since, based on the company's current profitability, it is able to pay its bills on time and therefore enjoy preferential status with its suppliers.

The company grappled with high inflation in the Russian economy by pushing up wages. Prior to 1992 the average monthly salary of SAP employees was approximately nine hundred rubles (a relatively high wage by national standards). By the end of 1992, however, the average salary had increased to six thousand per month. Salaries are now pegged to a local food basket to measure inflation and are adjusted monthly.

The company is continuing to build housing for its employees, utilizing local youth organizations to assist with the building program. Interestingly, its current efforts are focused on developing single-family housing. General director Alexander Yermishin notes that despite its associated costs, the building program is necessary to demonstrate to workers that the company is continuing to show financial success.

FUTURE CHALLENGES

SAP clearly got a head start on the privatization process by making an early move to become a workers' collective. Despite the difficulties associated with the collective ownership format and subsequent legislative changes that created uncertainties about legal structure, SAP's decision to take advantage of the opportunities presented in the initial Soviet economic reforms enabled it to capitalize on subsequent reforms and to make the transition to a joint-stock corporation without waiting for the implementation of the government's privatization program. As a result, SAP was among the very first Russian companies that could claim to be privatized and entirely employee owned.

As for SAP's decision to become one of Russia's first large, employee-owned manufacturing companies, the SAP management is confident that it has made the right choice and believes that it is at the forefront of the effort to revitalize Russian enterprise. At the end of 1992, SAP was one of only two former defense industries in Saratov that were in a positive and optimistic financial condition. Company management can also point to productivity improvements, improved financial performance, a waiting list for employment at SAP, and a growing sense of pride and flexibility among its workers as evidence of their success in revitalizing the company. The interest shown by the SAP employees in using their limited financial resources to purchase the shares of the company is perhaps the most telling evidence of the company's success in making the transition to a privatized, employee-owned company. SAP employees hope to capitalize on that success.

Achieving ultimate success will not be easy. In addition to the macroeconomic and political problems afflicting the Russian economy, continuing problems at SAP include conflicts with the managers of the small enterprises, who resist efforts to bring them back under the main legal structure, and a lack of sufficient computer capabilities for effective financial management of separate profit centers. Despite making great strides in restructuring the corporation to facilitate a market-based approach, management and workers still have trouble with new concepts of stock, different dynamics of corporate governance, and new legal structures. In addition, years of centralized power and a lack of accountability have made many workers skeptical of power structures. Much work is still needed to develop trust between workers, managers, and the company's board of directors, and extensive education and training programs are needed to provide workers and managers with the critical skills they need to operate effectively in the new environment.

Market competition will undoubtedly increase as Western businesses enter the Russian market, and SAP's management will be challenged as never before to respond to the new economic realities. It remains to be seen whether the flexibility SAP has as a 100 percent privatized and employee-owned company will provide it with sufficient advantages to stay ahead of the competition in marketing planes and attracting foreign investors. SAP management knows that it will undoubtedly be a long and rocky road to get individual production workers to begin to respond to market conditions and to improve productivity and accountability. Ultimately the value of their investment in SAP will depend on their own performance.

Employee ownership is, of course, no guarantee of success in a hostile economic environment. However, providing Russian workers with a personal economic stake in the success of the enterprises where they work will be a critical element of Russia's efforts to promote the establishment of a free-market economy. Employee-owners, motivated to work for the success of their enterprise, can help produce the short-term efforts needed to ensure economic survival and, most importantly, will receive individual economic benefits through ownership as the Russian economy stabilizes and grows.

NOTE

1. Saratov Aviation has also been the subject of a series of studies by the Center for International Security and Arms Control at Stanford. See Bernstein and Smith 1992; Bernstein and Perry 1993; Higgins and Binns 1994; Hendley 1992; and McFaul and Bernstein 1992.

11 Transforming a Russian State Enterprise: Krasny Proletary

John Simmons and David Hanna

Now, all of us think how to make our work more effective and how to be more productive. We have developed a strategy for expanding the company's efforts. With our new management methods, we have been able to focus most of the personnel of the company, including the profit centers, on solving one major problem—what our new products should be. . . . Employee ownership will be an excellent incentive to help us achieve high performance.

—Yuri Ivanovich Kirillov
General director, Krasny Proletary

◆ EARLY in 1988, Yuri Kirillov saw that in the near future the USSR would convert to a market economy and enterprises would be free of state control and state subsidy. He realized that this meant Krasny Proletary (KP), where he served as general director, would have to transform the way it operated. The country had taken a major step toward privatization with a new Law on State Enterprises that President Mikhail Gorbachev and the Supreme Soviet had put into effect on January 1. Krasny Proletary, a machine tool plant making lathes and turning machines, would have to compete successfully with four hundred other plants in the same business or go under.

Located in Moscow, Krasny Proletary is rich in tradition. The company was founded in 1857 by the Bromley brothers, German industrialists. It grew rapidly in czarist times, and its subsequent history parallels that of the city. Its workers supported and died for the revolutions of 1905 and 1917; the war memorial outside the company's old plant on Malaya Kaluzhskaya in downtown Moscow lists the names of the five hundred workers who fell during

World War II; pictures of the plant from the war years show women at machines assembling shells (for Krasny Proletary's history, see Nekrasova et al. 1986). Many of its current employees are the children and grandchildren of Krasny workers. But none of this history—nor its legacy in employees' pride in their work—guaranteed an easy transition to the market economy.

Until recently, Krasny Proletary focused on the production of lathes from eighty-five kilos to thirty tons, and was one of the world's largest lathe producers. One of three lathe operators in the former USSR works on a KP machine. While the company makes a total of ninety different models, three models now account for 90 percent of the value of the production. Despite its introduction of new products with the development of a market economy, including oil field equipment, nails, metal doors, toys, and a portable brick-making factory, in July 1993 Krasny Proletary employed 4,300, down from 6,000 in 1989.

Thirty years ago, Krasny sold 40 percent of its production on the open market abroad. Today it is unable to do so because of marketing problems and the failure to make technological advances. "While 45 percent of our engineers," said Kirillov, "could work to Western standards, the quality of our product is often poor. Few employees are enthusiastic. They need training and a change in their mentality."

To understand better how to meet the modern industrial world on its terms, Kirillov began to visit German plants and eventually established a joint venture with EMAG, a machine tool company in Salach, on several projects. With several of his managers, he attended courses in Western management methods in Germany and Britain that included plant visits. He also began to develop his own vision of what the firm needed, not only to survive in Russia's future market economy, but also to be the best.

Despite his new contacts and growing knowledge, Kirillov was aware that he still did not know how to realize his vision. Over the next two years he sought assistance from six different Russian and foreign groups. He discovered some interesting concepts, but "the consultants," he says, "were too theoretical." They were unable to help him design and implement a step-by-step process for the changes he wanted to introduce.

Then, with the help of Yuri Dzhed and Maxim Iliin of Krasny Proletary and Professor Arcady Prigozhin, director of the Management Consulting Department, Academy of the National Economy, he located Participation Associates, a management consulting firm in Chicago. The firm specialized in assisting companies in the United States and abroad to become high-performance organizations, using the concepts of total quality, participation, and employee ownership. Participation Associates had been training Russian managers in both Russia and the United States for two years, but this was its first opportunity to help a Russian firm make the transition to world-class management methods.

This chapter describes how Krasny Proletary began its transformation from traditional management and state ownership to a high-performance business capable of competing in the global marketplace. The journey is at midpoint. We detail the basic steps the company has taken and the problems it has encountered in coming this far.

TAKING HIGH-PERFORMANCE CONCEPTS TO RUSSIA

In the past twenty years, companies in the leading market economies have begun to implement basic changes in the way they do business. When well-designed and implemented, these changes have brought companies that were often already performing well to the status of best in the world. While it usually took five years or more to achieve substantial and permanent changes, significant results were often achieved earlier. Procter & Gamble, Florida Power & Light, Xerox, Saturn, Ford Motor Company, Scandinavian Airlines, Swedish Handelsbanken, Imperial Chemical Industries, Shell Oil, Rhom and Haas, Sony, Toyota, and Cannon are only a few of the larger companies that have demonstrated what can be done. A significant group of smaller companies, such as Columbia Aluminum, Quad/Graphics, and Johnsonville Foods, have also reached world-class performance.

While the high-performance concepts often carry different names, they focus on four ideas: meeting and exceeding the needs of the customer; empowering all employees to solve problems—and providing the skills to do so; using new incentives like employee ownership; and continuously improving all systems every day. To implement these ideas successfully requires the redesign of the social and technical systems of the organization by the people who work there.

Since the customer wants high quality at a reasonable price, high-performance companies focus on quality and its continuous improvement, rather than on achieving high profits. The profits will come as a result of the customer focus. To achieve continuous improvement requires continuous learning. As much as 15 percent of the work week may be spent training and coaching people at all levels of the firm in new concepts and methods.

The high-performance system, often called "the new workplace," assumes that lower-level employees can increasingly self-manage to achieve company and team objectives. They relate best to these responsibilities when they are able to participate in decisions that affect their work and in the ownership of stock in the company. As a result, fewer managers are needed. In contrast, traditional Taylorist "scientific management" systems assume that lower-level managers and workers do not want responsibility, have little ambition to improve, and need to be told what to do.

In the new workplace, traditional managers, instead of just giving orders, become leaders who can develop high-performing teams and coach individuals who are committed to the company's objectives and management philosophy. Managing people based on this assumption releases more energy and creativity from the same people. The redesign of an organization focuses on the continuous improvement of leadership, participation, and quality.

There are three basic steps in redesigning a company for high performance. The first is assuring the readiness of the organization for change. The second is a process of study and redesign that concludes with a plan of action for the entire organization and agreements from all key players. Third is the stage of implementation and continuous improvement.[1]

Each step in the process has four or five key activities designed to deepen the understanding of the basic concepts and tools of high performance, first among managers and then among professionals and workers. With this information they are able to carry out the company's transformation. The role of the consulting team is to provide the process, begin the transfer of the skills through training, and reinforce continuous learning with examples from around the world.

Since the redesign of a Russian state enterprise had not been done before, this posed a major challenge for us. While the consulting team had significant international experience, neither of us spoke Russian. In addition, though we were confident that high-performance concepts and tools could work in different countries, the Russian conditions were unusual.

When we began working with Krasny Proletary in January 1991, the Russian gross national product was already in steep decline. Supplies were interrupted, and inflation was beginning to rise. The government issued daily decrees for enterprises that were often vague and contradictory, and the best employees were leaving the plant. Krasny was affected particularly by the collapse of the Soviet defense industry; state orders ceased from defense plants and their suppliers, which used to be Krasny's largest customers. Kirillov's priority was survival, and he realized that the only way to accomplish it was to rethink the way Krasny operated.

Our plan to assist Krasny Proletary began with a diagnosis of the way the organization operated, including what people liked and did not like about working there. The senior management team evaluated our summary of the information we collected and our recommendations. Based on what they learned about how world-class organizations functioned, they developed a shared vision for what they wanted the firm to become and prioritized the barriers that stood in the way of achieving their vision. Working in groups, they learned and then applied new concepts and tools in developing solutions to problems. These problems covered the full range of management issues from a market-oriented strategy and the restructuring of decision making to crisis planning and incentives.

During the first year we met with them about every two months. The senior group of twenty department directors and staff reported on their progress, and we adjusted our interventions to help them overcome priority barriers as they appeared. Our intention was to raise their awareness about how world-class companies were managed and help them learn the concepts and tools while applying them to the barriers they were trying to overcome. They would learn by doing.

Work during the second year focused on the council of profit-center leaders and the reorganization of production teams into profit centers and on the continuous improvement of one profit center as a model of changes that would reach down to the shop floor. Assistance also continued on the preparation for privatization and a companywide strategy for training.

Early Concepts and Principles

Kirillov had developed a vision of the new Krasny Proletary or, as he began to call it, the "Prekrasny Krasny Proletary," the "Excellent Krasny Proletary," a play on the rhyming sound of "prekrasny" and "Krasny." For the organization to move forward, the senior managers needed to develop a shared vision.

Initially, however, Krasny's senior team had difficulty working together in small groups and applying a six-step problem-solving model to the problems they identified. They lacked motivation, and Kirillov was not pleased with their performance.

Work beyond the senior management team could not begin until a significant number of its members had demonstrated their understanding of the basic high-performance concepts and their ability to play a leadership role in the organization. This is a key principle of successful redesign. Too many organizations rush to implement new ideas at lower levels of the organization before its top managers have either adequately understood or begun to practice the new ideas themselves. When this happens, lower-level managers and workers see the top leadership talking one way—about delegation of decision making or the importance of quality—and walking another.

To convince Krasny's managers that these new ideas could work, it would have been useful for them to visit high-performance factories abroad. Since that was too expensive, we suggested that they visit Veshky, a Russian company on the outskirts of Moscow. The firm had privatized under the leaseholding law in 1989. Veshky's general director, Valery Voronov, was implementing a vision of the new Veshky which was very close to Kirillov's vision: an organization where all the employees were owners who were fully committed to meeting the needs of the customers while respecting the needs of their fellow employees.

At first, the Krasny Proletary managers refused to make the visit. They had a dozen excuses: "Veshky has three hundred employees; we have five thousand. What can we learn from them?" "They make simple kitchen furniture; we make sophisticated machine tools." "We just do not have time." We suggested that they send only two people for a half-day to explore the Veshky vision and methods. They still refused. Not until we offered to give back a day of our fee if the two felt they had wasted their time did they reluctantly agree.

The two managers came back impressed. They sent more managers. These invited the Veshky managers to make a presentation at Krasny Proletary.

What had impressed the Krasny managers? At Veshky, they had seen employees who cared so much they came to work on their vacations. They had seen a company that had transformed itself from making kitchen furniture to one that was successfully making and selling new products such as sweaters, tennis shoes, and prefabricated dachas. They had seen responsibility for decision making delegated to work teams through the profit-center concept. Profits were being reinvested in the company or used to build apartments for workers' families that were three times the size of the average Moscow apartment. Veshky had even attracted foreign investors, something government officials had claimed was not possible when firms became employee owned.

The Krasny managers were so interested in what they saw that they decided, without our suggesting it, to visit a company in the Ukraine they had heard about because of changes it had successfully introduced. They came back impressed, especially with the Ukrainian company's profit-center model. This decision was one of the first signs that Krasny management had begun to take responsibility for its own learning about high-performance organizations. It was a key first step in the transformation process. No longer were we consultants the only teachers; they had begun to teach themselves.

Continuous learning lies at the core of organizational redesign because it is the source of continuous improvement. The Krasny experience reveals other key principles as well. The leadership of a company must first understand high-performance concepts and be fully committed to making them work in every part of the organization. In addition, it must lead the process of education and redesign through the rest of the company. Work at the lower levels of Krasny Proletary could not begin until these conditions at the top were fulfilled.

Diagnosis Process

On January 5, 1991, our Chicago office took an unusual call. "This is Pan American Airlines calling. Your flight to Moscow has been canceled.

The Pentagon has ordered the plane to take American troops to the Persian Gulf. We are sorry for the inconvenience." The United States was about to go to war, and we were headed to Moscow for our initial two-week meeting with our new Russian client. Few Americans were flying anywhere, even inside the United States, because of the risk of a terrorist attack. Our families were not happy. But we made it.

On our first day on the job at Krasny Proletary, Moscow radio announced that Soviet troops had just killed fifteen people in Vilnius, Lithuania. The following Sunday a million people rallied near Red Square to protest, and troop movements were rumored on the outskirts of Moscow. In the meantime, the war in the Persian Gulf had started.

Krasny Proletary was also in crisis. It had not received any state orders for its lathes in the past two years and had to find its own customers. The company's best workers were leaving to work in new private firms, called cooperatives, where there were no restrictions on what they could earn. Salaries at cooperatives were usually double those of the old state enterprises. Inflation was rising, credit was tightening, and suppliers were running out of inventories. Krasny's people did not know what to do; they did not know what the future held for the firm. Would the firm survive?

Our goal during this first visit was to help the senior management group begin building a strong foundation for designing a high-performance system over the coming years. We began with a diagnosis of the current conditions in the company. With the assistance of Dr. Gregory Kuntzman, now with the Management Consulting Department of the Academy of the National Economy, and four graduate student interviewers, we collected data from over forty interviews held at different levels of the firm.

The questions were based on the key elements of the high-performance model. Questions included goals, decision making, customers, recognition and incentive systems, trust, communications, and quality. How did people react to new ideas and how were changes made? What improvements needed to be made? What did people like about working at the firm and what did they not like? Finally, we asked, "If management does nothing else, what are the three things the firm should improve during the next year?"

We had discovered during preliminary interviews that people tended to blame outside influences, such as the government, for causing their problems. While these forces were important, the Krasny workers had little control over them. We wanted to focus their attention on things they could improve. Some of the key observations that people who worked at Krasny Proletary made about their company were published in *Dvigatel* (*Engine*), the firm's newspaper, as part of a series of articles on the work of the consulting team which gave all employees access to information. Here's how the workers and managers who were interviewed saw the problems of Krasny Proletary:

- The shop equipment was modernized, but its management was not.
- Not a single problem is being solved at the shop level. Everybody takes problems to "the top level."
- The needs and requirements of the customers are irrelevant to most producers (workers); the quality problem is often ignored by employees.
- Top-quality specialists are leaving the factory.
- Production is on the verge of collapsing and emotions are boiling.
- One can often see idle or even drunk people wandering around the factory.
- Paper work is excessive. Papers are being shifted from one desk to another, often without any reason at all.
- Top management does not control people and events but vice versa: management is being controlled by the environment.
- Too many people go to meetings.
- It's quite common to break promises and routine work schemes.
- New ideas are often ignored or not carried out.

Analyzing KP's Organizational Performance

To help us analyze the interview data, we began with the principle that all organizations are perfectly designed to get the results they get. This means that each result or output of the organization is caused by a uniquely balanced system of strategy and design elements. To change the results, people who work in the system must first understand how these key elements interact to produce the current results. If employees want to modify the strategy and design elements, they need to develop an understanding of the root causes of their problems. This usually means changing their understanding of how organizations work, that is, making a paradigm shift. With this knowledge people then will be able to change the results they get.

In our analysis we were looking for the major causes of the results, both good and bad, that Krasny was getting. Based on these data, and working closely with managers, we could more easily identify the key parts of the management system to improve. We call "leverage points" those few things that could move the entire system to a higher level of performance. Since each organization is unique, the analysis of leverage points is central to designing a successful improvement strategy.

We used the model of organizational performance in Figure 11.1 to understand better the data we had collected and to present results to senior managers. Working clockwise around the diagram, we listed the needs of the "business situation" and the "business results," used the interview data to answer the questions in each box, and then compared them. One business need that could be better satisfied was the customers' desire for improved quality. While Krasny had a reputation for good-quality lathes, its real focus had been on meeting annual production targets. One of the results was mediocre quality as measured by the complaints of customers. We then identified the actual work behaviors that influenced the results, such as the statement "Too many people here do not care about doing a good job." We recorded these behaviors in the "culture" box.

Other important business needs in Krasny Proletary's environment included instability in supply, mutually contradictory regulations, lack of knowledge about whether KP was meeting the customers' needs, confusion caused by the closing of military production, replacement of large customers by small ones like state farms, difficulties for employees in buying consumer goods, and lack of engineers and good workers.

Additional data went into the culture box. When we analyzed the interview data, we asked what things prevented the company from being as good as it could be. One senior manager said, "I devote 80 percent of my time to trifles. It is the same for my deputies and department directors." We suggested that this resulted from people pushing responsibility up the organization, rather than accepting it themselves. This was a key element in the culture of the organization.

Another director said, "Taking initiative around here is like a brick that you throw in the air. It can land on your head." This helped us understand why people pushed responsibility up the organization. KP's culture was shaped more by fear of making mistakes than by trust. Fear not only discourages people from taking responsibility, it also prevents the development of the creativity that is crucial to high-performance organizations.

"The culture box," Kirillov said, "makes me very frustrated. For seventy-three years we have operated this way. Even after three years of perestroika, our people have still not begun to take initiative. They think they are still a monopoly. These attitudes cannot continue."

"This is an example," David Hanna replied, "of the organization getting the results that it is perfectly designed to get. If everyone understands that they are still thinking this is a monopoly, then you can do something about it. Genuine understanding is the first step to high performance. Working together with your deputies, you will be able to change the way you think."

We asked each manager to imagine that he was a fly on the wall of the plant. What cultural behavior would the fly see that produced the results

Figure 11.1
Organization Performance Assessment

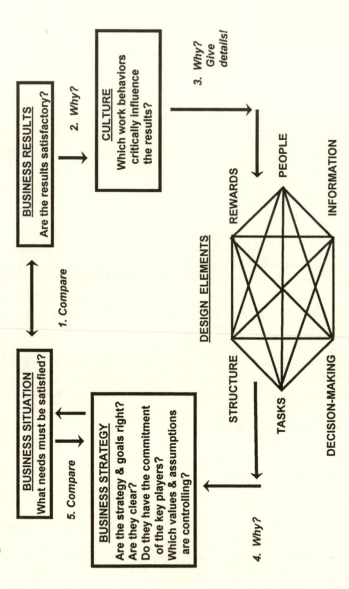

Source: David Hanna

All organizations are perfectly designed to get the results they get.

that the firm was getting? Our flies saw a great deal. People paid attention to the informal reward system. While there was a strong belief in teamwork, employees felt that the boss made all the decisions. Some people did not trust their colleagues at all. Too many people—sometimes as many as forty—attended meetings, and while those attending said they would pass information on to others, they did not.

To encourage the senior management group to learn from these data, we broke the group of about twenty into two smaller groups and gave them two questions. First, can Krasny Proletary be adequately described by the information in the culture box? Second, what is the influence of the culture on the results?

One group reported that external factors contributed to 90 percent of the problems the company was having; behind the lack of consumer goods was the lack of incentive to produce them, and the quality of the products that were manufactured was poor. Neither group answered the question about the influence of the company's culture on its results. The groups had taken ten minutes to get organized, and four people of the twenty had disappeared from the room! They did not want to have to answer the questions.

We then turned to the "design elements" of the model. We asked why each work behavior listed in the culture box occurred. Each answer was then listed under one of the six design elements. To determine why the organization had made these choices about design, we outlined the "business strategy" that the firm was currently using. As part of this analysis we listed the key values and assumptions that control daily work at Krasny. For example, "People should only get the information they need to do their specific job; they do not need to understand the firm's objectives or financial results."

Finally, we compared the actual business strategy with the needs of the business situation. This revealed the gap between what the business situation had shown must be done and what Krasny was actually doing. This analysis also revealed that there was a formal business strategy and an informal one. The formal strategy focused on increasing output and meeting the plan targets. The informal strategy was suggested in statements such as "our sales are guaranteed"; "the organization will take care of me"; "if we improve the old methods, we can be successful"; "they [always someone else] are responsible for making changes"; and "we do not have to invest in developing our people; they will take care of themselves." Some changes seemed counterproductive. Managers had been trying to give more responsibility to the heads of the brigades, the shop-floor work groups, but there was not enough monitoring and control: "When we gave full authority to the brigade," as one director said he had done, "it did great harm."

When we asked which tasks on the diagram were not being done, the responses were equally revealing: "Someone else, not myself, has to make the changes." "We know we must radically change to meet our customers' needs, but the system says we should just try and do a little better. We feel that workers' opinions do not count for much in this system."

Again we divided our twenty senior managers into two groups and asked them to choose top priority tasks to work on. One group prioritized their tasks as follows:

1. Strategy.
2. Structure. What would be optimal for the strategic solution? For example, the incentive that employee ownership would provide.
3. Improve continually the competence of the staff through training and coaching, including problem-solving skills.
4. Improve the wage system and social protection, including better care of pensioners and housing. (We should try and do better than the cooperatives are doing in this area.)

The other group listed the following priorities:

1. Achieve employee ownership as the main incentive for continuous improvement.
2. Remove overlapping responsibilities.
3. Delegate responsibilities and clarify the boundaries among departments down the organization.
4. Improve the information and feedback systems.
5. Training and coaching at each level.

After noting the substantial overlap in the priorities of both groups, we charged each with the question: What can we apply to Krasny Proletary from what we learned at the morning seminar and the diagnostic? The group working on strategy reported to the full group that "maximum profit is the goal. The customer is always right. We need the best information. We need to determine what to manufacture."

"If we pursue the above decisions, this will lead us to a new structure and a new workplace. It will include reducing the number of levels of management. Social stability and social factors will lead to stability in the team. All these things will lead to changing the workers' psychology. Employee ownership will encourage people to take more responsibility."

To conclude the analysis of the firm's performance, we asked Kirillov what he thought of the diagnosis of the firm depicted on flip chart sheets taped to the wall. "I can see myself on the wall," he said. "This is very impressive."

REDESIGNING KRASNY PROLETARY'S ORGANIZATION: 1991

Toward the end of this meeting we asked the group to think about what they most wanted to change about the way they worked. To establish priorities quickly, we introduced the group to tools for brainstorming and "Chicago voting" (so-called because you get to vote more than once). Here are the items that were the highest priority for them:

- There should be more independence in decision making both from the government externally and from senior management internally.
- More responsibility should be delegated to the brigade leaders.
- Senior managers should spend more time developing strategy and less time on the daily problems.
- People throughout the firm should be treated with greater fairness and justice.
- A reward system should recognize people who work better.
- Bureaucracy and paperwork should be greatly reduced.
- Everyone should become an owner of the enterprise.

Kirillov agreed that the next step was to begin work on KP's vision, strategy, and management philosophy.

Vision

Before the firm could develop a strategy for dealing with its current problems and establish longer-term goals for the coming market economy, it needed to establish a vision of what it ideally wanted to be in ten years. The senior management group needed a shared vision which they could communicate to all employees. Here is how Krasny Proletary's internal newspaper, *Dvigatel,* reported the process to employees:

Dreaming is not harmful. Make yourself comfortable in a cozy armchair, close your eyes, and challenge your imagination.

It is the year 2000. You come up to the gates of your plant. What can you see? What has changed for the past ten years? . . .

Having closed your eyes, you mustn't scrutinize and reason logically. Do not think what we can achieve, and what we cannot. Just try to draw an ideal picture of what you'd like the company to be in your imagination.

Every member of the senior management group in the workshop got this assignment. . . .

So what is our top management's vision of our plant on the threshold of the twenty-first century?

The Krasny name is a guarantee of high quality. The main criterion of the work is the satisfaction of the customer's demands within the scope of the single world market. Krasny is a reliable and prestigious partner.

A job at Krasny is an element of personal happiness. It helps people to provide for themselves, gives social protection to both the employees and the veterans, and helps people to develop their creative abilities. Every employee says that Krasny is his second home.

Krasny is a joint-stock company based on employee ownership principles.

There is full unanimity among the employees. Every one of them understands the common objectives, works to achieve them, feels himself an individual, and is not just a screw.

The plant has restructured. The production process became flexible and supple. It has been broken down into separate autonomous sections, the authority having been delegated down the organization.

The plant sees to its employees' professional training and has its own reserve of personnel. The best traditions have been preserved and are fostered. There is an atmosphere of friendship and mutual assistance.

Would you like to work at a plant like that? As for me, I would. (Kishinets 1991)

Strategy

The next step was to develop a strategy to achieve this new, shared vision of senior managers. First, we discussed with them the research on high-performance companies by Professor Michael Porter of the Harvard Business School which determined that five strategic elements had the most important influence on the profitability of a firm: the threat of new competitors; the struggle with the present competitors; the possibility of choice among and bargaining with the suppliers; the possibility for the customer to choose between Krasny and its competitors; and the pressing threat of new goods and services making Krasny's production outdated and uncompetitive.

"These elements may seem a bit far-fetched for our Soviet industry at present," commented *Dvigatel.* "There's not the slightest trace of competition under the general shortage of goods and monopolistic pressure of suppliers. But keep in mind that we're considering the strategy for many years ahead. Who can guarantee that the plants of the former military complex won't become our competitors in the near future, or there won't be an influx of goods from the West? How would we feel then?"

While Porter's research indicates that three different strategies can deliver a competitive advantage,[2] to attempt all simultaneously was to guarantee failure. "Only if we choose one of these can we outrun our competitors," commented *Dvigatel.* "And this makes it very important to estimate our advantages relative to the other machine-building firms."

In the strategy workshop, Krasny's managers argued that the firm's ace was its assembly-line production of machine tools. Hence KP's unit costs were much lower than those at the other plants, offering KP a potential competitive advantage. If they could improve marketing, they saw immense opportunities to improve performance and profits. Management concluded that a winning strategy for Krasny should focus on low-cost production, while seeking greater flexibility in production, which the plant's assembly process permitted, to achieve faster response to the changes in demand.

After agreeing on strategic principles, all participants were divided into four groups to work out plans for improving organization design, personnel training, employee motivation, and communication to employees in the context of the vision and strategy statements. Two hours of group work produced some interesting proposals in each area.

Perhaps most crucial was the proposal for a general overhaul of the management system. The top level of the organization was to focus on selecting managers; on basic policy issues like outlining economic, technical, and social strategies; and on finance. Operational management would be delegated to lower levels. Inside the plant, divisions would operate as economically independent units, defining their own personnel policies, solving their production problems independently, and retaining a percentage of their profits. While part of the profit would be used centrally for reinvestment and company social programs, the independence of operational units inside the plant was to be the main thrust of organizational redesign.

Management also concluded during the workshop that the company's stock should be mainly owned by its employees, and it proposed to link compensation to company performance through profit sharing at the company and operational unit level and through dividends on employee stock. Further, managers proposed pay for improving knowledge and skills and new incentives for initiative as well as rewards for seniority, pension bonuses, and continuing free medical service and social security.

Management Philosophy and Behavior

Central to the success of high-performing companies is a common approach to managing people. To develop this management philosophy and work on other problems that the firm faced, we suggested that the Krasny leaders plan a five-day retreat for the senior management group.

Since none of them had ever been on a retreat before, we recommended that they find a rural setting close to Moscow with good sleeping accommodations and meeting rooms. After reviewing several possibilities, they settled on the Three Little Birch Trees, a sanatorium in Domodedovo owned by the Ministry of Finance. This would provide the relaxed atmosphere needed to study and reach agreement on the major problems facing the firm, and it would help the senior management group deepen their trust in each other so that they could better work together. To develop a management philosophy for the firm, we asked them at the retreat to share with the group their own management experiences, both good and bad, while they were moving up the ranks. We asked them how they wanted to be managed and how they wanted to manage the people who report to them. We identified core values from their own experiences. These could also be seen as principles for designing high-performance management: teamwork, honesty, trust, open communication, cooperation, fairness, and respect for individual differences.

After the managers had developed this list of what was important to them, we told them that some of America's highest performing companies had based their own philosophies of management on the same core values they had just identified. The Krasny managers were impressed by this similarity.

We asked several of the managers to volunteer to take flip chart notes and draft a statement that others could critique. Here's what they came up with:

Philosophy of Management

We build our relationships as a team of people driven by common values in an atmosphere of trust and respect, based on the principles of integrity, fairness, equality, and mutual assistance. This is the only way that leads to the common goal.

We then asked each of the directors to discuss this statement with their subordinates and get their opinion on it. One of the directors reported at the next meeting that his people were "enthusiastically in favor of it. They asked, however, what the senior management team meant by each word in the statement."

At a meeting in February 1992, the senior team approved the final draft of the statement and then agreed that they were responsible for implementing it in each of their departments. While there would be articles in the company newspaper and information on the bulletin boards about the management philosophy, it was the responsibility of each group leader to explain it to his group. Most important, each director was expected to hold the philosophy as the standard for his or her own behavior.

Each employee is responsible for seeing that the philosophy is implemented. If they feel that someone is not being honest with them, for example, they are encouraged to question him and remind him of the statement of philosophy. This process provides valuable feedback for employees at all levels. It encourages people to "talk back to the boss" and to understand that talking back is part of the job.

When people understand the core values of the philosophy and can use the tools of feedback, the organization has a powerful method to increase the speed of continuous improvement.

At the same retreat, the senior managers began to learn Stephen Covey's "seven habits of highly effective people," derived from Covey's twenty years of research about what makes some people much more effective than others. They are part of a training program that has helped thousands of managers and workers around the world. The seven habits are as follows:

1. *Be proactive.* We, not our environment, are primarily responsible for our success or failure.

2. *Begin with the end in mind.* We must begin with an end in mind. We become what we think about.

3. *Put first things first.* Success comes from putting first things first and not allowing ourselves to give our time to urgent, but nonproductive, activities.

4. *Think win-win.* A win-win philosophy is the only viable one when working with others—even when circumstances suggest one must win and one must lose.

5. *Seek first to understand, then to be understood.* By seeking first to understand others before selling our own ideas, we not only learn more, but also gain influence in our relationships.

6. *Synergize.* The fruit of these habits is synergy: creative breakthrough solutions to even seemingly impossible predicaments.

7. *Renewal.* We achieve continuous improvement by renewing ourselves physically, mentally, spiritually, socially, and emotionally. This is what maintains a high level of personal contribution. (Covey 1989)

Kirillov and his group were so impressed with the insights they achieved into their own behavior and that of their colleagues that they requested that all KP employees receive training in the seven habits. "It has been a long time since we have learned such important lessons, and it was hard work," said Kirillov. "This is a real shift in paradigms for us."

Employee Ownership

The last thing the senior group did at the retreat was to begin to study the principles for design and implementation of successful employee ownership. Based on the experience of over ten thousand American companies that had used employee ownership, the Krasny leadership began to explore American lessons and make choices as to what would be best for their own needs. They were encouraged to bring all the employees into the design process, especially the 350 elected employee representatives.

The leadership studied the experience of Weirton Steel, Quad/Graphics, Columbia Aluminum, Mondragon (Spain), and others. They discussed their needs with managers of American employee-owned companies such as Lowell Marshall, president of Republic Storage Systems in Ohio. As a result of this study, they decided that they wanted the full participation of employees in ownership. While they wanted outside stockholders who could bring valuable know-how or technology, they wanted to retain control inside the company. By the end of 1991, they drafted a charter to guide their new company.

The charter drew upon ten principles for designing the most successful employee-owned companies in the United States. These principles are as follows:

- Deepen the trust among all employees of the enterprise.
- Sell stock to outsiders, but retain control.
- Involve future employee-owners in design decisions.
- Have employees pay for and vote their stock.
- Participate in the election of the board.
- Retain in the firm a significant share of the profits.
- Opt for majority ownership rather than minority.
- Buy back stock when employees retire.
- Include all new employees as owners after a probationary period.
- Develop laws that encourage rather than discourage employee ownership.

In short, the first twelve months of our work at Krasny Proletary focused on helping the senior management group assess their own strengths and weaknesses as managers and learn how world-class companies manage themselves. They developed the foundation for moving Krasny ahead: a vision, a strategy, and a management philosophy. To help develop the vision, they visited other Russian companies that had implemented employee ownership and understood that it could work for them. Through the seven habits and other training in the concepts of total quality, teamwork, and effective meetings, they began to improve their skills.

They learned the principles of the "Z" process described in Chapter 15 for transforming the performance of firms, which shows how change can be introduced into an organization, starting at the top. Senior managers must first understand new ideas and then practice them. When management has demonstrated what it has learned, it is time to cascade the concepts and tools down other levels of the organization—the higher level teaching it to the level which reports to it.

As a result, the senior group at Krasny began to shift paradigms. It began to change the way it thought and acted. It also began to study the restructuring of the firm into smaller units or profit centers. And it began to see the value of learning new skills as a result of American methods of training—in which people learned more by doing, seeing, and talking than by listening to an expert talk.

Because of this foundation, often acquired painfully and slowly and with strong resistance from senior managers, the work the second year began to gather some momentum. If it had not been for Kirillov's continued strong support for the learning process, despite some senior managers calling it a waste of time, the work could not have gone forward.

GATHERING MOMENTUM: 1992

In 1992, Krasny Proletary made some significant breakthroughs in reforming management and getting results. Early in the year, the senior management group agreed to break the firm into fifteen profit centers, six months before it had been scheduled. The quality of Krasny products began to improve, as measured by the absence of complaints from its customers. A team of experts from the World Bank visited the plant and called it a model of the changes that could be achieved in large state enterprises.

CNN, the American television channel, broadcast a segment about Krasny's progress. The *Wall Street Journal* and *Business Week* noted it. Russian Channel 2 featured Krasny Proletary with three other companies as examples of firms making the successful transition to "people's capitalism." At the Machine Tool Exhibition in Chicago in September, Krasny sold all the machines it brought and left with $2 million in orders, its first sale in the United States. While in Chicago, the Krasny team had the opportunity to visit a world-class company which uses the profit-center approach: Allied Signode, a division of Illinois Tool Works.

For 1992, the management improvement effort focused on several key areas, including the following:

- Work with the people who were likely to become the profit-center leaders, including strategy for establishing the profit centers and leadership training.

- Implement the basic improvement concepts and tools in two areas that would become profit centers as models for the rest of the firm.

- Work with the senior management group in their efforts to deepen their understanding of high-performance management, including employee ownership, and their effort to spread the vision and strategy throughout the firm.

- Continue the development of a strong internal consulting team so that each profit center had at least one person who was learning to be a trainer and facilitator.

Team-Building Workshop

In March 1992, in an attempt to operationalize the new strategy, Krasny sponsored a team-building workshop for the engineering and marketing departments which was led by Sally Craig from Participation Associates. The nine engineers, many of them third-generation KP employees, had a combined service of more than 250 years. They were deeply distrustful of the new marketing department, which had only been established in September 1991. The chief engineer stated that he did not see the usefulness of the marketing department–especially since he was faced with the near-term prospect of laying off close to a quarter of his workforce. The marketing department, on the other hand, expressed nothing but buoyant enthusiasm. The two teams were clearly far apart in their thinking.

The participants gradually loosened up as they played the corporate survival game "Lost at Sea," a classic simulation exercise designed to show how group decision making can produce superior results and to teach the value of synergy. The first day ended with each team assessing their level of internal teamwork: How well do they communicate their expectations to each other? What kind of problem-solving mechanisms do they use? How much understanding do team members have for the strategies and goals of the team and the company?

The engineers were not used to being asked their opinion about anything other than strictly technical matters. The marketing group still had not defined its priorities, nor did it have a clear sense of its mission—and it had yet to establish its value in the eyes of the engineers.

On the second day, a series of small-group experiential exercises demonstrated the importance of trust. The message was clear: trust depends on an individual's being trustworthy, and trustworthiness is an indispensable element in creating a positive work environment. The group was then led through an exercise in group problem solving. Three small groups—engineers, marketers, and a mixed group—used brainstorming methods and discussion to define problems and develop strategy. They then developed action plans for resolving them. The joint group of engineers and marketers shared a major breakthrough in how they will work together in the future.

The positive results of this workshop could be seen months later. No longer do the two departments mistrust and withhold information from each other. The marketing department has been legitimized and is now respected by the other departments, and the mid-level managers of both departments are much more likely to work synergistically in a win-win mode than previously.

When profit-center leaders began to see the benefits of learning new skills themselves, they wanted these for their centers. This demand was what we needed to assure that the training would not be wasted. With the assistance of the leaders of the internal consulting team, Maxim Iliin and Elena Kishinets, Krasny developed a training plan that would teach middle- and lower-level employees the key skills that senior managers had learned, including organizational diagnosis, strategic planning and visioning, teamwork, effective meetings, total quality concepts and tools, the seven habits of highly effective people, problem solving, feedback, and work redesign.

To support this training effort, the profit-center leaders were each asked to choose one person who would become a facilitator and trainer. Iliin and Kishinets came to the United States for training at the Covey Leadership Center and the Employee Ownership Center, Kent State University. Albert Markov, the director of marketing, attended the executive management program at Duke University for two weeks, then visited American firms for a week. Sally Craig and Andrei Voronkov joined the external consulting team. The joint consulting team began to concentrate its efforts on training employees who would become trainers.

Profit-Center Leaders Speak Out

We interviewed profit-center leaders to find out what they had done with their new independence. Sergei Sergeev is a profit-center leader who runs the quality control complex (three hundred employees) with five laboratories and a new servicing operation that works directly with customers. They have been systematically collecting feedback from their customers for the past year. They are using a statistical process control and are seeking to decentralize responsibility for quality back to manufacturing units. Certification of quality is new to Russian business, and Sergei feels it will take them up to three years to meet ISO 9000 quality standards now demanded by European buyers.

He is especially enthusiastic about the new participatory approach. "Before we were closed like oysters, especially the higher-ups. You Americans are not solving our problems for us. You have helped improve our self-esteem and have helped us to define our values and see what we really want. I belong to a new generation of leaders. The changes you are introducing are not hurting me like they are the old ones. Our people were raised on the idea that *nothing* depends on them." He said that reorganization of his department had led to a flatter reporting structure and tighter discipline. He had refused to accept some additional employees that company management had wanted to assign to him.

Alexander Pozdyaev is the chief of the precision lathes plant (420 employees) and a highly articulate and forceful young leader. He has assembled his own leadership team in the profit center with two direct assistants, both experienced production workers, and four department heads, all more experienced and older than himself. The technology function has been centralized and no longer reports to individual shop foremen. He has also created two new departments: accounting and planning. Supervisors of these two functions at first did not want to work in a centralized service, but they are gradually learning to work together.

Pozdyaev has enthusiastically accepted the directive to develop his line of business. They are just completing an order of three very complex lathes for China, on schedule, on budget, and with an expectation of more orders to follow.

Pozdyaev's department also has a new product. A year earlier, two engineers came in off the street, offering Pozdyaev a design for a self-contained and portable brick-making plant. In a joint venture with the engineers' company, they produced three prototypes. It was the hit of a building trade exposition in September, with President Yeltsin hailing its promise. Orders began to roll in for delivery in 1993. Pozdyaev was able to motivate his workers by explaining the financial advantages to them if the product is successful.

Nikolai Salomatin runs the largest profit center, universal lathes (950 employees), and Sergey Avtomonov's group makes consumer goods and robotics. The new plant was designed to produce 5,000 robotics units annually. Its maximum output reached 3,400, and now they are only produced by order in small lots. The group is now producing small, consumer-oriented "universal" lathes and even toys. When asked about toy production, Avtomonov says that they were ordered to produce toys by Gosplan during perestroika and that they have kept it up because they can do it easily and they have a ready market.

Substantial independence for profit centers is a recent thing, and Salomatin says that he is frequently asked in team meetings why the company was divided into profit centers. This is evidence to him that the workers haven't begun to see any results of this yet, and he feels that the main task is to clarify advantages of the profit centers to employees and to be able to show them concrete results. "Before, our main headache was to fulfill the plan; now everything has changed, and we have to think about sales, and so on." Avtomonov interjects that they need economic tools to compare profit centers.

Avtomonov continues to speak to the need to have a sanctioned process so that once an order is fulfilled, his profit center can continue to produce, sell, and retain the profits. Salomatin adds that his profit center can provide services to other plants. They used to make only new products and now they do some repairs for customers. They are also producing and selling nails, whereas before they were producing them only for their own purposes.

The profit-center leaders are beginning to see the results of their work to redesign the company. Their own attitudes and behavior are changing toward themselves and what is becoming the company that they own.

PRIVATIZATION: 1993

In the spring of 1993, Krasny Proletary privatized.[3] As in the privatization of state enterprises in general, this involved a two-step process: (1) the conversion from a state enterprise to a corporation with 100 percent of the stock initially owned by the state and (2) the subsequent sale of this stock to nonstate entities including employees.

Krasny Proletary completed the first step in its conversion from a state enterprise on March 23, 1993, when the documents establishing KP as a joint-stock company were finally signed and sealed. The initial capitalization of the new company was established as the July 1, 1992, residual asset value of plant and equipment[4] in 1991 (that is, preinflation) rubles plus working capital (including raw materials and inventory); the total amount was 191.6 million rubles. The company therefore issued 191,600 shares with a nominal value of 1,000 rubles each.

The second step required sale of this stock by the state. Three lengthy meetings of KP's representative conference[5] culminated in a recommendation for Option 2 of the privatization law, and in September 1992, KP's work collective—all its employees—cast 82 percent of their votes in favor of

Option 2. This option allows current and former employees[6] to purchase up to 51 percent of the stock. The remaining 49 percent is reserved for sale to other entities, including a portion to be sold on the stock exchange. Employees may also purchase some of these shares.

The rules for the purchase of the 51 percent reserved for employees were established by the State Property Committee (Goskomimuschestvo, or GKI). These rules called for a private purchase of stock at a value equal to 1.7 times the shares' nominal (that is, preinflation) value of 1,000 rubles each. Thus, 97,716 shares were available for employee subscription for vouchers at 1,700 rubles per share. By choosing Option 2, which gave them a controlling interest in their firm, KP employees precluded their receiving the free shares that would have been provided had they opted for Option 1, which offered 25 percent of the stock as nonvoting preferred shares.[7] If the employees subscribed for less than 51 percent under Option 2, the remaining shares reserved for the employees would be sold to outsiders as well.

The GKI rules for employee stock purchase permitted each eligible participant to offer to purchase up to 5 percent of the company. If the subscription produced offers totaling more than the 51 percent available, subscribers would be sold the amount of stock equal to the proportion of their subscription relative to all subscriptions. All subscribers were assured at least one share.

Employees could use vouchers to purchase stock; at least 50 percent of each individual's purchase of shares and at least 80 percent of the full closed subscription had to be paid for in vouchers. The voucher system was created by the Russian government in an effort to distribute state property evenly among all of the people, whether they worked in enterprises being privatized or elsewhere. An estimate of the asset value of all state property was made in 1991 and then was divided by the number of eligible Russian citizens. This calculation produced a ten-thousand-ruble voucher for each man, woman, and child in the country, and the vouchers were distributed in the fall of 1992. At the same time, however, inflation averaging 20 percent a month rapidly devalued the currency and virtually eliminated savings for most citizens. Many people, not believing that their vouchers were worth anything, sold them on the street. One could purchase a voucher with a ten-thousand-ruble face value for as little as four thousand rubles.

Notice the implications. In practice, in the spring of 1993, with four thousand current rubles, one could buy a voucher capable of purchasing six shares of stock which were worth six thousand preinflation rubles in the employee closed subscription. All market theory to the contrary, a voucher representing your share of the national patrimony was trading for the price of three or four bottles of vodka.[8] Under these circumstances, the voucher system permitted a very rapid concentration of wealth to the extent the vouchers could be used at preinflationary values, as they could in closed subscriptions.

While the work collective at Krasny Proletary voted for majority employee ownership, the management believed the subscription rules might produce dramatically different results. Unlike the managers at many firms, they hoped to see a fairly equitable distribution of shares among as many employees as possible, not a concentration of shares in the hands of a small group of managers. Under the GKI rules, as few as ten eligible participants could offer to purchase 50 percent of the company. Since their offers would be so large in proportion to those requesting a more modest number of shares, they would end up with the bulk of the company, leaving the majority of would-be shareholders with only one share each; moreover, there was fear that employee participation in the stock purchase would be low, and perhaps the employee shares would be undersubscribed.

Where would ten employees come up with enough vouchers to purchase 50 percent of the company? Since the GKI rules precluded the enterprise from forcing employees to reveal where they had gotten the vouchers, an employee could serve as a front for a wealthy investor who had acquired a large amount of vouchers on the street. Indeed, the rules—in the name of the free market—provided an open invitation to the "black market mafia" to acquire dominant positions in legitimate business.

To avoid this possibility, KP's board in February 1993 decided to impose internal recommendations, suggesting subscriptions to be limited to 200 shares per individual, instead of the 9,580 shares that the 5 percent rule would have permitted, and guaranteeing each subscriber a minimum of 6 shares. When the first round of the subscriptions revealed that ten employees[9] had subscribed for more than 200 shares, management approached these ten subscribers and asked them to reconsider. Each then voluntarily resubmitted a subscription for the 200-share maximum.

At the board's initiation, the company undertook a campaign to get workers to participate in the purchase of stock. At the beginning of its new ownership training program, the company held meetings for all employees to explain the process and what was at stake. The text of the flier used in these meetings gives a clear sense of the argumentation for participating:

EMPLOYEES OF KRASNY PROLETARY!

On March 23, 1993, our enterprise has been registered as the JOINT-STOCK COMPANY KRASNY PROLETARY!

To become the owners of our company, we have to buy 51 percent of Krasny shares.

What does it mean to us?

It means that we protect vouchers and money from inflation by investing it in real assets.

It means that we can buy ownership at a very low cost (twenty to thirty times lower than its real value). We have this advantage because we are buying the shares of our company. No bank or investment fund would offer us such a great deal!

It means that we are creating the capital that will protect our well-being and the well-being of our children. Future dividends will depend on the company's profit and on how many shares you get.

It means that we receive the right to participate in making major decisions within our company, and also the right to elect and to be elected to the managing positions.

> The fate of our company
> and of our workplaces
> will be in our hands!

As a result of this campaign, 4,115 of Krasny Proletary's current and former employees participated in the closed subscription on April 7, 1993, subscribing for 133,601 shares, far more than the 97,716 shares available. This forced the company to prorate the shares among the subscribers accordingly. Every subscriber got the right to buy the minimum of 6 shares (one voucher) and then 67 percent of the remaining shares requested. While 767 subscribed for only 6 shares, the other four-fifths had their subscriptions prorated. Thus those who subscribed for 12 shares (two vouchers) got a right to buy 10, 18 shares (three vouchers) got 14, and so on. Those who subscribed for the maximum of 200 shares—and there were ultimately 141 of these—ended up with the right to buy 139 shares each.

Ownership of the remaining 49 percent of the company's shares is to be made available to current shareholders or sold on the market. A holding company set up by the Ministry for the Machine Tool Industry will retain 20 percent of the shares for three years; this block of shares will then be sold on the stock market. Fourteen percent of the shares will become available for purchase in 1994 in a competitive, closed subscription by other entities connected with Krasny Proletary, such as suppliers, customers, and foreign partners. Ten percent of the shares will be sold to small investors for vouchers through a public auction process in 1994; employees can bid for these shares. The final 5 percent of the shares will belong to the Shareholder Fund of Workers of the Enterprise, which holds them on behalf of the employees.

The consequence of this process is that majority ownership of Krasny Proletary is vested at least temporarily in its employees. Shares are broadly spread among the roughly 75 percent of employees who participated; the

141 largest employee shareholders hold only about 20 percent of the employee shares. Employees will probably end up with some additional shares as well. On the other hand, the absence of restrictions on the sale of shares by employees to outsiders will probably lead to increased outside ownership over time.

While shares will eventually be voted on a one-share, one-vote basis for the board of directors, in an interim period there is a four-member board that includes the general director, who has two votes; an elected employee representative (a manager), with one vote; a local government director (from the *rayon* [district] government), with one vote; and a director from the GKI (the GKI represents the ministry's shares on the board of directors), who holds a vote and the so-called "golden share," that is, the right of veto power for the state for the first three years. Thus, while a majority of the shares of Krasny Proletary are already in private hands, the government will maintain more than a modicum of influence over the firm in the immediate future.

KRASNY'S FUTURE

Ever since starting the work with Krasny Proletary, we have felt that we were racing against the clock. Could the firm introduce the new methods fast enough to escape the devastating effects of the declining Russian economy? Could Krasny Proletary develop new products, and new markets for their old products, fast enough to pay the bills and keep the plant operating?

At this writing, at the beginning of 1994, we do not know the answers. The Russian gross national product (GNP) declined 20 percent in 1992, while inflation spiraled to over 5 percent a week in the last five months of 1992 to hit 10 percent a week in December. In 1993 the GNP fell another 14 percent. Inflation gradually declined to 15 percent per month at the end of the year. The minister of finance, however, resigned in January 1994 and predicted hyperinflation, more than 40 percent per month, by midsummer.

A capital goods producer, Krasny Proletary was hard hit. While some new products were selling well, demand for most products was minimal. In the past three years, Krasny has cut more than 30 percent of its workforce through layoffs and voluntary resignations. The prognosis for 1994 is not promising.

The workers and managers at Krasny, however, feel they can survive. Many hadn't thought they could survive the past three years, when almost half of the four hundred machine tool companies folded. Krasny's employees have worked overtime and weekends to develop and market new products. Today, many believe they are the masters of their fate, a major shift from three years ago. The new energy and creativity that have come with this understanding could help the company to be first a survivor and then a world-class player.

NOTES

1. These steps, which we call the "Z" process, are diagramed in Figure 15.2 and discussed in detail in Chapter 15.

2. These strategies are to seek to be the *low-cost producer*, manufacturing with the lowest costs in the industry; to pursue *product differentiation* to meet critical customer needs better than the competitors do, a strategy usually permitting a premium price; and to undertake a *segment focus* targeted at a narrow group of the customers' needs, based on either cost or quality.

3. Dan Bell, of the Northeast Ohio Employee Ownership Center, Kent State University, assisted in the preparation of this section.

4. Residual asset value is equal to the acquisition price of plant and equipment less depreciation.

5. The representative conference acts for the work collective much as a representative town meeting acts for the citizens in those New England towns which have gotten too big for town meetings of all citizens. In September 1992, KP's representative conference was made up of 307 delegates among the company's 4,862 employees, or about 1 for each 16 employees. They acted more as mandated delegates than as independent representatives. The final vote in the representative conference was 255 for Option 2 and 21 against, with 2 abstentions and 29 absent.

6. Eligible participants included all current employees, all pensioners, former employees with ten or more years of seniority (if men) and seven and a half or more years of seniority (if women), and certain vendors providing logistical support to the company.

7. Interviewed in July 1993, Yuri Dzhed noted that the debate in the representative conference had revolved around the fact that the free shares under Option 1 were nonvoting and that it was unclear at the time what the basis for the price of the additional 10 percent of shares would be. Had it been known that the Option 1 shares would subsequently be given voting rights and that the price set on the additional stock would have been based on nominal value (i.e., 1,000 rubles per share), Dzhed thought the result might have been different.

8. To put this in terms of wages, a voucher would buy assets valued at twenty-four months' worth of preinflationary wages at the average industrial wage in 1991; but vouchers could be bought on the street markets for a week's worth of the average industrial wage in February 1993. From an exchange rate perspective, in the summer of 1991, 32 rubles bought one dollar. In February 1993, 650 rubles bought one dollar. So the equivalent of about $6 in cash (4,000/650) could buy $187.50 in assets (6,000/32).

9. One was a manager; nine were not. During the pilot of the ownership training program's first class, the audience protested vehemently against prorating shares when employees offered five or fewer vouchers. The first five vouchers were come by honestly, employees emphasized, not purchased or acquired otherwise. KP managers had, in fact, sought to exempt all subscriptions for thirty or fewer shares (i.e., five or fewer vouchers) from proration, but the GKI turned the proposal down.

12 Leading the Transformation of Krasny Proletary

Yuri I. Kirillov

In this chapter Yuri Ivanovich Kirillov looks back on the progress that Krasny Proletary made and how they did it. In June 1992, eighteen months after the intensive improvement effort had begun at the firm, Kirillov described his experience. Since the transformation process is at an early stage, this is a progress report from the man who was a champion of the new methods of high-performance management, total quality, teamwork, employee ownership, and continuous improvement.

Krasny Proletary, a state-owned firm with 4,300 employees, used to make only lathes, primarily for the defense industry. Now it has added over a dozen new products from oil field equipment and brick-making machines to steel doors and nails. In September 1992, the firm sold its first lathes in the United States.–Editors

◆ IT took us some time to realize which direction to follow. At the beginning we lived by probing and making mistakes. It was the time when Gorbachev came out with his program of perestroika for reforming the country. When 1988 began, we saw for the first time some of the practical results of his program. The new Law on State Enterprises, for example, went into effect in January. It was intended to give the firms greater autonomy from the state and democratize hierarchical management.

Many of us at the firm realized that if we did not take some concrete and realistic measures, and did not take them soon, we would be unforgivably lagging behind. After several years of trying different approaches with little success, we have now achieved significant results.

RESULTS

Our foremost result is the changing mentality of our senior management team. This started eighteen months ago. The new paradigm that we've acquired of thinking about the customer, quality, and restructuring, for example, is a first step toward being ready for the market economy.

Changing the mentality of the management team was not easy. At the very beginning of our discussion of the possible establishment of profit centers, several senior managers were vehemently opposed to splitting the plant into autonomous blocks. Today, if you tell one of them that profit centers were not his idea, he will fight you; he really does believe that it was his idea.

The second achievement is that senior management has started to work as a single team. Now we are sharing the same ideas. First, we began with about fifteen people from the senior team who were given consulting services, including seminars, diagnosis, and coaching. Then this group expanded to include the leaders of our new profit centers. To give the process of continuous improvement at the plant a good push, there is now not just one general director—there are two, three, and many more.

Third, we've developed a strategy and vision of the future for Krasny Proletary. Now we are building our work on the basis of our vision.

A fourth important result is that the initiative for improving the way we work is now coming from below. The paradigm shift which started with the top management team has moved down to middle management.

The most interesting results are from the bottom of the organization. The bulk of our workers were able to get acquainted with everything our American advisers taught us through the many articles we published about our new methods in our plant newspaper, *Dvigatel (Engine)*.

While working on our "crisis plan," which called for the development of alternative products, we tried to involve each team at the bottom. By using the methods of brainstorming, several profit centers developed over one thousand ideas for new products. Then they prioritized them by applying criteria such as which products would be quickest to produce the most profits. Our new marketing department assembled the new product ideas and assisted the profit centers.

In Avtomonov's profit center, for instance, they are making instrument nozzles for electric drills. New products will enable the nozzles to be used for various purposes including grinding, polishing, and trimming. They also started making small individual concrete mixers with both hand and electric drive for country cottages.

Now, when we meet to discuss a burning issue of the day, instead of two or three people talking at the same time, we are sure everyone will have a chance to express his personal opinion. All of us acquired a habit of listening to other people. When everything is discussed and different points of view are considered, we usually come to a consensus.

What is more interesting is that this process has moved beyond the senior management team: now we can finally speak about the merger between the top management interests and the interests of profit centers' chiefs and the middle management. Before there was quite a gap between a top official of the company and a middle manager. The first looked upon the second with a slight condescension. That gap was very hard to close. Due to the help of American specialists we finally managed to overcome this barrier. The result is a psychological climate with more open communication among all the levels. Nowadays not a single person of the work collective believes that we are trying to split up the factory and to ruin the company.

Now, all of us think how to make our work more effective, how to be more productive. With our new methods, we have been able to focus most of the personnel of the company, including the profit centers, on solving one major problem—what the alternative products should be. Before we only knew how to produce metal cutting lathes. Today, market demand for them dropped down considerably, and we have to design something else and put it into operation so that it will enable us to survive under market conditions.

Nevertheless, we still have a long way to go to accomplish a whole program of reforms. We are just at the beginning of the privatization process. This fall (1992) we have to create a joint-stock company. We'll have to solve quite a few complicated organizational and economic problems to turn our newly established profit centers into efficient and profitable subdivisions of the company.

We plan to set up our own bank to finance the profit centers. We'll have to expand our training courses for the personnel of the profit centers, so that people can learn new concepts and tools, rotate jobs, and combine some similar occupations.

We'll have to fight for ourselves under the conditions of a free market with highly competitive firms, which we believe will soon appear.

At this stage in our change process, the most important achievement is that the initiative is coming from the workshop level. The days are gone when people worked by a directive which was sent from the top. Now the people themselves come up with new initiatives. Today they solve a lot of important problems on their own, such as hiring and reducing personnel of the profit center and suggesting alternative products. Now the senior management team only considers the most important policies and issues.

At the weekly meetings of the profit-center directors, our goal is to achieve mutual understanding and effective coordination in the spirit of creating win-win agreements. This is a decision process where both parties are satisfied, which we learned from studying the seven habits of highly effective people.

MY CAREER AT KRASNY PROLETARY

In December 1974 I came to Krasny Proletary. I was a young specialist having just graduated from the Moscow Technological College of Machine Tool Building (Stankin).

My first responsibility was engineering and technological projects in the department of the chief technologist. In 1978 I became the chief of a small group of twelve technologists who were working on putting into operation the mass production of multipurpose lathes using assembly lines. They suggested I take the job of deputy chief of a workshop. I had worked there for less than a year when I had another job as the vice technical director. It was basically the same application, mainly technological and engineering problems, but now it was within the framework of the whole enterprise involving the issues of organization, production, and general control.

Two years later, in 1983, I was appointed to supervise the construction of a new factory not far from this office in Cherjemushki. There I performed as facilitator of the engineering of the whole enterprise. I had to build not only the technological process for manufacturing our basic product, but I also had to design the management system. We started with a bare piece of land.

For three and a half years I dealt primarily with construction at the new site and commissioning new types of products. I was appointed vice director of the new site. Since the general director of Krasny was located at our plant near the center of Moscow, for most of the time I was left on my own at the new site.

I subsequently became the chief engineer of the whole enterprise, both the old and the new plants. Thus, my office was moved back to the old building. But within half a year a most unfortunate event took place: our old general director Sergei Ivanovich Pavlov died.

For a year I kept the job of technical director. Then in January 1988 our first elections were held under a new system of management introduced by Mikhail Gorbachev. According to the new Law on State Enterprises, all the top management nominees had to be voted upon at a general meeting of the enterprise employees. I got the majority of votes and became the general director of Krasny Proletary. Since then I have been the chief executive officer of the company.

My election was basically due to a psychological factor: the magic of the authoritarian system of management which still prevailed in those years. On election day, a former general director, O. A. Korolev, who had held the post for thirteen years until the end of 1985, came to the company.

Korolev had been very popular among the workers. He resigned of his own accord to work as a consultant on Boris Yeltsin's team. When he came to the factory, there was a meeting of the top management with the trade union organization and the veterans' committee, which is made up of the workers with the longest seniority. In this meeting he said: "I really see there's only one candidate to assume the post of general director. There's no other appropriate alternative."

Due to his recommendation, therefore, I was the only nominee included on the list of candidates at the general employee meeting. I was elected by a decisive majority. The minister of machine tool building signed my appointment as well.

Since 1988 we have had quite a few changes. The system of electing the top manager of the company was canceled by a governmental decree. A new Russian ministry emerged—and it reconfirmed my authority. As all the property of Krasny Proletary belongs to the state, it is the state, personified by the Ministry of the Machine Tool Building Industry, which appoints me general director of the company.

Now, in June 1992, we are very close to another stage. We are privatizing by setting up a new joint-stock company. Who will be the new general director is unknown. The person will be chosen and his functions defined by the council of the joint-stock company that we are creating.

KIRILLOV'S VISION

What is my own vision for the company in the year 2000? When you come and visit us then, you will not see an idle worker in a workshop hanging around, smoking a cigarette, or having a chat somewhere in the corner. You will see only one idle man at the company: the general director. He will be jobless and desperate because the level of efficiency will be so high that there will be nothing left for him to do! Probably, the general director's main activity by the year 2000 will be writing memoirs and occasionally going on excursions around the grounds of the factory, just as one goes to a fine arts museum.

The profit centers will be independent and will be producing a very wide assortment of products, both our traditional metal cutting lathes and new products—consumer goods, wood-processing equipment, construction material equipment (cement, reinforced concrete, brick components equipment), the necessary equipment for gas and oil drilling, automated assembly lines for the automobile companies, hand-manipulated electric equipment, and tools to work on wood and metal. All these products will be of very high quality, will have low production costs, and will be quite competitive in the world market. All the necessary components that we do not produce will be purchased abroad, such as electric rotary ball bearings, so that they will not spoil the overall quality of our product.

But the final product will be assembled, tested, and produced at Krasny Proletary. The personnel will be highly trained and will be top professionals in their trade. They will be most hospitable to their customers and local partners. You will see a smile on everyone's face. This will be the result of the general strategy and philosophy of management we worked out.

I hope by that time we'll be living in a real market economy. I hope that the local Russian ruble will be convertible enough for the domestic market if it is not a totally convertible currency. I hope that we shall not have to deal with the monopolistic suppliers of our components, that our profit centers will have a chance to buy these components and all the necessary equipment themselves in accordance with the market laws of competitiveness.

I hope the profit centers will have a chance to investigate the market to sell their products. I think many of our traditional partners supplying us with spare parts and our customers will actually become our shareholders as well. We will sign not only long-term contracts but also win-win agreements with them.

SEEING WITH OUR OWN EYES

As far as the process of my personal improvement along my "self-perfecting maturity continuum," as described in the seven habits, a most significant role was played by establishing contacts with European companies. Since 1988 we have had some very close links with EMAG, a West German company, and a joint venture was founded. It helped us a lot. With our own eyes we saw a very different system of management for approaching and tackling problems.

I made a number of trips to West Germany and I visited German companies. With the help of EMAG and our ministry, we took a three-week course in Germany in which German specialists taught us many of their methods and techniques. Those workshops were varied and included classroom lectures and excursions to the production lines. They explained their organizational structures, accounting, and finances. Although we seemingly spoke the same language, when we discussed some basic business issues we did not understand each other.

The next year we had a three-week training course at a London business school where they spoke to us in detail about Margaret Thatcher's privatization reform. It looked so similar to what Mikhail Gorbachev was undertaking at that time that we were deeply interested. Other foreign training courses and plant tours, while useful, were not effective enough. A director went somewhere, picked up some information, and then told his people about it when he came back. It did not sink deep roots in people's minds.

When we came back from Great Britain, we began inviting Russian specialists to come over to Krasny and help us with our problems. We tried six different groups. Moscow University was our first choice. Then we invited a group of consultants from other educational research centers, such as the Plekhanov Academy of People's Economy and Management, to teach us to embark on the program of restructuring the company in accordance with the basic general reforms which were being carried out in the whole country.

Unfortunately, we wasted a year on these training courses, not to mention the money. The outcome was thoroughly useless. What we found out was that the experts we dealt with knew the market economy and Western management methods from books only. They had a purely theoretical understanding. They had very abstract ideas of how to make a gradual transition of the company into a joint-stock one. Instead, we needed practical answers to all our questions.

They investigated us at all levels, including a general look into the whole structure of the company and a couple of local investigations at shop level. The results of these investigations were not very helpful. For example, we learned that not a single boss of any department was "good enough" to keep his position. Once we had a group of specialists who spent over a year here. Their final recommendation was "You have to switch over to the third model of self-accounting." What on earth did they mean by that? What is the general director supposed to do with these "profound, scientifically trustworthy" statements? What should be your response, your reaction? It was at that time we first thought about inviting foreign specialists to help us.

It was Maxim Iliin and Yuri Mikhailovich Dzhed who came up with the suggestion of finding someone who could really help us out of this complicated situation. Maxim said that I should meet an American and talk to him about the possibilities of arranging consultations. The American was John Simmons, president of Participation Associates in Chicago.

I remember when we first met at the new site in Cherjemushki in July 1989. It was about six o'clock in the evening and John looked very tired. He was to leave for the States the next morning. We had a conversation, and Maxim took him through the plant. But he gave no concrete answer to me. John probably needed some time before he decided he was going to help us. We then reached an agreement by fax. Perhaps he found it a challenge to speak two different languages. I do not mean English and Russian: I mean understanding the different psychological and economic ways of thinking of Russian and of European or American managers.

Gradually, our senior management team became involved in the American workshops and assignments. Taken at face value, the results of the initial stage of work together were very discouraging. People from the team used to say, "Oh, come on, what are we doing here? We know it all; we knew it for a long time. And we are in no need of any advice from Americans on the subject."

REDESIGNING THE MANAGEMENT SYSTEM

In the past our senior managers did not work together as a team. We had a lot of disagreements as to how to implement recent policies of the government. Should we change the organizational design of the plant? What should we do about the management system? We saw that we had too many managers. At the same time every senior manager was concerned only about his section of the job. Three-quarters of the team were against whatever changes were proposed.

Before perestroika every time we had a meeting the final decision had been made by the general director. The 1988 Law on State Enterprises required democratization, and I didn't want to use the old authoritarian methods. We began to use consensus. This took time and energy. Let me cite one example. At first one director was dead-set against splitting the factory into separate profit centers. His main argument was "If we subdivide the company into independent profit centers, the company will not be able to survive. It will collapse." After lengthy discussions, he became a supporter of the idea.

Step by step, the mentality of the management team gradually changed. It was a very interesting process to observe. By the end of the first year there was a paradigm shift for most of us. We began to think differently about the plant and ourselves. Not all of us did, of course, because there are always some people who are so strongly opposed to the very idea that I do not even try to change their mentality. While these people are useful to the company in their own style, nowadays we focus our attention primarily on the young generation, the middle management, and the newly appointed chiefs of profit centers. Progress is much more noticeable with these people.

David Hanna and John Simmons did not tell us what we should make or whom we should hire. Instead they provided us with a process for thinking about who we were and what we wanted to become. This process—the high-performance system—was one John and David had used to improve companies in the United States and elsewhere. We studied other companies' experiences. We learned concepts and tools such as vision, strategy, structure, quality, teamwork, and management philosophy that the best firms had used to achieve world-class performance and continuous improvement.

We have only begun to make the necessary changes in the way we work, and now I would like to speed up the process. The profit-center leaders who have changed their mentality must quickly push the new methods to the workers on the floor. This is a long, continuous process of training.

Each worker must change his attitude toward quality. Each worker must understand that quality is the only route to survival under market conditions. People at the bottom must also learn how to work with the customer and to understand his needs. All employees must understand the management philosophy of our firm. People must be polite to each other and wear a smile, as we've stated in our philosophy of management:

> We build our relationships as a team of people driven by common values in an atmosphere of trust and respect, based on the principles of integrity, fairness, equality, and mutual assistance. This is the only way that leads to the common goal.

The senior team developed this statement. With John's help, we developed a vision of how we wanted to manage. We discussed several drafts. We examined each word and the implications it had for how we would have to change the way each one of us managed. We then helped others to understand.

The values stated in our philosophy are the basis for our successful transformation. Without them we would not have an excellent team. Team spirit is very important for creative work. Team spirit is when people share the same ideas. We should no longer behave like a pack of wolves. For seventy years we had been taught to fight some enemy. This idea united us. Now everything has changed. People are at a loss and they don't know what to do. Where is the enemy? Whom should we fight now? That's why the philosophy of the firm is so important. It is like the religious values that are taught at the monastery which is not far from here.

One must have certain spiritual values, some inner core. It could prevent people from negative and extreme behavior.

CUSTOMERS FIRST

We have begun to put the customer first. We are trying to meet and then exceed our customers' expectations of our products and service. In the past we focused on meeting the quantity of lathes required in our plant goals. Very few people were concerned about the customer.

What got us all started thinking in this way was that after 1988 we had no more state planning commissions and no state orders for our lathes. Today we have to sell what we produce. The best thing for us would be if all our workers could go and see our customers. Since only a part of our staff can meet with the customer, we use various kinds of information such as our plant newspaper and meetings.

As was stressed at our workshops, this kind of information needs improvement. To do this, we must first carry out serious analysis. One of the examples of how the teams are being informed is the Report of New Product Ideas. The original list of proposals made by the people was five times as long as this one. The staff in the marketing department scrutinized it and reduced it to this fifty-page report. Then they sent it back to the teams. People in the profit centers now will know which product can find a market, at what price, and at what estimated profit.

RESTRUCTURING INTO PROFIT CENTERS

We came to the profit-center structure because we had to break the logjam in decision making at the top of the organization. We had too many people waiting outside my office and those of the other top managers. We needed to delegate responsibilities from the one man at the top to the lower levels. To do this, we created fifteen profit centers. Profit-center leaders now must teach their managers inside the profit center our new methods and delegate their responsibilities to them. The profit-center leader is responsible essentially for the financial success of the profit center. In the long run responsibility will reach the shop floor and every worker.

After our workshop on profit centers, we drafted ten pages of guidelines that described the rights and responsibilities of each profit-center leader. The profit centers are not legal entities yet. They have just a subaccount at the plant, in our internal bank. The leader of the center is appointed by the general director, and this leader assigns his staff.

The greatest problem we have encountered implementing the profit-center idea is accounting literacy. When we transferred to a profit-center structure on April 2, 1992, the profit centers were not yet ready to do accounting, bookkeeping, or transfer pricing for contracts among the profit centers. We had no trained personnel. We used to have a central accountant's office before, and it made all necessary calculations for other divisions. Now all the profit-center leaders have hired staff to do the job. We have sent people to courses for bookkeepers and accountants.

At first one profit-center leader declared that creating profit centers was a phony business. The restrictions we were discussing meant the lack of autonomy: profit-center leaders wanted to be totally independent. Then I said, "All right. We are ready to give full autonomy to those profit centers which are ready to do the bookkeeping and pricing and to conclude contracts. You are welcome." All talk ceased at once; everybody said, "Well, let's restrict it for the time being." Now everybody understands that the process of gaining autonomy should be developed over time.

The profit centers are not responsible yet for their own marketing. They will use the services of the marketing department. But as their mentality changes, they have begun to think how to do the marketing by themselves. In the meantime, some of them have started to do market research.

Forty percent of the profit is left with the profit center. We had a win-win discussion at a workshop with all profit-center leaders and we agreed on it. They named this figure themselves. They said, "It's enough for the time being."

LAYOFFS BEGIN

During the general meetings and conferences throughout the plant in 1990 and 1991, the top management adhered to the method of "shock therapy." We kept saying to everyone in the plant that the quality of our product was not good enough. We would not be able to sell as much to our customers as we gave away to Gosplan. This meant that we were unable to sell a sufficient number of lathes to cover our expenses and get some profit.

We made the people realize they were approaching the stage of lowering their income and reducing the working personnel. For the first two years we simply tried to frighten them. But by the end of 1991 we really had to carry out some threats, and the first reduction in force took place. The demand for our production had continued to slide. Initially we produced 6,500 computerized lathes annually; now we were producing only 3,000. Fortunately, we had forecast the drop and spent almost a year preparing to produce some alternative products.

Thus, it was a very gradual transition into the new conditions of the market.

At the initial stage we laid off five hundred people, but fortunately, three hundred of them simply changed jobs. They were able to find other jobs at the same factory. There was no great panic; they simply shifted their places. A worker was not needed at one place but he was needed at another, so he retrained and started to do another job, but he kept his position at Krasny Proletary. Then we decided to reduce staffing by another five hundred people over the period of half a year and panic broke out, since there were no more niches left to be filled up. Besides, whatever vacancies there were did not seem too tempting to the majority of workers. Most of the job openings were hard physical work and rather dirty as well.

But that situation helped us greatly to raise the labor efficiency and quality level of our product even higher. Each worker realized that he could lose his job if he was not good enough at it. The first stage of reductions basically concerned the technical personnel of the factory; the second stage involved the workers from the shops themselves. All of us are grown-up people after all, and we do see what's going on in the whole country. We watch our televisions; we read our newspapers.

CHANGING ATTITUDES

The real process of shifting people to new ways of thinking and acting–shifting their paradigm–takes place through training. This training happens in two ways. The first is in American-style seminars. In these two-to-five-day workshops, we learn by doing. We put the new high-performance concepts and tools into practice. They have been essential to our progress. The second occurs informally when I suggest that the profit-center leaders use our new management methods. They then coach the people who report to them and so on, cascading down to the workshops.

Training in technical skills is also very important if you want to have personnel able to do their jobs well. Say you want a bookkeeper. Train him, if you don't have one. Bookkeepers, accountants, and lawyers are in short supply today. Thousands of private enterprises have been set up lately and they all want people with these skills.

We have learned that continuous training is a key to success. In fact, it's hard to overestimate its importance.

Incentives and recognition also play a key role in changing attitudes. In the past two years we have developed new ways of recognizing people for making improvements by using mainly material incentives. Moral incentives had been traditional in our country, but there were too many moral incentives and too few material ones. In the past, we presented certificates at meetings so that the person should feel rewarded. Money, however, was not allowed. Today, of course, we are not neglecting moral incentives. We certainly celebrate birthdays in the teams and give flowers. We visit families. We try to be even more considerate when someone is ill. We arrange days in the firm where the teams elect their best members. We arrange a dinner party for them and invite artists to give a concert.

Now we pay bonuses to all the members of a team as well as to individuals for achieving some special result. This year, for example, we've allotted 40 million rubles for bonuses. We gave the money to the leaders of the profit centers to distribute with the advice of the shop supervisor and the leaders of production sections.

The profit-center leaders are now thinking about ways to reward and recognize the efforts of everyone who works in a profit center. This will be an incentive for everyone to take more responsibility for meeting the needs of our customers.

We feel that when we become a joint-stock company and all employees become owners, employee ownership will be an additional incentive to work smarter and harder. We have learned this from the managers of American employee ownership companies who have visited our plant.

We have also found that getting people at all levels of the firm more involved in setting goals, making plans, and solving the problems that directly affect their work is both an incentive and a reward. Greater involvement gets them to take more responsibility for achieving our goals. Asking them to get more involved recognizes our increased confidence and trust in them.

As the profit centers develop and better understand their needs, we will continually improve our incentive and recognition systems, which are a key part of our effort.

LESSONS FOR MANAGING CHANGE

During the past eighteen months of work with our American advisers, we have learned some lessons about managing the change process here at Krasny. First, based on my experience in Europe and from the workshops here on American companies, I think that Russian employees have a similar basic mentality to Americans. The difference is in the management methods.

I would recommend that the directors of Russian enterprises not rush to achieve immediate results. Instead they should plan the changes over a longer period of time, say one to two years.

For me personally it was very important when I saw there were some changes in the team. First I had some bad feelings about our having invited consultants from America and seeing that the senior management team did not take it seriously. But in about half a year–after about three workshops plus tasks to do between workshops–some people began to show certain interest. We involved each member step by step. First people did not believe we meant real business. They took it as a kind of game. It took them a year to understand what it was all about and to take the work seriously. When this finally happened, it was the most positive moment, a real breakthrough.

They finally got serious for several reasons. First, they realized that the general director attended each seminar. This forced them to be attentive and to concentrate their efforts. But, most important, the new information which had been accumulating evolved into a new level of understanding about our problems and what to do about them. It forced managers to apply the new understanding in the workshop. It took time for every person, sometimes six months, sometimes eight, to reach this deeper understanding.

The volume of new information made a big difference. Our workshops on the customer and quality were very important. The whole team got an assignment that was very helpful. They began an analysis of the crisis we were in. They had to outline five main directions for improvement at Krasny. They then had to point out our barriers to moving in these directions. First they were rather cynical about it. They didn't want to work on the directions. But soon they outlined the issues by themselves. When they had done the job, it was all their ideas. They began to get involved. This job became a kind of practical platform which helped involve them in the process of learning and growing both as individuals and as managers. Doing practical work forced them to start to think and to study.

The senior management team saw that it was not Dave or John who just gave them some theoretical knowledge and examples. They had created this analysis themselves, and it would guide the future direction of the plant. When they experienced this kind of workshop, then they started to believe they also can plan and influence the process of creating our future. They began to take more initiative and more responsibility for the future of the plant. They implemented the first of the seven habits of highly effective people which they had learned: be proactive.

With these changes in mentality, we launched our strategy. We made some structural changes, including the profit centers. This helped prepare the senior managers for this practical mission. At each seminar they began to take more and more responsibility for planning and managing our future. This big load pinned them down to the ground and helped change their mentality. Today all of them have put on heavy rucksacks of responsibility—they have become the directors of the profit centers.

Finally, we learned that changing our mentality, learning new management concepts, and trying new tools were difficult. We encountered a lot of resistance from the senior people. I think it might be very hard for people to do it by themselves. I would recommend inviting consultants and signing a long-term contract with them. I don't mean just any consultants. We had a lot of consultants who were not helpful at all. Russian enterprises need consultants who possess the tools for paradigm shifting, for the changing of mentality, and who have acquired experience in practical consulting, not just theoretical ideas.

In conclusion, it seemed in the past that the senior managers always pushed the responsibility up to a few of us. It had always been like that. The chief engineer or technical director had to solve all technical problems. The general director had to solve the problems of finance, investments, banks, and marketing.

Some days ago one profit-center director came to me. They are now preparing a new product—an automatic brick-making machine. "Mr. Director, you know what? We've just signed a contract for thirty units with a wholesale firm. This means that our profit center can now go into full production. We also decided to do market research. We found additional segments of the market where these machines can be used."

Both managers and workers in the profit centers are no longer concerned just about production, but about future sales as well. They think about marketing problems. Now they are bringing solutions to us at the meetings, not problems. Their mentality and the future of the firm have changed.

PART THREE

LESSONS OF AMERICAN AND RUSSIAN MODELS OF OWNERSHIP AND MANAGEMENT IN EMPLOYEE-OWNED ENTERPRISES

13   Introduction: On Not Reinventing the Wheel

John Logue

◆ ONE of the ironies of Russian economic reform has been the tendency of reformers to take ideological positions that ignore empirical reality. From "shock therapy" to "voucherization" to storming the privatization quotas, Russian economic reform policies often seem to have been driven more by wishful thinking than by empirical analysis. Those who are charitably inclined are reminded of the genetic "triumphs" of T. D. Lysenko and their unfortunate consequences; those less charitably inclined draw comparisons to the collectivization of agriculture in 1929–30 and its results. The result has been the continued triumph of politics over economics and of theory over practice, with continuing regrettable consequences for ordinary Russians.

Much of the debate about employee ownership in Russia has revolved around foreign, particularly American, experience. Too much of that debate has had a polemical cast that generated more heat than enlightenment. Clearly, the striking differences between the American context (or that in other Western industrial market economies) and Russian circumstances require that all foreign experience be adapted to fit Russian circumstances.

The American experience both with employee ownership and the redesign of management offers useful lessons as Russians struggle to redesign enterprises to meet the demands of the market economy. While American and Russian differences at the macro level in terms of law and of market infrastructure (in particular, the absence of a commercial banking system in Russia) are significant, the similarities at the level of the enterprise are obvious and important. In particular, the processes of motivating workers by giving them an ownership stake and developing an ownership culture and of redesigning the enterprise's management to fit the market's demands for flexibility and efficiency are similar in both countries.

Since the passage of the Employee Retirement Income Security Act (ERISA) in 1974 provided tax advantages to Employee Stock Ownership Plans (ESOPs) as qualified employee benefit plans, the United States has become a laboratory of direct employee ownership unlike that anywhere else in the West. By 1994, some 10,000 companies were at least partially employee owned; of these, at least 2,500 were majority employee owned. The flexibility of American law permitted a wide range of employee influence and participation in the management of these firms, as well as countless variants of the short-term rewards of ownership; only the long-term rewards (ESOPs are a pension plan) were regulated by federal law. As a consequence, it has been possible to compare both participatory and nonparticipatory employee-owned firms as well as to compare employee-owned firms with their conventionally owned counterparts. The evidence from about twenty studies over the last decade establishes conclusively that participatory employee-owned firms outperform both nonparticipatory employee-owned firms and their conventionally owned counterparts.[1] The American evidence is persuasive that more democratic forms of organization outperform less democratic ones in the economy—as well as in politics.

Part III of this book begins by examining the American experience with participatory ownership and management and what lessons may be derived from this experience for Russian economic reform. Chapter 14 summarizes the American experience with employee ownership and focuses on the empirical lessons from American firms which may be of utility under Russian conditions. Chapter 15 reviews the American experience with developing high-performance workplaces and draws conclusions that are relevant for Russian employee-owned firms. Both chapters rest on the assumption that broadly shared ownership of firms by working men and women and broad employee participation in decisions on the job lead to a more democratic society with widely shared prosperity and are therefore preferable to a system in which ownership is highly concentrated in the hands of a few and managerial absolutism is supreme. Both are also deeply rooted in the American empirical experience of the last several decades: firms which combine broad employee ownership and participation with appropriate training systematically outperform their conventional competitors in the market economy.

The concluding chapter of the volume goes back to reanalyze the Russian case studies in Part II in this comparative context. There are lessons here for the twenty thousand or more Russian firms which became at least nominally majority employee owned prior to the June 30, 1994, witching hour for voucher privatization and the expiration of the 1992 privatization law and model. There is much in both the American and Russian experiences with employee ownership that is instructive for these firms. There is neither reason to reinvent the wheel nor to repeat the mistakes of others.

NOTE

1. Cf. Michael Conte 1992. Since the American Capital Strategies Employee Ownership Index was established in 1991, public companies which are more than 10 percent employee owned have systematically outperformed the Dow Jones, the Standard and Poor 500, and the Wilshire 5000 stock indexes. See "Employee Ownership Index" 1994.

14 Employee Ownership in the Market Economy: Lessons from the American Experience

John Logue

◆ IN the last two decades, there has been an explosive growth in employee ownership of businesses in the United States through Employee Stock Ownership Plans (ESOPs). Pioneered in the 1950s, ESOPs provide a mechanism for ownership of part or all of a firm's stock by its active employees. Prior to the passage of the first favorable federal legislation in 1974, there were a few hundred ESOP companies employing less than a hundred thousand workers. Today some ten thousand companies employing about 11 million people (or almost one-tenth of the American labor force) are partially or wholly owned by their employees through ESOPs.

Although employee ownership in America has received much publicity in connection with its use to avert the shutdown of large manufacturing facilities, such as Weirton Steel, or in airlines under pressure, such as Northwest, TWA, and United, over 95 percent of ESOPs are established in profitable firms. Partly or wholly employee-owned firms can be found in practically every sector of the American economy: manufacturing, construction, retail, wholesale, financial services, health care, and so on. They include both large publicly traded firms, such as Mobil Oil, Procter and Gamble, and American Telephone and Telegraph, which employ hundreds of thousands, and small, closely held companies which employ from several dozen to several hundred.[1]

One should not exaggerate what these numbers mean. Employee ownership ranges the gamut from ownership of a fraction of 1 percent of the

An earlier version of this chapter appeared as Logue 1991b.

company to 100 percent ownership, and employees are often minority shareholders with little influence in many "employee-owned" firms where the ESOP is simply an additional employee benefit plan. In theory these firms represent a partnership between the employees and outside shareholders, but in practice they are generally indistinguishable from conventional firms except that some of their shares are owned by employees who thereby benefit from capital accumulation in the firms. Most of the large companies which have ESOPs fall into this category.

Yet there are also perhaps 2,500 majority employee-owned companies in the United States which employ more than 1.5 million workers.[2] These include such major firms as Avis, Publix Supermarkets, Republic Engineered Steels, United Airlines, and Weirton Steel; United alone has some 80,000 employees. While some 200 companies were bought to avert shutdowns, the overwhelming majority have been profitable plants or firms bought by employees from retiring owners or from larger corporations divesting a plant or division. Many of them have undertaken conscious efforts to create genuinely democratic structures of enterprise governance. While these firms constitute only a tiny sector within the overall American economy, they compete successfully with conventional companies in the market economy. They offer valuable lessons for other American employees and companies and, perhaps, for employees and companies outside the United States as well.

The American experiments with employee ownership offer the most significant body of experience about successful worker ownership in modern market economies. That experience suggests that firms which are substantially employee owned and which involve their employees in decisions systematically outperform their conventional competitors. The keys to creating successful, democratic employee-owned businesses include the structure of ownership of the firm, the structure of worker participation in decision making, and the provision of training so that employees can take an informed role as owners. But before we turn to those issues, let us examine the anomaly of how employee ownership, long proposed unsuccessfully by the political left, became a mainstream practice promoted by both conservatives and liberals alike in the United States.

IDEOLOGY AND WORKER OWNERSHIP IN AMERICA

In the latter part of the nineteenth century, the idea of direct worker ownership of the means of production through production cooperatives was part of the ideology of organized labor. The Knights of Labor, the precursor of the American Federation of Labor, energetically promoted the organization of production cooperatives. Between 1878 and 1886, at least 135 Knights of Labor cooperatives were established. While most did not survive as businesses, the idea survived in the craft unions. The preamble of the Machinists Union constitution of 1891, for instance, cites the organization of cooperatives as one appropriate means, alongside economic and political organization, to achieve the goal of "restoring the commonwealth to all those performing useful service to society."

For the better part of a century, the growth of co-ops was stymied by a structural problem. Those co-ops that failed in the market disappeared for the obvious reasons. But those that succeeded disappeared too. The problem lay in the design of ownership: each member owned one equal share. If the co-op did well, all shares appreciated in value. When founding members wanted to retire, new workers could not afford to buy the retiring members' shares. Success was as fatal as failure: retiring members sold to outside buyers, and the cooperatives were converted into conventional corporations.

Despite this difficulty, the concept of co-ops was revived regularly in crises as a means to put the unemployed back to work. The Depression generated hundreds of co-ops; the oldest surviving worker-owned businesses of any size in the United States, the plywood co-ops in the Pacific Northwest, were purchased by their employees to avert shutdowns beginning in the 1930s. The structural problem in transferring ownership between generations was finally solved by the internal account system developed by the Industrial Cooperative Association (now the ICA Group) in Boston and patterned on the Mondragon cooperatives in Spain.

Cooperatives gradually disappeared from labor's agenda as industrialization advanced. While setting up co-ops was realistic in the traditional crafts, it was hard to see how it could work in mass production. How do you start up a cooperative steel mill or auto plant? After the turn of the century, radicals in the labor movement, such as the Industrial Workers of the World or the unions in the Congress of Industrial Organizations, focused on fighting the bosses instead of replacing them. The real economic gains from collective bargaining so far outweighed the hypothetical benefits from production cooperatives that, by the 1950s, the concept had virtually disappeared as a subject of union interest. Moreover, workers achieved sufficient influence over wages, hours, and the conditions of employment through collective bargaining that some theorists of American industrial relations, such as Milton Derber (1970, 1977), have argued that collective bargaining itelf is industrial democracy American-style.

The issues of democratizing the workplace and democratizing the ownership of productive assets did not disappear, however.

Unlike Western European countries where the push for industrial and economic democracy came from the labor movement, labor and the left did not put worker ownership on the American political agenda. The prime legislative proponent of the concept was Senator Russell Long, a moderate Democrat from Louisiana; the principal theoretician of the movement was investment banker Louis Kelso. Both sought to stabilize the capitalistic system, not to overthrow it[3]; they saw the increasing concentration of capital in ever fewer hands as a threat to capitalism. For the capitalist system to survive, it needed more capitalists, and where were they to come from if not from the ranks of workers?

The demand for economic equality in America has not been couched in collective terms, as was generally the case in Europe, so much as in individualistic ones. From Thomas Jefferson's ideal nation of independent farmers and artisans through the populist revolt of the 1890s up to Huey Long's "share the wealth" campaign of the 1930s, even American radicals idealized the economically independent producer. Thus employee ownership strikes a chord in the overarching Jeffersonian ideology that America is—or should be—a land of independent producers in town and country. That is obviously not possible in a pure form in an advanced industrial economy, but employee ownership approximates a contemporary equivalent of the Jeffersonian view. It is fitting that Robert Dahl, the principal theorist of pluralist democracy in the postwar period in the United States, concluded in the *Dilemmas of Pluralist Democracy* (1982) that the size and power of major corporations threatened to undermine the workings of pluralism—the modern form of the founding fathers' checks and balances; his remedy in *A Preface to Economic Democracy* (1985) is to democratize the ownership of the large corporations.

That, in a nutshell, is why the concept of employee ownership enjoys the broad political support of public figures from Ronald Reagan on the right to Jesse Jackson on the left. Belonging to no political party or faction, employee ownership belongs to all.

STRUCTURING EMPLOYEE OWNERSHIP

The most common structure for worker ownership in the United States is that which Long and Kelso promoted: the Employee Stock Ownership Plan. An ESOP is a form of joint equity by employees in the company that employs them. It is formally set up as a trust—a legal entity which is separate from the company—which holds the stock that is allocated to employees individually and which is administered by a trustee who acts on their behalf. Thus it combines joint ownership of part or all of an enterprise by its employees with individual property rights and financial benefits.

Employee Stock Ownership Plans are "qualified employee benefit plans" under federal law, created by company contributions which are allocated to individual employee accounts within the trust. As in other qualified employee benefit plans, employees' property rights to their ESOP accounts are restricted while they are working; the primary financial benefit is realized when the employee retires. However, ESOPs differ from other qualified employee benefit plans in two notable ways: (1) they invest primarily or solely in stock of the sponsoring company and (2) they can borrow money. These characteristics make them an ideal tool for employees to purchase part or all of their business.

Designed by Congress to spread the ownership of productive wealth in America, the ESOP uses the lure of tax breaks to tempt companies to give their employees a share in capital formation. When a company contributes company stock (or cash to buy company stock) to the ESOP, the contribution is deductible from its taxable income. As a consequence, every corporate dollar contributed to buy employees stock through the ESOP saves about forty cents in federal and state taxes. This, in effect, permits tax-free retention of company earnings—but in the hands of employees, not outside shareholders.

Each year's contribution of stock or cash is allocated to individual employees' accounts within the ESOP trust on the basis of hours worked, pay received, or some other labor-based formula. (American law gives companies several choices for allocation, but once the firm has made the choice, it must use the same rule for everyone—managers and production workers alike.) ESOPs do not provide equal ownership for all employees; rather, they provide approximately equal shares annually for similar service in the course of the year. The effect of annual allocation of shares to employees is to reward seniority in the company. The longer you stay with the company, the more stock you accumulate.

To have a vested (i.e., guaranteed) right to the stock, the employee has to meet the years of service required by the plan; by federal law, the vesting period cannot exceed seven years. The stock forfeited by employees who leave the enterprise without being fully vested is reallocated among the remaining plan participants.

Individual employees cannot sell or mortgage the stock while it is in the ESOP trust, but when they leave the company or retire, they have a right to receive either their stock or cash. If there is a market for the stock (that is, if it trades on the stock exchange), they can sell it when they choose. But if the company does not trade on an exchange, and practically all small and most medium-sized companies do not, then the company or the ESOP is required to repurchase the stock at the fair market price. That price is set annually by a valuation by an independent third party. The company usually contributes the repurchased stock again to the ESOP, so additional stock is available every year for allocation among current employees. Thus newly hired employees also come to share in ownership and, in their turn, accumulate stock over time.

In effect, each employee receives both a money wage and a capital wage from his or her labor in the firm. The fact that the capital wage remains bound in the firm for the duration of the worker's employment permits the accumulation of a significant and stable capital pool while it ensures a permanent ownership stake in the firm for all (or most) full-time, permanent employees.

Capital Accumulation for Labor

Over time, value accumulates in the individual employee's account for two reasons: (1) the contribution to the ESOP made by the company which is allocated to individual accounts each year and (2) the growth in value of the individual employee's previously allocated shares through reinvestment of earnings in the firm and through the firm's improved performance.The example in Table 14.1–Reuther Mold and Manufacturing–may help explain how this works. Reuther Mold is a family-owned business that manufactures rubber and plastic molds and large industrial fans. Its ESOP, established in the firm's 1988 fiscal year, currently owns 30 percent of the stock in the company. Reuther is very close to the Ohio median ESOP in terms of percentage of stock owned by employees, employment, and sales, and somewhat below the median in rate of ESOP contribution.

Table 14.1 shows what the average Reuther employee has received since the ESOP was established. An employee who has worked all six years has accumulated 688 shares. Employees who have worked fewer years have fewer shares: for example, an employee with three years would have 254 shares and a new employee who worked only in the most recent plan year would have 100 shares–if the newer employees were as well paid as those with more seniority.[4] For the employee who has been at Reuther since the ownership plan started, the difference between the value of the shares when allocated ($10,700) and the total value of the individual's account in 1993 (almost $12,000) reflects the individual worker's share in the improved performance of the firm.

Thus while value generated in production continues to accrue to capital, workers share in its distribution to the extent they participate in ownership. In the case of Reuther Mold, for example, 30 percent of the surplus retained goes to employee-owners; 70 percent goes to family owners. In the case of 100 percent employee-owned firms, 100 percent of the retained earnings go to employees' capital accounts.

Rethinking Labor's Income in Employee-Owned Firms

Employee compensation in both conventional and employee-owned firms in the United States can be divided into three segments: base

Table 14.1
Accumulation of Shares and Value for the Average Employee-Owner at Reuther Mold and Manufacturing

Date Allocated	New Shares Allocated	Shares by Forfeiture*	Total for Year	Share Value	Dollar Value	Shares Previous	Total Shares**	Total Value
2/29/88	232	0	232	$12.99	$3,016	0	232	$3,016
2/28/89	121	6	127	$15.60	$1,974	232	359	$5,597
2/28/90	70	5	75	$17.05	$1,279	358	433	$7,382
2/28/91	71	13	84	$18.18	$1,527	433	517	$9,399
2/29/92		70	70	$17.15	$1,200	517	587	$10,067
2/28/93	100		100	$17.30	$1,730	587	687	$11,885

Note: Figures reflect rounding.

* When employees leave without being fully vested, their unvested shares are subsequently redistributed among the accounts of the remaining employees.

** This assumes that the employee was working for Reuther Mold when the plan was established in 1988 and continued working for Reuther Mold without any breaks in service. Of the original 112 participants in the Reuther ESOP in 1988, by February 28, 1993, 18 had quit or been terminated, 13 had retired, 2 had died, and 79 were still active employees. The 43 new employees who had joined the ESOP as of February 28, 1993, had, on the average, significantly fewer shares.

compensation (e.g., current wages and benefits), deferred compensation (e.g., pensions and retiree medical benefits), and variable compensation (e.g., bonuses). In employee-owned firms, the mix between these three components changes. While base compensation tracks that of conventional competitors, deferred compensation grows automatically because of the company's contribution to the ESOP (and, hopefully, because of rising share values); and variable compensation (which now includes dividends and profit sharing as well as bonuses) tends to increase relative to base compensation. This larger variable element in the employee-owned company's compensation ties both the employee's total current income and the company's total labor cost to the economic success of the company. That is a powerful tool to motivate employees, and it also makes it easier for the company to weather market downturns.

What does this change in compensation actually amount to? In the Reuther Mold case cited above, base wage and benefit levels have not been affected by the ESOP. Additional deferred income in ESOP contributions over six years has amounted to about $10,700 and there has been an additional $1,200 in capital appreciation; that total averages about $2,000 per year. In additional variable income, dividends were small (for example, about $18 per employee-owner in fiscal 1990), but worker-owner profit sharing was a more significant 20 percent of profits; to use the fiscal 1990 figures, dividends amounted to $18 and profit sharing to $663 per employee-owner.

In 100 percent employee-owned businesses, 100 percent of the profits belong to the employees. What proportion should be reinvested in the business in new equipment and what proportion should be paid out immediately to worker-owners? It is worth noting that because employees share individually in the collective capital accumulation and eventually realize the value of their shares, American employee-owned firms have high rates of capital formation. They do not seem to have the problem with employees choosing to drain capital from the company through excessive current compensation that plagued the Yugoslavian system of workers' self-management.

STRUCTURING EMPLOYEE PARTICIPATION

While the growth of employee ownership in America has been due primarily to the broad range of tax advantages, there is clear evidence that employee ownership has a positive impact on corporate performance. A number of studies over the past fifteen years have found that ESOPs are positively correlated with improved productivity, profitability, and job retention and creation (see, for example, Long 1978; Conte and Tannenbaum 1978, 1980; Russell, Hochner, and Perry 1979; Marsh and McAllister 1981; Rosen and Klein 1983; Wagner 1984; Quarrey 1986; Rosen, Klein, and Young 1986; Logue and Rogers 1989; Conte 1992; Logue and Thomas 1994). There is, however, substantial question about what aspect of the ESOP phenomenon is responsible for the positive findings: is it ownership per se, the rate of increase in individuals' ESOP accounts, or increased employee participation? Or is it some mixture of the long-term benefits of ownership, short-term financial incentives, and employee participation?

The last seems to be the case. The most extensive and methodologically best study of ESOP firms, conducted by the U.S. government's General Accounting Office (1987), found no association between employee ownership by itself and corporate performance but did find that employee ownership *coupled with employee participation* was related positively to firm performance. In the tradition of American pragmatism, employee participation is encouraged not because it is good in itself, but because of its practical economic benefits.

There are other reasons for maximum feasible employee involvement in the company. As owners, the employees expect to be involved. Moreover, employee participation gives employees some control over the everyday work process.

American laws concerning employee ownership protect employees' financial rights within the ESOP trust, but unlike European laws they do not require or even encourage employee participation in managing the firms that they own. Thus most ESOP firms' governance and management structures are identical with those of conventional enterprises. Federal law, however, permits participation, and many majority employee-owned firms have experimented with various structures for participation and democratic governance. What works seems to depend on the history of the company, the work process, the employees, and the management.

What is developing out of empirical practice in a number of the most advanced majority employee-owned firms is a modification of the governance structure of the conventional American corporation, supplementing it with new structures appropriate to greater employee involvement. This empirical model of what I have elsewhere called "feasible enterprise democracy" (Logue 1991a)–Table 14.2–uses the legal structure of corporate shareholder and ESOP governance to provide employee input into long-term planning and oversight over management. It supplements this structure with a plant steering committee which has jurisdiction primarily in overseeing the current status of the plant and solving plantwide problems. Finally, it provides participation on the shop floor in laying out the daily work process through problem-solving groups, work teams, self-managing work groups, and the like. For enterprise democracy to be successful, it is also necessary to create a culture of ownership in which employees act

Table 14.2
Structures of Feasible Enterprise Democracy

Structure	Composition	Scope of Decisions
Board of Directors	Balance among managerial employees, bargaining unit representatives, nonbargaining unit representatives, and mutually acceptable outsiders	Long-term planning, major investments and oversight of management
ESOP Administration Committee	Chief Financial Officer and nonmanagerial representatives of employee-owners	Oversight over economic rights
Company Steering Committee	Representatives of management, departments, problem-solving teams; or bipartite union-management	Current company operations and problems
Shop-floor committees	All relevant nonmanagerial employees and supervisors; or voluntary member. Organized on functional or departmental basis	Day-to-day production problems

like owners on a daily basis and managers seek automatically to involve employees in all decisions that concern them directly.

Let us look in greater detail at these elements.

Employee Participation as Shareholders

In the traditional structure of the American corporation, the shareholders elect the board of directors. The directors select a top manager (a president or chief executive officer [CEO]) who is responsible to the board. The CEO then selects the other management people. The role of the board is usually limited to oversight over management and long-term planning; it intervenes directly in the business only in times of crisis.

Although American law permits closely held companies to limit the voting rights of ESOP participants relative to those of other shareholders, democratic employee-owned companies write their ESOP documents to give ESOP shareholders full voting rights and, frequently, to guarantee nonmanagerial employee representation on the board. The most common model for distributing board seats that has developed in union-initiated employee buyouts calls for rough equality in numbers of worker and management directors and for the two groups jointly to select several outside directors. One warning: nonmanagerial employee board representatives often have trouble serving as good representatives for those who elect them because they lack experience with and training for the issues considered by the board.

ESOP companies frequently have an ESOP administration committee to oversee the actual administration of the plan. Membership on this committee involves a fiduciary responsibility, that is, a legal responsibility to act prudently to protect the financial interests of all participants in the ESOP trust. This committee should also have direct employee representation.

Even when employees have full rights and representation within the traditional corporate governance structure and on the ESOP administration committee, this is not sufficient to provide employee participation in decision making or influence over management implementation of decisions. The reason is that the key corporate structure—the board of directors—generally meets infrequently (four times a year is most typical) and is best suited for setting long-term policies. While the board exercises oversight over management, it usually steps in only after management has done something catastrophic. While employee involvement on the board is obviously important, it must be coupled with employee participation in ongoing plant decisions and on the shop floor.

Employee Participation in Running the Plant

Employee-owned companies hire managers to run the firm just as conventional companies do. But they need a structure to provide continual employee involvement at the plant level, and the board of directors rarely performs that role. Conventional American corporations and American law offer no models here.

A number of successful employee-owned companies have dealt with this problem by setting up internal steering committees that represent all or most employee groups. These enterprise steering committees, which include employee representatives and management, meet weekly or biweekly to discuss plant operations, sales, equipment, maintenance, capital improvements, employment levels, monthly results, and other key issues. In some companies, they are advisory; in other companies, they have the power to make binding decisions.

Steering committees are typically structured in one of two ways. In the first, employees elect representatives from their work groups to sit on the committee. For example, at a forge running three shifts in the hammer shop and one shift in the die shop and the office, that would mean elected representatives from the die shop, each hammer-shop shift, the organized office workers, the salaried staff, and perhaps maintenance and other groups on the steering committee.

In the second setup, the bargaining units select representatives to serve on the steering committee. A number of employee-owned companies have established joint union-management committees like this. It is preferable that representation not be limited to unionized employees but that nonbargaining salaried staff also be represented on the steering committee.

In either case, steering committees generally set ground rules which encourage seeking consensus, rather than simple majority decision, and which avoid issues that properly belong in the collective bargaining process.

Employee Participation on the Shop Floor

Board-level participation and plant steering committees provide employee input into long-term company planning, the hiring of management, and plant-level problems. The key factor in making most employees feel like owners, however, is to involve them in participation on the shop floor.

In the last two decades, "quality circles," "quality of work life" programs, labor-management participation teams, "problem-solving groups," and "total quality management" programs—in short, "participatory management"—have been heralded as the reforms that will make American industry more competitive internationally. While such programs are initially generally popular and achieve their goals, many do not survive. The reason is that most conventional programs are designed to involve employees' brains as well as their muscles in their work for the benefit of distant stockholders. Not surprisingly, employee enthusiasm runs down quickly when employees realize this.

But in wholly employee-owned companies, the shareholders and employees have identical interests because the shareholders are employees and vice versa. Workplace participation programs offer a real opportunity to involve employees as owners in improving work processes and job satisfaction. Both lead, in the long run, to higher productivity.

Shop-floor participation programs in employee-owned enterprises vary tremendously, and each company has to design its own to meet plant conditions. Such programs generally involve establishing either problem-solving groups or other employee teams within geographic areas in the plant, or functional groups that cut across work-group and departmental lines. The point is to get employees involved as owners and to decentralize decision making to involve those affected by the decision. In some employee-owned firms, such employee groups handle everything from newsletters and community relations to equipment design and purchasing, from picnics to preventive maintenance, from getting vending machines that actually work to rearranging equipment in the shop to get a better work flow. In the next chapter, John Simmons discusses how these ideas can be implemented in the firm.

A Culture of Ownership

Creating new structures for participation is a means to an end: creating a culture of ownership and participation in the plant. That is no simple task, and it takes years. It is necessary, however, if the firm is to reap the full benefits of employee ownership.

The prerequisite for creating a participatory culture in the company is that management is committed to employee participation and involvement. In addition to the basic character trait of fairness that every manager in an employee-owned firm has to have, managers have to be open, honest, and tolerant of criticism. Employees and their representatives likewise have to realize that ownership brings responsibilities as well as rights. Those responsibilities include making sure that the plant runs well, taking an active role in correcting problems—or better yet, preventing them from occurring—and keeping good managers happy.

To make employee ownership work well, both employees and managers have to change their old attitudes. That is much harder than changing the company's bylaws or structure. Yet the best-designed structure for worker participation in employee-owned firms will fail unless workers and their representatives understand the issues that they need to deal with. This requires three things:

1. *Information.* All workers need regular information about the economic status and business strategy of the firm. Employee representatives on corporate governance bodies need full access to company books.

2. *Factual understanding.* All workers need to receive some basic education in how employee-owned firms work in general and how their own company is structured. All employees need basic education in what makes the business tick. Further, worker representatives on company governance bodies need—at a minimum—training in (a) understanding the balance sheet and profit and loss statements, (b) understanding internal corporate accounting, and (c) basics of corporate finance.

3. *Group process training.* All employees—managers and hourly workers alike—who are involved in governance bodies and on shop committees need basic group process training. If employee participation is to be effective, committees and other bodies need to reach decisions effectively without the process breaking down in arguments about the past, personality conflicts, venting of aggression, or the various other ways in which human beings fail to work together.

Firms that are serious about worker ownership and governance should expect to devote substantial resources to training and education in the early years of worker ownership. The payback comes in making better decisions and in carrying them out more effectively because the democratic process produces general agreement on the reasons for the decision.

PROMOTING EMPLOYEE OWNERSHIP AS PUBLIC POLICY

Democratic employee ownership thus seems to have many advantages: increased productivity, competitiveness, profitability, capital investment, widely spread ownership, improved employee compensation, greater job security, and more social justice are among them. These desirable social and economic consequences are not, however, sufficient grounds to persuade conventional capitalistic firms to implement employee ownership. In the United States that has required two things: (1) the creation of tax incentives by the federal government that make it profitable for the firm, the previous owners, and the banking community to support establishing employee-owned firms and (2) education of business owners and managers about employee ownership by business consultants—attorneys, accountants, bankers, and others—who make money by providing the professional services associated with employee ownership. While employee ownership ultimately benefits employees, it has also provided handsome tax benefits for companies, owners, and lenders and equally handsome professional fees for those employed to establish plans. Employee ownership has spread quickly in the United States in part because there was money to be made from it for people other than employees.

While the importance of tax and pension law and the role of independent professionals do not pertain in Russia, other aspects of the American employee-ownership infrastructure may be more easily matched. These include (1) the creation of national, nongovernmental organizations to promote employee ownership and (2) the establishment of regional centers to provide information and technical assistance to establish employee-owned firms and to provide employee training in existing employee-owned firms.

The employee ownership movement in the United States is led by two national, nongovernmental organizations, the National Center for Employee Ownership and the ESOP Association. The former is a membership organization that enrolls both individuals and companies as members, and it plays a crucial role in information, outreach, and research through its publications, conferences, and workshops. The latter is the trade association of ESOP companies, and one of its crucial roles is lobbying the government for maintaining ESOP tax advantages.

Some twenty states have also enacted legislation to encourage employee ownership. Six have established state centers to provide information, outreach, training, and some technical assistance to employees interested in exploring employee ownership. While these programs vary in their funding and activities, as a group they provide three basic sorts of programs: (1) general information and public education through articles, conferences, workshops, and radio and television programs; (2) technical assistance to employees and enterprises seeking to implement employee ownership; and (3) training in the basics of ownership and participation in existing employee-owned firms. Such programs are in many ways analogous to the agricultural extension system, the technology transfer system in American agriculture that has produced such dramatic improvements in farm productivity.

LESSONS FROM AMERICAN EMPLOYEE OWNERSHIP

The legal form that employee ownership takes in the United States is so intertwined in the American pension law and tax code that it is not suitable for export. The degree of flexibility and experimentation at the company level means that there is not one American model of employee ownership but many. Still, some common principles may be distilled from the American experience.

1. The combination of joint ownership of the means of production by current employees with individual accounts for each employee within a trust can provide incentives for workers and a sense of real ownership. This requires two things: (a) combining the long-term incentive of capital accumulation with short-term incentives in the form of profit sharing, bonuses, or dividends on stock and (b) creating channels for employee participation and providing the information and training necessary for employees to act as informed owners.

2. American law provides only a broad framework for employee ownership, laying down certain principles of fairness and standards to prevent fraudulent transactions. Within this framework, companies have wide latitude for developing systems that work within their own traditions and market niches. This flexibility has been crucial to the success of American employee ownership. The latitude for experimentation has led to a rapid accumulation of empirical experience that has been far more instructive to American employee-owned firms than the best expert advice could have been twenty years ago. Had Congress sought to be

highly prescriptive in its legislation, employee ownership would have been frozen into a single mold; it would have been far less dynamic and creative.

3. The ability to borrow money through the ESOP trust makes it possible for employees to purchase firms from sellers—whether private corporations or public entities—and to build new plant and modernize capital equipment with borrowed money and repay the debt with future pretax earnings. Given the Russian voucher program and the preferential prices on sales of stock to employees, borrowing played no role in the first stage of Russian privatization through June 1994. The American mechanism, however, may have some use in future Russian privatization and in the vital recapitalization of already privatized Russian enterprises.

4. The American ESOP permits considerable economic inequality among employee-owners based on differences in pay and in seniority. Both reflect actual contributions to the firm: the former, in terms of skill level; the latter, in terms of years worked in the firm. Individual accounts tend therefore to grow with input into the firm in skill and seniority. Between firms, inequalities reflect differences in worker productivity and demand for products, assuming a market (or quasi-market) economy. They do not reflect speculation or exploitation. In 100 percent employee-owned enterprises, only those who work in the enterprise accumulate value—and they do so because they work there. This is not only advantageous in terms of promoting social justice and limiting social conflict, it also clearly encourages reinvestment and productivity growth. Again, while this is not relevant in the initial phase of Russian privatization, it is clearly relevant in the postprivatization phase. Interestingly, some of the early Russian firms to privatize, for example, KEMZ, spontaneously created equivalent structures for sharing capital formation and those structures have proven successful under Russian circumstances.

5. The legal structure of ESOP ownership—a trust that holds stock within a corporation—permits employees to form partnerships with outside owners while retaining control. In the United States these are almost always private, domestic, individual shareholders, but they could also be (a) public entities (in fact, one of the first ESOPs established in the United States was at Conrail; for more than a decade, employees owned 15 percent of Conrail through an ESOP while the federal government owned the other 85 percent), (b) foreign investors, (c) other employee-owned

businesses, or (d) other legal entities. Retaining employee control is more difficult with individual direct employee ownership of shares. In the postprivatization period, control is certain to become a key issue quickly for Russian employees, not least in dealing with speculators and with foreign firms.

6. Creating a culture of ownership among employees is vital for improving performance, and it does not happen spontaneously even in the United States, where ownership is a well-established concept.[5] Creating a culture of ownership among Russian employees will be even more difficult. In our experience, Russian workers in well-managed firms are as distrustful of management as are American workers in firms with histories of bad labor relations. Management is hard work in employee-owned companies. It requires that managers add employee participation, communication, and ownership training to their job descriptions.

Employee ownership is not a panacea in a market economy. Ownership entails risks. The firm can fail, with the attendant loss of jobs and accumulated capital. It can muddle through, doing poorly and paying its employees less than they might earn elsewhere. Ownership offers no guarantees. Yet at the same time, the American experience suggests that the combination of employee ownership and employee participation from the shop floor to the boardroom can be a powerful tool to increase the productivity of the enterprise and the prosperity of its employee-owners.

The reason is simple: democratic employee-owned enterprises involve their employees—who understand the business—to use their initiative, energy, and hard work to improve their own economic situation. To succeed, however, requires a fundamental rethinking of authoritarian Russian managerial practices—just as it has of American management.

NOTES

1. For broad analyses of employee ownership in the United States, see Rosen, Klein, and Young 1986 and Blasi 1988. For employee ownership in closely held businesses, see particularly Bell 1988. For employee ownership in public companies, see particularly Blasi and Kruse 1991. The legal and financial complexities of ESOPs are described in detail in Smiley and Gilbert 1989.

2. Estimate by the National Center for Employee Ownership; an additional 10 percent of current ESOP firms will eventually be majority employee owned. Our 1992–93 study found that 30 percent of Ohio ESOP firms are currently majority employee owned, and 37 percent will be so within five years.

3. The titles of Kelso's books promoting employee ownership are symptomatic of his aims—as well as of the American political debate: *The Capitalist Manifesto*, with Mortimer

Adler (1958), and *How to Turn Eighty Million Workers into Capitalists on Borrowed Money*, with Patricia Hetter (1968).

4. Of course, new employees are, on the average, paid less than more senior employees. Since Reuther Mold allocates 70 percent of stock on the basis of earnings and 30 percent of stock equally, the average employee in the plan for three years has 221 shares while the average employee with only one year in the plan has 74 shares, assuming that both made the average wage while at Reuther.

5. The relative enthusiasm among American employees for employee ownership through ESOPs stems from a culture of ownership rooted in individual ownership of small businesses, not from stock ownership itself. The traditional American model of corporate stock ownership yields a culture of inactive, absentee ownership, not the active ownership and responsibility that employee-owners ideally should demonstrate.

15 Making Employee Ownership Work: American Lessons about Reaching High Performance

John Simmons

♦ "UNLESS we can quickly turn around the performance of our firm," the general director of a large Russian textile factory told me just after it had been privatized in January 1993, "our six thousand people are going to be on the street." He then asked, "What is the best way to manage a company like ours where most of the employees are owners of the shares in the enterprise?"

For more than six years my colleagues and I have been working with Russian managers and workers on that issue. We feel that both larger Russian enterprises, like Krasny Proletary in Moscow and Saratov Aviation in Saratov, and smaller firms, like Veshky Enterprises and MOVEN, both in the Moscow area, are beginning to provide answers to this and other questions on management reform. These Russian firms, which have achieved remarkable results under the most difficult conditions, have learned from their own experience and from that of others. They have established a shared vision of what values and behaviors they think are essential to the way they would like to manage. They have studied how the best firms in the West and Asia improved performance, created new products, and better met the needs of their employees and customers. While they have been successful thus far, they do not have much experience with employee ownership.

In America many companies—both conventional and employee owned—are struggling with problems caused by competition that are similar to those affecting Russian firms. As President Bill Clinton declared in Chicago in July 1993, "a major revolution" is taking place in American companies.

In an effort to win back lost market share and become more competitive, thousands of firms have reexamined the basic principles of management and ownership that they have been using. The changes are so profound that they are reinventing the way corporations function.

This chapter looks at the strategy, concepts, and tools that the best American companies have used to improve their performance radically; it also describes the steps that the leadership of those firms took to make the transformation from traditional management methods to new ones. During the past twenty years these companies have been studying and adapting the best ideas they have discovered in worldwide research on high-performance companies. Their transformation has not been an easy process; it has required years to accomplish. If Russian companies can learn and apply the principles of high-performance organizations, their transformation process may be quicker and easier.

PRINCIPLES FOR HIGH PERFORMANCE

From the first day they open their doors, all organizations try to improve their performance. However, some organizations in the 1980s and 1990s pulled way ahead of their past performance and their competitors. How did they do it?

Managers and workers at these companies discovered a new way of looking at how to improve, and they became committed to implementing it. The method that they uncovered is not that mysterious; any senior manager or union leader can discover and implement it. It does not take special personality traits such as charisma or a high IQ. Reading and listening are the two key skills required to get started—along with making the decision to open up time in the schedule.

The new way of looking at improving revolves around four principles: leadership, participation, quality, and continuous learning. (See Figure 15.1.) These principles have provided the foundation for helping many American companies reach high performance. All four require that people are motivated to learn and continuously improve. The fifth element, called the "Z," is the process that adapts the four principles to the specific needs of an organization and helps implement them.

It does not have to take a crisis—although a crisis often seems to be the thing that jolts people out of their current ways of thinking—to get leaders to poke their heads out of the sand and actually see what other organizations are doing, sometimes just across the street. Several years ago I traveled three thousand miles to give a two-day workshop on high-performance teams to a company in San Diego. Out of the window of the meeting room was a TRW plant, a company I was using in my presentation. I asked the thirty people if any of them knew about TRW's

Figure 15.1
The High-Performance System

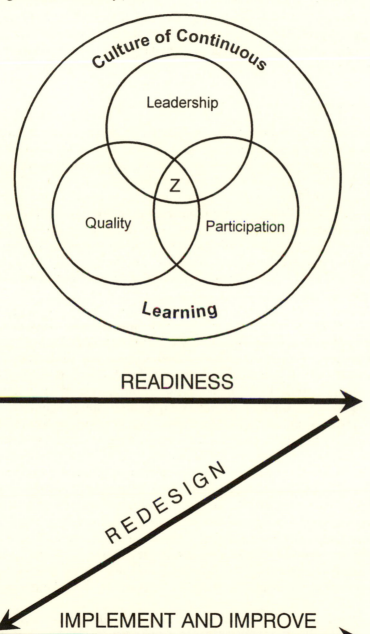

experience or had even talked to anyone in the plant across the street. No, they said.

Sometimes the answers are right in front of us, but we do not even realize it. The key lessons about leadership, participation, and quality that I have seen at companies that are high-performance organizations are similar: after reading through them, you may realize that they have been in front of you for some time.

Leadership

The road to creating a high-performance organization begins with questions by leaders at the top: Are we doing as well as we could be? How do the best companies in the world continuously improve performance? What do they focus their employees' attention on?

The answers reveal, for example, that leaders often need to learn new skills, such as effectively communicating their vision, becoming better listeners, and "walking their talk," to help lead the improvement process. They also need to understand how to develop a consensus for building a high-performance organization and how to follow through to make sure that the vision is implemented. None of this is easy, but being a leader never is.

The leadership of the high-performance firm needs a clear vision of what they want for the company. Trying to make the old ways work better will not help firms break through old barriers to reach new levels of performance. As Albert Einstein said, "We cannot solve our problems with the same level of thinking that caused the problems." There are several lessons that leaders need to learn before they can implement their new visions. Among them are shutting up and listening, developing a commitment to the new vision before implementation, staying involved in the vision's implementation, and being committed (walking the talk) to the new vision on the first day of its implementation.

"The most meaningful lesson," wrote John Hudiburg, chairman and CEO of Florida Power and Light, the first winner of the International Deming prize for quality, "of all my education [during the transformation process] was to shut up and listen" to both customers and employees to "let them help you identify and solve the company problems." Give people a chance to "show how good they can be. Stop falling over your own ego," said Hudiburg, "and begin to have more respect for people. Not only I, but every one of our managers had to learn this lesson" (Hudiburg 1991: 95).

Hudiburg warned that firms should proceed with such an improvement effort "only if they and their top management were absolutely convinced that this was what they should do." They would encounter barriers and doubts along with the way. "Therefore, they should be convinced that it was the right thing to do before they started" (Hudiburg 1991: 111).

Successful companies have avoided the trap of calling the transformation process an "experiment." The experiment label tells everyone that management is not sure about what they are doing, and many will rush forward to pick it apart. At Florida Power and Light, the senior management team decided that what they really needed to focus all employees on was customer satisfaction. After that decision, they never talked about "productivity, efficiency or cost control." Those all resulted from a zealous pursuit of customer satisfaction (Hudiburg 1991: 110–113).

The new leadership of Columbia Aluminum—a Goldendale, Washington, aluminum smelter which had been shut down because of inefficiency but which was reopened by the employees and an outside investor—started by developing a shared vision of what they wanted to achieve, and it is worth summarizing. They envisioned becoming number one in their industry and making money while doing it. This vision included (1) a corporate culture in which everyone worked together to achieve common goals and in which every employee looked forward to coming to work every day—an ambitious goal in a smelter where the temperature is 120 degrees Fahrenheit (150 degrees Celsius); (2) a fair reward system tied to results (employee ownership was the main vehicle for achieving this objective); and (3) a company in which every employee was committed to implementing the company's mission.

Their vision had other components. They wanted to use both the hands and the head of every employee, whether they were clerical, engineering, or out in the smelter. For too long, people had not been asked to think on the job. Achieving this required a new philosophy of management. They developed the concept of employee involvement teams to cover the entire organization. They wanted to push the responsibility for quality and customer satisfaction down to each individual employee.

Management and the union leadership used off-site meetings and outside help to develop a process to clarify four specific areas: (1) developing a vision shared by the entire company; (2) performing an analysis of the current problems; (3) brainstorming the barriers to achieving their vision; and (4) developing action plans to overcome these barriers. They spent several months implementing these four steps. Managers and workers traveled to other employee-owned companies and firms with high employee involvement to study the results and lessons of those companies. They communicated their ideas to all employees to help implement the vision. Now they are introducing total quality throughout the company. That Columbia Aluminum went from the worst performance of any smelter in the United States to the best in less than three years is a testament to the approach they used.

Developing a commitment to the new vision through study, debate, and agreement will give the leadership group the answers to some basic questions. How much are we aware of the key problems? What should we do about them? If the audit of the system is properly done, it will most likely reveal that management is the cause of 80 percent of the problems, as Edwards Deming, the quality expert, was fond of saying.

Although an audit will not say so, the leadership needs to recognize that its strategy for reaching high performance cannot be delegated. Delegation immediately sends the message that this is less important than the other activities that the chairman has not delegated. Of course, groups across the organization need to get involved in planning and implementation. But the top team needs to set the course and then regularly check the progress through monthly "policy reviews" to be sure the ship is still headed in the new direction.

Max DePree, past chairman of Herman Miller furniture company in Zeeland, Michigan, established employee ownership and involvement because he "felt that it was the Christian way to manage."[1] Since the ESOP's establishment, the company stock has had a 48 percent annual compounded return on equity, which made it the fourth most profitable of the Fortune 500 companies in the mid 1980s. In fact, *Fortune*'s editors named the firm "America's best-managed company" three years in a row. The company has been so successful because, in DePree's words, "we've practiced inclusive capitalism, where people have a real say about their jobs and get a fair share of the results." His book about his philosophy, *Leadership Is an Art* (1989), has been a bestseller.

The Herman Miller company is also an example of what can happen when there is a downturn in the market. A few years ago, they had an 8 percent decrease in earnings. Some of the senior managers wanted to return to a more authoritarian approach to save the company and deal with the market problems. But because DePree was still involved in the ongoing change toward more employee involvement, he was able to assert his leadership. His decision was "to push employee involvement even harder." Rather than going back to the old way of managing, the company's leadership reinforced the empowerment and employee involvement that they had been working toward. DePree went to Herman Miller's employee teams[2] and asked for help. Within a year, the teams had cut $12 million off operating costs in a $200 million company. That was double what they had been able to achieve the previous year.

As the Herman Miller example illustrates, the effective implementation of high-performance systems requires the demonstration of some basic skills at the top of the organization. This is important because people at the lower levels often feel that the top is not addressing the key problems that need to get solved if the organization is to achieve its objective. This is particularly true in government agencies where the people at the top levels may be political appointees with their own personal and short-term agendas.

The people at the lower levels have seen many new "programs" to improve the operations be announced with great fanfare and then six to eighteen months later quietly disappear. They are replaced with another solution to as yet ill-defined problems. Thus, people are not only skeptical about whether what the top recommends will have an impact, but many are also bitter that the top is wasting their time when they could be getting on with the job.

For example, it was 1988 before the executive group of General Motors realized they were a major part of the GM problem. One sign of this was that they did not work well as a team. This was fifteen years after they had committed the rest of the corporation to a new team-management style. As a result of this insight, they went through team-development training to help them walk their talk. Roger Smith, the chairman, hired a full-time consultant to help him with his own anti-team behavior.

Finally, leaders of Russian employee-owned companies need to look closely at their own compensation and the firm's incentive system. Widening the gap in salaries between the top managers and workers, for example, can demotivate the majority of the workforce. Japanese firms, which are only beginning to use employee ownership, have relied on profit sharing to provide material incentives. Profit sharing in Japan is for all employees, not just managers, which happens in most Western firms. In years of high efficiency and sales, 30 to 40 percent of the annual income of Japanese employees will come from profit sharing. In poor years, the employees receive nothing extra. It is, therefore, a major incentive for all employees to work smarter and harder in the future. A few American firms are beginning to follow the Japanese example by reducing high salaries for top managers.

Most organizations should make some improvements at the top before senior managers proceed to tell the rest of the organization how to change. In short, to develop the credibility needed with the rest of the organization to launch a high-performance process, the top needs to begin to fix some of the problems they are responsible for and to practice what they are preaching. They need to learn how to become effective leaders of the transformation process.

Participation Systems

Once the leadership has agreed on a joint vision, it needs to begin implementing it. This often involves the creation of a participation system where all employees are encouraged to participate in decisions which affect their work and are rewarded for it. Many companies start their participation process by teaching all their employees quality tools like statistical process control or flow charting, or they send every senior executive to a workshop for a week. While they learn important information in such training, unless they begin to apply it, the half-life of what they learn is about three months. Such training is often a solution in search of a problem that has not been adequately defined, let alone acknowledged by the senior management team.

Unless an organization already has a participative culture, it is more cost effective to start moving the culture toward more cooperation and teamwork than it is to start learning quality concepts and tools. There are two main reasons. First, the quality tools are most effectively learned in a team setting where continuous learning, problem solving, feedback, cooperation, and coaching are already well-developed skills. In this environment, departmental barriers to better solutions are already beginning to fall. Second, the quality tools are most effectively used in an organization where all employees are clear not only about the corporate vision, mission, and management philosophy, but also have participated in developing a vision for their own department and work units that is consistent with the corporate vision. Their effectiveness is also enhanced when the corporate policies about reward and recognition have already been revised to support high-performance objectives of customer satisfaction, total quality, and a new management philosophy.

Remember that the improved quality systems that many American organizations first started to use were based on the Japanese experience where the corporate culture already fostered teamwork, cooperation, and respect for all employees. These were organizations where virtually all employees were committed, often zealously, to the achievement of company goals. When Honda employees who are laid off from assembly jobs go out to sell cars door to door, we have a new definition of commitment.

Joe Walkush, president of Science Applications International Corporation (SAIC), in San Diego, California, also knows something about committed employees. "It is not uncommon," he says, "to find half-full parking lots in the evenings and on the weekends. Employee-owners of all levels, not just upper-level management, want to put in extra effort to do the best job possible." SAIC's employee-owners have a reputation for hard work and high-quality service to their customers. The results of this commitment have been remarkable. In the 1990s, the compounded annual growth rate of the company's stock has been 23 percent. If an employee had bought $500 worth of stock in 1969, when the company was founded, it was worth $932,000 in 1990.

Unfortunately, too many companies look at the Japanese or American examples, decide that teams are the answer, and then tell everyone they are a team. It is great hype, but it is also nonsense. Once the teams are created, some companies think that they can reach new levels of performance by increasing the number of meetings and buying some flip charts and markers. But having these things in place is only part of the answer. People need better skills in problem solving, listening, feedback, conflict resolution, and goal setting. Procter and Gamble, which already provided substantial training, doubles the amount of training that its people get when a plant starts to implement a high-performance system. The plant manager at Digital Equipment Corporation's best plant, in Enfield, Connecticut, estimates that 15 percent of a team member's time is spent learning, usually through informal coaching on the job.

Total Quality

While leadership and participation are essential elements to developing a high-performance system, all employees must have a broader knowledge of their customers and must better understand what their customers—both internal and external—need. Furthermore, they need to develop personal relationships with them. A salesman at one high-performance firm was visiting an old client who said that he was going to buy the competitor's product, which was 30 percent cheaper. The salesman decided that he would act like a consultant rather than a salesman. He began asking the client about the problems he was having. The salesman asked a question about the quality control process on the incoming material that had not occurred to the client. The client was so impressed that he placed an order for the salesman's more expensive product. Another company, whose clerical staff had been learning that they had to put the needs of the customer first, got a $250,000 order because the potential client was so frustrated by the rude treatment that they got from the clerical staff of their competitor.

Harry Quadracci, the CEO of Quad/Graphics, which has been called the world's finest printing company, is clear about his focus. He puts understanding and meeting the customer's needs as the company's number one priority for every employee. How does he get this to happen? He leads by example. "I spend," says Quadracci, "90 percent of my time with the customers."

While a focus on quality is essential, some companies miss the point by focusing on the quality guru, not themselves. In fact, some people are beginning to say that they have been "Juraned" or "Deminged"! This means that they have been trained in the techniques of one of the quality masters. They can tell you why the other gurus do not match theirs.

This approach is nonsense. First, it does not reflect what actually happened in Japan or at the leading American companies. The Japanese drew heavily on at least three American experts in the early 1950s, Joseph Juran, Edwards Deming, and Walter Shewhart. By the 1960s, the Japanese had already developed their own experts, both inside and outside the plants, who created, taught, and wrote about their precepts. This included models and concepts that were developed in firms such as Canon, Toyota, and Sony.

The gurus have an important perspective on the nature of the problem and the solution. However, it is only one perspective. The well-designed high-performance system draws on a full range of theories and models, including the excellent work of Juran and Deming. Most important, leaders at these companies apply and mold existing knowledge to their own company's particular circumstances.

MAKING IT WORK: USING THE "Z"

The central point at Herman Miller, Columbia Aluminum, and the other examples is this: at an early point in the transformation process, first the champion and then others in the leadership group saw that to accomplish their ambitious vision for the future, they needed to make a paradigm shift in the way they thought about their company and the way they were leading it. To make the kind of improvements they wanted, they could no longer fine-tune the existing methods by trying harder, working longer hours, or hiring better people. They needed new ways of thinking about the nature of their business, the needs of their customers, and the role of their employees in meeting those needs. Table 15.1 summarizes the factors that change as companies shift paradigms from a traditional management approach to the high-performance system.

In the high-performance firm, everyone, not just the boss, is responsible for achieving the objectives of the firm and the team. This means that problems get solved more quickly and effectively, because the people closest to the problem are responsible for the solution. Also, higher-level managers get involved less often. The boss can then use his time to work on strategic issues; and he has time to spend with key customers. In this system, everyone becomes a leader by taking responsibility for meeting the customers' needs.

Training in new skills becomes essential. As people become empowered to solve problems and make decisions which the boss used to make, they need new concepts and tools to work in teams. Employees who did not care about the success of their firm become proactive in their jobs—one of the seven habits of Stephen Covey's training program.

The incentive system changes. Instead of being paid just to show up for work, people get paid for the results the firm achieves. Employee ownership can be a strong incentive: when the value of the stock and dividends

Table 15.1
The High-Performance Firm: Key Factors That Change

Key Factors	Traditional Firm	High-Performance Firm
Responsibility for success	The boss	Everyone
Improvement	The boss and occasionally engineers	Everyone continuously
Leadership	Authority by top	Everyone shares the vision and is empowered to achieve it
Managers	Watchdogs	Coaches/teachers
Manage people by	Boss's control	Their own commitment
Culture	Rules	Core values
Product quality	Inspected-in	Built-in
Customers	Who cares?	Reason for being!
Training	Limited	Continual
Job design	Single task	Whole job
Organizational structure	Top-down	Work teams
Incentives	Hourly wage	Pay for results
Ownership	Outside owners	Employees/partners
Recognition	Infrequent	Often
Decision making	Top only	All levels
Employment security	People expendable	Minimal job loss
Attitudes	Do not care	Practice seven habits
Labor relations	Conflict	Cooperation

increase, employees earn more. Regular information and training are needed for employees to realize what their responsibilities as owners are and to help them begin to act like owners. Through a monthly gain-sharing bonus, employees can also benefit from the productivity improvements they make.

Any improvement effort begins with questions. What is the best way to manage the firm? What are our choices? How do we make the transition from where we are today to what we want to become?

To answer these questions in a way which is best for their own firm, a company's leaders should use a step-by-step process. This helps to assure that they will first understand and become committed to the high-perform-ance method before beginning the implementation process. With this understanding, they will be able to design and implement what they want. This step-by-step process, which we call the "Z," has three phases: first, getting the leadership ready for making changes; second, getting others to join them in redesigning the structures, policies, and systems; and third, involving everyone in the implementation of the changes and continuous improvement. The "Z," as shown in Figure 15.2 can be described as continuous improvement by everyone through continuous learning. People and organizations learn best by seeing what the best firms are doing and then trying it out. Through the "Z" process, the leadership develops agreement across the organization about what changes should be made before they are implemented.

While many organizations in the United States today are trying to make changes in the way they work, they usually go about them in an uncoor-dinated way, not following a process similar to the "Z." Leaders need to understand that if they skip a step in the "Z," they jeopardize the success of their transformational effort.

The causes of most failures to make the transition begin in phase one. These are (1) an inadequate understanding by the leadership of what is needed for making the changes and (2) a failure to provide training for people throughout the firm to learn the new skills that are essential for high performance. In practice, leaders often jump right into the process even though they have only a vague understanding of what they want—high profits and better pay, greater market share and higher sales. Moreover, the leaders are frequently ignorant of the principles and tools that will help them achieve their goals and lack a clear idea about their own roles in designing and implementing a transformational process.

This often leads to communication breakdowns (people responsible for one area rarely talk to people responsible for the other areas), people not "owning" the improvement process, and the effort losing its momentum. Most senior managers who want to reach high performance fail in the attempt. They know the results they would like, but they do not know how to achieve them. While managing the change of organizations to get the desired results is a complex process, it can be learned.

A key principle for the successful management of change is that we own what we help create. If people participate in rearranging their office furniture or in ordering new equipment, then they understand why the changes were made. They are more committed to making the new system work. As a result of involvement, the company also gets a more effective office design and machines that are better used. The same is true for changing the way the company is managed. People will own the changes if they participate in the change process. Each of the three phases of the

Figure 15.2
Following the "Z": The Steps for Achieving High Performance

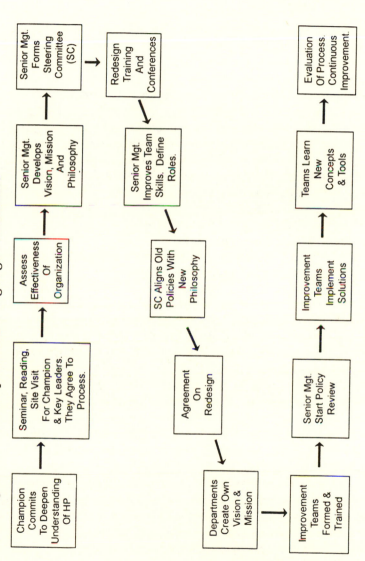

"Z" has key activities that are essential for a successful result. Utilization of the "Z" process can help a firm get employees involved in the change effort.

Phase 1: Readiness

The senior management group needs to get ready to lead major changes in their firms by clarifying what they want the firm to become. There are five elements needed to assure readiness: champion, site visits, assessment, vision, and steering committee.

Successful change usually begins with one person at the upper level of the organization who feels that there is a better way of doing things than the firm is now using. He or she is the initial champion. This person does some research on high-performance methods and becomes convinced that the new ideas could move the firm to a new level of performance. The champion then begins to help other senior managers understand what he or she has just learned. The champion often hires an external consultant to help plan and manage the important effort. Change can also begin in the lower levels of the organization, but those people must find a champion at the top to assure long-lasting results.

Once the champion begins the effort, the leadership should make on-site visits to high-performance companies. The study process may take several months and include reading, discussion, and attending workshops led by experts. The leaders learn how other firms have planned and implemented new concepts of leadership, quality, and employee participation in ownership and problem solving. The most important part of this awareness process is site visits to two or three firms that have been successfully using new methods for at least three years. It does not matter that they are not in the same industry as the firm making the site visit.

To reach the new levels of performance they saw at the firms they visited, the leadership needs to understand the key strengths and weaknesses of their organization. They need an assessment done by outside consultants who collect the data through interviews and focus groups formed from employees across the firm. The consultants then present an analysis of the data and make recommendations to the senior management group. The group reviews the amount of time which is needed to make significant changes and the budget implications. The group reaches an agreement that they want to design and implement a high-performance system over the next several years, and they plan the next steps.[3] They understand that there is no quick fix.

To provide a clear direction for all employees to share, the senior management team develops and agrees on a vision, mission, and management philosophy for the firm. These clarify the objectives and the core values which provide the basis for how people will manage and lead. Will they, for example, use many rules and regulations to shape behavior or will they trust people to make decisions that are best for the company and the customer?

The senior management team then plans a process by which the draft of the mission and management philosophies is taken to the next two levels of management for discussion, understanding, and revisions. At the start of Phase 2, the three documents describing the firm's vision, mission, and management philosophy are cascaded down the organization. Each manager holds meetings with the people who report to him or her to discuss the documents and to gain their understanding. The initial reaction of some employees is often skepticism because they have seen "changes" before that brought few benefits to them. This discussion process is a major step in helping all employees understand the changes that are beginning to take place in the company.

Firms often form a steering committee to lead the transformational effort. The steering committee usually includes people from the top two or three management levels from across major areas of the company. In a unionized firm, it includes the union leadership as full partners. In large American companies with different plants or locations, each plant will have its own steering committee.

The end of the readiness phase of the "Z" comes when the steering committee reaches agreement on the results they want to achieve and the process for achieving them. They are convinced that the high-performance methods could help their firm. With this agreement they are ready for Phase 2.

Phase 2: Redesign

The redesign phase of the "Z" begins to get people from the middle and lower levels of the organization involved in first understanding the new directions for the firm and then having the responsibility for shaping and implementing them.

Once people understand the new vision, mission, and management philosophy, redesign conferences can begin. In larger companies the redesign work will focus on two or three plants first. In smaller firms, those with under five hundred employees, the redesign can cover the whole company. A hundred or more people may participate in the conference process. It analyzes the environment, including the markets the firm will work in, and the social and technical requirements of the work. The role of the steering committee is to set the guidelines for the transformational effort and to approve the recommendations offered by the redesign conferences.

All employees begin to deepen their understanding of the new directions of the company and of their new roles as well as their rights and responsibilities as owners. In training sessions they learn how to read profit and loss statements and balance sheets. They learn the concepts and tools of better meetings, teamwork, and total quality. These sessions are best co-led by workers and managers who have some training skills. Managers are then encouraged to communicate regularly with their people to increase the amount of information employees have about their customers and the progress of the business.

To lead the effort effectively, the senior managers usually need to learn new skills to work together better. They need to define their roles in leading the transition to using advanced concepts of understanding customer needs, the redesign of work structures and systems, incentive systems, quality, participation in problem solving, and employee ownership. They begin to model the behavior they would like employees and teams lower in the organization to practice, such as regular meetings and retreats, strategic planning, feedback, and team building. They become coaches to the managers who report to them, not "givers of orders." They initiate a policy review process that takes them to sections of the company on a monthly basis to verify that key policies are being implemented. They learn the barriers to implementation that they can help to remove. Finally, the leadership gets coaching from the external consulting team.

As all these steps are being taken, the steering committee begins to examine existing company policies in order to align them with the new philosophy. The reward and promotion systems, for example, need to recognize the importance of teamwork and reward managers for building outstanding teams. Training programs need to be aligned with the new needs. Managers and workers do more of the training instead of specialized trainers or internal consultants. The structure of the organization begins to change to fewer levels of management and less hierarchy. Possible new incentives such as gain-sharing programs are evaluated and introduced.

Phase 3: Implementation and Continuous Improvement

Based on the company vision, mission, and management philosophy statements, each department and team creates its own vision and mission related to its specific responsibilities. They use the same process of discussion, revision, and agreement that was used by the senior management group.

As departments define their vision and mission, teams are formed both within and across departments and work groups. One type of team is the people who work together on a daily basis, including their supervisor. A second is cross-functional or cross-departmental teams, like marketing and engineering, which work on mutual problems. Other teams can include suppliers and customers along with the employees. The teams are trained in total quality concepts, problem solving, flow charting, group facilitation, consensus, feedback, and other group and technical skills. If teams are to take on more responsibility for meeting the customers' needs and working directly with suppliers, then they need additional interpersonal and technical skills. The supervisor's role changes from telling people what to do and maintaining discipline to being a coordinator, coach, and teacher. The team leaders then help train their members.

Once the teams are trained, they can spend two to six months applying the problem-solving process to a specific problem the team is having. Using the process helps them to get approval for their solutions and to obtain the resources needed to implement them. Management needs to support the work of the teams, especially when the solutions are being implemented. The results need to be communicated in the company, and the teams need to be recognized for their work. The teams are constantly learning new tools and concepts. As much as 10 to 15 percent of their week is spent in learning or coaching others about new methods.

An essential part of the process is evaluation and continuous improvement. Are the new policies and philosophy being implemented in each department? The senior managers spread out across the company to initiate a monthly review of the implementation. What has the progress been? What are the barriers? How can the managers help teams and departments remove them? The managers insist on reviewing key measures of financial and management performance. All employees seek to continuously improve the systems and processes that they are using through feedback from their external and internal customers. They understand that continuous learning leads to continuous improvement.

The time required to implement all the steps in the "Z" varies with the size of the organization and the willingness to schedule the necessary work. Normally, some teams can begin implementing solutions after nine to eighteen months from the time Phase 1 begins. Another two to three years are needed for refining the processes, training the internal consulting team, and coaching the leadership. Leaders need to realize that while they will begin to see changes within the first year, the transformational process from old to new methods usually takes three to ten years.

The steps of the "Z" are designed to build awareness, understanding, and commitment from the top of the organization down to the shop floor and back office. Policy review, individual feedback, and continuous improvement are key feedback loops to assure that the new management systems are getting the information they need to correct themselves.

SOME AMERICAN EXPERIENCES

American managers have learned important lessons about how best to manage employee-owned companies. Russian managers have as well.

Alexander Mironov, the general director of the Moscow Ventilator company (MOVEN), observed in April 1991: "When people became owners of our plant, their attitudes began to change quickly. If we had not made them owners, the changes they made in two years would have taken decades."

Employee ownership has grown rapidly in the American economy. In 1993, there were about ten thousand employee-owned companies in the United States, employing about 11 million Americans, up from only a few hundred companies twenty years before. As Professor Michael Conte's review of more than twenty years of research on employee-owned companies demonstrates, studies have consistently confirmed that they equal or exceed conventional firms in performance (Conte 1992).

Studies by Professor Joseph Blasi have shown that these firms have higher growth in their stock value than companies that do not have employee ownership. In 1992, for instance, the value of the one thousand publicly traded employee-owned companies, as measured by the price of their shares traded on the American stock exchanges, increased 23 percent, while the value of the other six thousand companies increased only 4 percent (Blasi 1992).

Eighty percent of American adults believe that workers at employee-owned companies pay more attention to the firm's financial performance and to the quality of their products and services than employees at companies that are not employee owned. Sixty-nine percent think workers at employee-owned companies work harder than workers at non-employee-owned companies (Bureau of National Affairs 1987: 17). This 1987 survey, done for the Bureau of National Affairs, in Washington, D.C., demonstrates that employee ownership has broad support in the United States, and that support is growing.

While employee ownership has been used successfully in Western firms for more than one hundred years, it has only been in the past thirty years that it has been used successfully in larger enterprises. Some employee ownership enterprises in the United States, France, and Great Britain have more than forty thousand employees. United Airlines, based in Chicago and the world's largest, has eighty thousand employees. By 1990, 10 percent of all employees in the United States and the United Kingdom worked in employee-owned companies. Codetermination, a practice in all but the smallest German firms by which one-half of the seats on the board of directors are occupied by representatives of the workers, provides many of the benefits for performance that employee ownership does. The idea is also spreading in China and other developing countries. According to Professor Conte, the American experience shows clearly that in companies where all employees own shares, financial performance is either equal to or better than that in companies where all employees do not own shares.

Many firms have become successful employee-owned companies. Employee ownership, however, can also fail, and that experience is very instructive. A ball-bearing manufacturer, Hyatt Clark, in New Jersey, was purchased by employees with the help of an outside entrepreneur. After years of losing money, the company saw profits increase by 9 percent in the first year of employee ownership. The board of directors decided to reward its managers with a bonus for this achievement. The rest of the employee-owners did not receive a bonus. Six months of discussion and argument ensued. When the board dug its heels in and refused to pay a bonus to the rest of the employees, they went back to their old work habits. Productivity and quality began to decline. Eventually, the plant had to close down. While this incident was not the only problem that the company had, it was symbolic of the fatal absence of a core value: fairness.

Employee ownership also eventually turned sour at the South Bend Lathe Company in Indiana, another early example of employee ownership. Initial results were excellent: in the first year of employee ownership, profits were up about 10 percent, productivity was up 25 percent, and the company received the largest contract in its history. However, an outside expert hired by the company to analyze the firm talked to managers and employees and found that while 36 percent of the management felt that employees were now more involved with problem solving and decision making, only 3 percent of the employees agreed. Richard Boulis, the firm's president, had created a management process in which the employees had no voice and he made most of the decisions. Despite being the majority owners, the employees could not directly vote their stock.

Within three years from the start of the ESOP, the employee-owners went on strike concerning wages. The strike made the evening television news across the country, showing the owners carrying placards out in front of their plant. The newspaper headlines read "Owners on Strike Against Themselves." On the surface, the strike was about wages, but the underlying issues really were poor communication and lack of involvement in the problem-solving and decision-making processes. After a ten-week strike, without reaching an agreement, the employees decided to go back to work. Boulis established a communications committee, which had him meeting monthly with the twenty-five department heads. He initiated limited pass-through voting, which involved consulting all of the owners on issues concerning expansion of the company. He also established a problem-solving team to meet for an hour a week.

The problem at South Bend was that Boulis wanted the workers to act like owners, but he did not give them genuine ways to take on this responsibility. Boulis did not realize that by changing the ownership, he was changing the whole philosophy and culture of the company. If he had treated the employees as genuine owners, he would not have had these problems.

What occurred at South Bend Lathe and Hyatt Clark is typical in one way. There is a honeymoon period for a year or two, during which productivity goes up, profits are better, and everybody feels great. Then the second phase kicks in, in which employee issues are not being addressed well enough and problems result because the employees still feel as powerless as they did when the ownership plan was started. The fundamental question is how to institutionalize the honeymoon.

SIXTEEN PRINCIPLES OF "Z" MANAGEMENT FOR RUSSIAN COMPANIES

Successful employee-owned companies in the West have used sixteen principles in designing their system of ownership and creating their company charters or bylaws. Following these principles helps them to avoid the mistakes made by South Bend Lathe and Hyatt Clark. Employee-owned companies in Russia which are doing well, such as Krasny Proletary, Veshky, MOVEN, and Saratov Aviation, are already applying some of these principles. Other Russian companies that are trying to make the transition to high-performance organizations may want to consider these principles before investing too much time and resources in the effort. (Note: Employee ownership means that all employees own voting stock in the firm, not necessarily that they own all the shares or even a majority of the shares.)

1. *Deepen the trust among all employees of the enterprise.* Trust is the foundation for long-term business success. To get ideas for improving trust at an enterprise, ask the people at all levels what they would suggest. They will suggest more frequent and honest communication, a shared philosophy of management, greater involvement in solving problems and reaching decisions that affect their jobs, and managers who "walk their talk" (i.e., people who do what they say they will do).

2. *Sell stock to outsiders, but retain control.* Russian enterprises often need outside investment but, like American firms, they do not necessarily have to give up control of their company to get the investment. To retain control, firms can structure the stock ownership by having different classes of stock, one for the outsiders and one for the insiders. The outsider, or preferred, stock pays dividends but does not carry any voting rights. The insider, or common, stock has voting rights and dividends. Firms, of course, can also sell voting stock to outsiders. If the majority of voting stock goes to outsiders, however, the employees lose control.

It is worth noting, however, that in the past decade larger American firms have increasingly bought stock back from outsiders so that they could regain control of their firms. Similarly, the Mondragon enterprises[4] in Spain do not have outside investors because of the financing infrastructure they have created. Instead, they have established a common bank which they own that makes loans and provides the advice that outside investors often provide.

3. *Involve future employee-owners in design decisions.* Some Russian companies have not yet privatized. For these firms to achieve the best long-term results, the process used to design the charter, including the employee ownership plan should include representatives of key stockholder groups: managers from different levels, professional and clerical staff, and workers.

Several key decisions, such as "Do we want employee ownership?" and "If we do, what will be our rights and responsibilities?" should be widely discussed in the enterprise. It is recommended that the decision about employee ownership be put to a secret ballot of all employees. Another vote should be taken to approve the charter or revisions of the charter. These votes achieve two purposes: (a) trust is deepened when everyone participates in the approval of the decision and (b) even more important, the discussion deepens understanding among employees about what ownership means to them and the organization. While the time for doing this may be short, there is no substitute for open debate in helping to build an understanding of the new, employee-owned enterprise.

Other Russian enterprises have become joint-stock companies, but they cannot yet approve their own boards of directors. They must wait to do this, according to the law, until all the shares of stock are sold, including those shares held by the government. When all the stock is sold, these joint-stock companies need to revise their charters and align them with these principles.

4. *Employees should pay for and vote their stock.* People place less value on something that they get for free than on something that they pay for. Employees in companies who have not paid for the stock they receive will not initially understand the ownership concepts as well as those who did have to pay. They are not as committed to achieving the firm's objectives. Until the value in rubles of their stock begins to become significant, employees are not so concerned about what the responsibilities of ownership are. This may take five to ten years!

Because of American tax and securities law, American employees rarely pay for their stock directly. In some firms people have taken 10 to 20 percent cuts in wages as a substitute for paying for the stock. American employees would unquestionably have a stronger sense of ownership initially if they *had* paid directly for a portion of their stock. Paying even the discounted price, as the Russian law provides, can have a positive effect in stimulating a sense of ownership.

Option 1 in the Russian privatization law of June 11, 1992, gives employees nonvoting stock. The Russian companies that follow this option may find that it will create significant problems for them. When employees become owners, they expect to have greater say in solving problems and making decisions. That is what ownership is all about. When they do not get these rights, they turn against the managers as they did at South Bend Lathe and other companies. The nonvoting option only creates pseudo-owners.

5. *All stockholders participate in the election of the board.* The most successful employee-owned companies have a board of directors which is elected by the employee stockholders. The board approves the firm's basic strategy and policies and selects the general director. The general director has the full responsibility for the operations of the company.

The employee views are represented on the board in several ways. As owners of voting stock, they vote to elect members to the board. The direct vote of all employees is required when there are major decisions under consideration, such as closing part of the company. At some ESOPs, employee representatives sit on the board and sometimes are even the majority. Elected councils of employees, as in "conference" in Russian enterprises, with people representing different departments and levels of personnel, are consulted by the board and the general director. Until the June 11, 1992, law is amended, or their firm's charter is revised, employees from Russian companies which chose Option 1 will be denied participation in the vote for their firm's board of directors.

6. *Retain a significant share of the profits in the firm.* Enough profits should be set aside for purposes of reinvestment. Some should be used for a depreciation fund. Russian accounting practices about depreciation may not set aside enough money to replace old equipment and buildings. Additional funds are also needed to handle the budget deficits often caused by the cyclical downturns in the market economy. This is something that Russian firms will soon discover. This reserve fund can be drawn upon during difficult periods for the business. Firms also need to have a repurchase fund to assure that enough money is available to buy back the stock of retirees.

7. *Majority ownership is better than minority.* When employees own more than 50 percent of the stock (i.e., they have majority ownership), they have greater control over the company's future. Majority control also assumes that no single employee or group of employees holds more than 5 percent of the stock. Majority control gives the communities where the companies are located greater assurance that the plant will not close. (Outside investors have less interest in the economic health of the community than do the people who live there. Outsiders are therefore more likely to shut a plant down and sell what is left for their own profit.) At the same time, to

achieve high performance, it is not essential for the employees to own 100 percent, or even 50 percent, of the stock. Regardless of the percentage of stock owned, it is essential that the other principles discussed here be implemented for the enterprise to achieve high performance.

8. *The company should buy back stock when employees retire.* While current Russian law may encourage employees who retire to retain their stock, this could lead to significant problems. Potential outside investors could appeal to retired people to vote for higher dividends or for an outsider takeover rather than for reinvesting profits in the firm.

Alternately, the charter of Russian companies could require the repurchase of shares by the firm when people retire. This is what American firms do. The charter could also exchange voting for nonvoting stock. Ideally, the charter should require that the firm buy back the stock from retirees at a fair price over a three-to-five-year period. This spreads the firm's financial liability to repurchase the stock over time while keeping control of the shares inside the firm.

9. *Include all new employees as owners after a probationary period.* The enterprise should avoid having either full-time or regular part-time workers who are not owners of stock. Include all regular workers to avoid the split between owners and nonowners which can cause conflict and poor performance. People who work for a temporary period, say a week or six months, and then leave are not defined as part-time.

10. *Develop laws that encourage rather than discourage employee ownership.* Enterprises should work together to protect and encourage employee ownership through new legislation. First, the value of the stock, for example, should not be taxable to the employee until he or she retires from the enterprise. Second, the June 11, 1992, law should be amended to eliminate the nonvoting stock provision for reasons stated previously. Third, the creation of employee ownership centers in major cities should be encouraged to provide information and assistance to enterprises. Such centers should organize conferences and workshops where companies can share information about the best practices and learn from foreign experience.

11. *Design a process for the enterprise to continuously improve its performance.* The enterprise needs to develop a process like the "Z" mentioned above for designing and implementing the four principles of high performance. This process should include diagnosis, action planning, monthly policy review, and evaluation. It would include the tools of total quality management, gain sharing, teamwork, and employee participation in problem solving.

12. *Employees have to learn to be owners.* Employees need to learn their rights and responsibilities as owners. They need to learn, for example, that they have a responsibility to stay informed about how their company is

doing. People need training in how to understand a balance sheet and corporate reports. They need to ask questions and get answers. To take responsibility and ask questions, owners need information and training on a regular basis.

13. *Communicate so that everyone understands the business.* Sharing information is a key to success. All the employees need to understand the corporate, departmental, and team objectives. The leadership needs to discuss regularly the financial condition of the company with the employee-owners. Understanding the enterprise's corporate strategy and finances will help employee-owners to become more effective workers and managers. At Reuther Mold and Manufacturing in Ohio, selected as an outstanding employee-owned company by the National Center for Employee Ownership, employees receive information about their company through seventeen different channels each month, from newsletters to meetings.

14. *Continuous learning is the key to continuous improvement.* All people need to learn new skills—both technical and teamwork. The company needs to encourage continuous learning at all levels if it is to reach high performance. In the best American companies, people spend 10 to 20 percent of their time each week learning.

15. *No cookbook exists.* People looking for a cookbook to follow to help them design the perfect employee-owned company will be disappointed. Rather than using a specific recipe, people are best guided by learning these design principles. This is because people need to study what has worked and not worked in other companies and decide for themselves what they think is best for their situation. Each firm is different. They need to debate among themselves the alternatives and craft their own solution. This process of debate will not only deepen their understanding, but also strengthen their commitment to their solution. Using a cookbook is no substitute for the benefits gained from the process of study, debate, and decision.

16. *Nothing is more important than leadership.* No factor is more important for the success of employee-owned companies than the commitment and understanding of the firm's leadership—the general director and the senior management group—to implement these principles. In fact, when employee-owned companies fail, the reasons for the failure can be traced to their leadership. Of course, there are external factors such as the weather or economic depression which are beyond the control of management.

The responsibility for making an employee-owned company successful, however, does not rest entirely with the senior leadership: the leadership needs to create leaders at all levels. If employees are to be effective working with suppliers and customers, then they need to think like leaders too. This requires empowerment and training.

Russian firms can learn from the experience that has often been gained only with great pain in American companies. If firms revise their charters based on these sixteen principles, it will help them avoid the problems of American firms such as South Bend Lathe and Hyatt Clark.

WILL IT WORK IN RUSSIA?

On June 11, 1992, the Supreme Soviet passed a law on privatization. Will Russian enterprises make the most of the opportunity it offers? How can Russian companies revise the charters of their new joint-stock companies so that they can benefit from the experience elsewhere? Will they make the same mistakes that Hyatt Clark and South Bend Lathe made? Such mistakes could create confusion and failure in Russian enterprises.

During the past six years that I have been working with Russian managers and workers, I have seen the privatization process deepen the mistrust in some enterprises. Employees ask, "Will foreigners buy our company, throw us out, and profit from the sale of the equipment and buildings? If some Russian managers buy a controlling block of stock, will they do the same thing and then retire to Sochi?" Since both of these results occur in Western companies, these are not irresponsible speculations.

Leaders of Russian employee-owned firms need to begin with the end in mind. They need to be convinced that employee ownership, along with the participative culture that is essential to get the most benefits out of ownership, is the best for them personally as well as for the company. If they begin with this commitment, they will build continuously improving firms. Our research has shown that many American firms with employee ownership have failed to apply one or more of the sixteen key design principles. Without better understanding of the international experience, Russian enterprises are likely to make the same mistakes.

As President Bill Clinton has noted, there is a revolution taking place in American firms and government agencies. It is changing the way people think about all aspects of their organization, their customers, and their suppliers. Will these ideas work in Russia?

They already are. While no single Russian example exists yet where all the new concepts are being applied, a growing number of firms are using many of them, as the case studies in this book indicate. The ideas are being adapted to work in Russian conditions and are yielding excellent results.

The issue now is how to speed up the process of diffusing the experiences to other firms and of developing some firms which are using most of the concepts. Russian management associations and business schools could use conferences, newsletters, networks, and television to raise awareness around the nation about the growing Russian experience with high-performance concepts. Hopefully, efforts will be made to establish a cost-effective strategy for these activities to happen.

In fact the crisis that many Russian firms are experiencing provides an incentive to try new ideas. It is possible that high-performance methods will spread more quickly in Russia than they have in the United States. Furthermore, Americans will have a lot to learn about the continuous improvements that Russians will make in the high-performance system.

High-performance management offers the Russian people and their economy a substantial opportunity. Western experience proves what some Russian firms, where employees have already owned stock since 1989, have learned. If well-designed and implemented, new methods of management and ownership can lead to higher productivity, quality, and profits. Employee ownership also leads to a fairer distribution of those profits. As other chapters in this book demonstrate, employee-owned Russian firms have attracted foreign investment and are exporting their products. If Russian managers and workers are willing to learn from the experience of other firms, both in Russia and the United States, they will benefit not only themselves, but their country as well.

NOTES

1. For an additional incentive, Herman Miller also has a gain-sharing program which divides the money earned from productivity improvements between the employees and the company. Every month, each employee gets two checks—a regular paycheck and a gain-sharing check.

2. All employees are members of teams which have learned new skills and tools. They meet for an hour every week to address problems.

3. For a detailed example of how this process worked in one Russian firm, see Chapter 11.

4. Located in the Basque region, the employee-owned Mondragon group includes about 120 firms which employ about twenty-one thousand and do about $2.6 billion in sales; about 25 percent of their production is exported.

16 A Second Revolution from Above?

John Logue, Sergey Plekhanov, and John Simmons

◆ W ITH the collapse of the Soviet Union in the fall of 1991 following the failed putsch against Mikhail Gorbachev, the gradual reformism of Gorbachev's perestroika gave way to the revolutionary aims of Boris Yeltsin's economic reform team. Yegor Gaidar and Anatoly Chubais, the architects of Yeltsin's policy, overtly sought a near instantaneous transition from a state-owned and state-planned economy to a privately owned market system. Russia was to have an economic revolution from above, comparable in scope—though not in methods or bloodshed—to the collectivization of agriculture and the introduction of centralized planning in the 1929–34 period that laid the foundations for the Soviet planned economy and ended the economic pluralism of the New Economic Policy period.

This second "revolution from above," promoted as "shock therapy," was to combine price liberalization, tight monetary and credit policies, structural reforms (permitting bankruptcy and encouraging competition and labor mobility),[1] and privatization. It is the last that has been our concern in this volume.

The methods chosen in the 1992–94 phase of privatization were to make all citizens property owners by issuing them investment vouchers and to give extraordinary preferences to workers and managers in purchasing their enterprises from the state. The former was espoused by Yeltsin's reform team to build political support for dismantling the old planning apparatus and system of state ownership. The latter they accepted, as Sergey Plekhanov details in Chapter 3, as an undesirable but necessary compromise to implement privatization.

Despite the reform team's preference, work collective after work collective in enterprises subject to privatization voted for majority employee ownership. Given the option of choosing between minority ownership without charge (and without voting rights) and majority ownership to be paid for by vouchers and cash, more than two-thirds of work collectives voted for majority ownership.[2] Thus direct employee ownership of the means of production became, at least temporarily, the predominant means of privatization and form of ownership in Russia.

While direct employee ownership of the means of production had, in Gorbachev's days, been a positive reform on the road toward market socialism, for the Yeltsin reform team employee ownership smacked of a failed, partial transition to capitalism. It was seen as a necessary evil to win political support for privatization in Parliament. Privatization from below through employee ownership was already under way through various forms of purchase and through widespread leasing by work collectives; this pluralism of forms of ownership that had been nurtured in the Gorbachev years could not be swept away by a stroke of the pen.[3] Meeting increasing opposition from both conservatives and reformers in Parliament in the spring of 1992, Gaidar eventually compromised to permit varying models of privatization. The talk among Gaidar's team and its American advisers about renationalizing leased enterprises to enforce uniformity of privatization through auctions was abandoned out of sheer political necessity. They accepted employee ownership as a transitional form until the "real owners"—foreign firms and investors and new Russian capitalists—appeared to run the Russian economy according to standard capitalistic principles. Employee ownership was an infantile stage to be outgrown quickly, not something to be nurtured as a basis for an efficient market economy and widely shared property ownership.

The government placed its hope in rapid development of public companies with outside shareholders, equity markets, and mutual funds. Capitalist economies demonstrably had stock markets, and these were, at least in the Marxist orthodoxy of the Soviet years, linchpins of the capitalist order. Thus the implementation decrees related to privatization time and again were seemingly motivated by the conviction that the rapid development of secondary markets for trading stock was crucial to the success of economic reforms. (David Ellerman's biting characterization of this stock exchange fixation as the "cargo cult" of the postsocialist world[4] seems all too accurate.) Companies privatized under Options 1 and 2 were required to be open stock companies (i.e., public companies), regardless of the vote of the work collective. Work collectives' efforts to restrict tradability of employee stock to keep it within the employee group were struck down in January 1994 by presidential decree; the previous form of collective ownership by the work collective as a whole was outlawed in October 1992. Perhaps most crucially in the 1992–94 period, the privatization vouchers themselves were made tradable; that created a widely held, tradable security and, almost instantaneously, a highly speculative secondary market.[5]

The government promoted the creation of "voucher funds" which were–at least in the optimistic spring of market romanticism–to be American-style mutual funds with professional management, prudent investigation of investment targets, and substantial willingness to enforce the harsh discipline of the market on Russian enterprise managers. Voucher fund managers ideally were to play a key role in washing out the inefficiency of the old state enterprises.

The heavily touted voucher funds were, in fact, immensely successful in attracting vouchers. In a poll done shortly before the end of the validity of vouchers in the summer of 1994, fully 28 percent of Russians reported placing their vouchers in a voucher fund, slightly behind the 30 percent who reported having sold theirs, but well ahead of the 18 percent who invested directly in companies.[6]

Ironically, the voucher funds, which were seen as the cornerstone of market efficiency, more characteristically turned out to be gigantic pyramid schemes. They promised incredible rates of return in massive advertising campaigns; these returns were actually paid to early investors out of the flow of vouchers subsequently coming into the funds. Rather than investing the vouchers in newly privatized firms, many funds simply sold the new vouchers (often to managers buying up shares of their enterprises or to speculators) to pay the promised dividends to previous investors, keeping additional vouchers flowing in. In the virtually unregulated conditions that the government had created as part of its free-market ideology, a number of fund managers simply stole the funds and shuttered their offices. It is estimated that the majority of roughly 650 voucher funds will fold in the near term,[7] with the loss of many citizens' investment of what was supposed to be their share of the national patrimony.[8]

Despite the abuses of "voucher privatization," it constituted an effort to spread ownership of productive assets among all Russians. It would have been more successful in this aim had the vouchers been nontradable (which would have militated against the reform team's aim of encouraging the "real owners" to emerge) and had voucher funds been regulated to ensure a modicum of honesty. Yet it did create a mechanism for widely shared ownership and rapid privatization in an economy in which macroeconomic policy had wiped out household savings.

Moreover, the peculiarly Russian approach to privatization pursued by the State Property Committee (GKI) of setting targets for privatization and then proceeding to "storm the plan" actually did privatize the bulk of small retail and service shops and some twenty thousand larger firms. This single-minded focus on achieving the planned level of privatization was reflected in the frank insistence of one official of the GKI in an interview with one of the editors that the GKI was unconcerned with the success of enterprises once privatized; the GKI's only proper concern, he argued, was meeting privatization targets.

This crash approach to privatization had the potential to create mammoth economic difficulties in relatively short order, as it in fact did. But it also overwhelmed the bureaucratic resistance in the ministries and enterprises that had impeded or derailed previous reform efforts from those of Khrushchev to those of Gorbachev. Moreover, it created virtually overnight a significant constituency of privatized firms and of managers who have a strong interest in consolidating the new economic system. Bad economics may make good politics.

LESSONS OF PRIVATIZATION FROM BELOW

In this context of politicized privatization, the empirical experience with privatization of the Gorbachev era simply did not count. What had worked and what had not worked were strangely immaterial to policy makers. As Anatoly Chubais put it in a televised debate in March 1992 with John Simmons, he saw no point in visiting one or another of the successful firms already privatized through employee ownership that were within an hour's drive of the Kremlin because he had already visited a collective farm. In this peculiarly Russian triumph of neoliberal ideology, empirical experience might be appropriate to illustrate the correctness of the government's policy but not to test alternatives to it.

Yet there is much that can be learned from this experience. The six enterprise case studies in Part II provide a living history of the process of privatization from below in Russia: from initial experiments with leasehold enterprises and cooperatives under Gorbachev in 1988 and 1989, through BUTEK members and beneficiaries of special ministerial decrees in 1990 and 1991, to privatization under the terms of the 1992 Russian Federation privatization act. It is a history in which many of the false starts and detours in the process have been glossed over; the full story of the actual privatization process at any of the firms in question could be the subject of a book by itself.

The case studies suggest certain commonalities at the level of the firm in the transition from state to private ownership and from a centrally planned to a market economy. Though this empirical experience had little, if any, influence on the government's privatization policy, it is worth our reflection. It mirrors the spontaneous effort to develop working, market-oriented firms under Russian conditions. Here are ten lessons drawn from that experience.

First, every firm undertook a radical decentralization of authority and decision making about operations in a relatively short time after privatization. This was both in reaction to the hypercentralization of the old system and in hope that decentralization to departments and work teams would increase individual responsibility and efficiency. The evidence from these case studies suggests that that generally was the case. Decentralization helped produce sharp gains in production and quality, the development of new products for the market, and higher incomes for workers. However, the process was far from easy. It also yielded major problems of coordination within the firm. Balancing decentralization of decisions with the demands of coordinated information and production became a characteristic difficulty in the postprivatized firm.

Second, decentralization was generally tied to new incentive systems which provided substantial material rewards for workers above and beyond whatever distant material rewards that ownership might provide. (In the firms discussed in Part II, ownership was initially vested in the work collective as a whole, not in individual form; Stroipolymer was an early exception with its individual accounts.) In general these systems led to relative improvement in wages and living standards, even after adjusting for inflation, until the economic meltdown of the capital goods sector occurred in 1993–94.

Third, despite the fact that all the firms in question were majority employee owned (and five of six were 100 percent employee owned), there is no evidence of the triumph of the new owners' desire for consumption over investment. Quite the contrary—the case studies demonstrate that the new owners used independence from the state plan to make heavy investments in capital improvements for new products and to renew basic production capacity, which had often been starved for capital for decades by the ministry in charge. Again, much of this may be attributed to the leadership of their general directors, and it is not clear that this emphasis on investment can withstand the collapse of living standards under the impact of the general crisis. Still, the case studies make it perfectly clear that majority or wholly employee-owned firms do not automatically "eat up their capital," as GKI officials had forecast.

Fourth, the firms combined a general culture of economic egalitarianism and formal democratic structures (at least in the formative stages of privatization) with significant real authority for the management that transcended the formal structure. That economic egalitarianism was not, however, always coupled with much respect by management for manual workers; indeed, in several cases there was strong managerial opposition to worker self-organization. In none of the cases studied was there any genuine countervailing power to management in the form of a representative union. Despite the formally democratic internal structures of the firms, they vary dramatically in their practice from Voronov's "enlightened despotism" at Veshky through Makharinov's "guided democracy" at Stroipolymer to Vrachev's "participatory democracy" at KEMZ. However, their formal structure did provide a relatively easy avenue to force a discredited general director from office. It is doubtful that the boards of directors in Russian public companies set up during mass privatization, which by decree have a two-thirds majority of outside directors who are often in practice handpicked by management, will be a comparable check on management abuse of power.

Fifth, to a man, the general directors in the firms studied seemed devoted to promoting the welfare of their employees. Indeed, they continue to show significant (and paternalistic) concern with the social-welfare role of firms—provision of kindergartens, housing, sports clubs, vacation camps, clinics, and the like for employees—despite the growing economic reasons to eliminate such unprofitable activities. These firms demonstrate much of the "social partnership" that Plekhanov argues in Chapter 3 is vital for the successful development of democratic privatization. That managerial paternalism extends to managerial pride in avoiding layoffs which may threaten the firms' long-term competitiveness.

Sixth, there was a significant understanding of the process of privatization among workers who had gone through the process personally. While their understanding was certainly coupled with skepticism (particularly in the larger firms), manual workers interviewed generally could explain something about the ownership structure. Many had a recognizable sense of ownership: that hard work and reinvestment on their part would yield material benefits that had not been available under state ownership. This sense of ownership, however, which arose from the considerable education that took place during the lengthy process of privatization in these firms, was not shared by new hires. It certainly was not spontaneously generated by a transfer of property rights. If employee ownership is to succeed in mass-privatization firms, some sort of ownership training, similar to that done successfully in America, is going to be necessary to help inculcate more of a sense of ownership.

Seventh, the firms generally sought to create an internal market for employee stock, at least for those who left the company or retired. The process of setting a value in these internal markets was arbitrary, reflecting generally a formula for adjusting asset acquisition values to inflation, rather than the value of the ongoing business. However, these values may still be more realistic than those of the highly illiquid and inefficient markets that the government is calling into being for the public companies under mass privatization. It certainly will be easier to adjust valuation practices for internal company markets to reflect "real values" (as understood in the West) than to create a liquid, efficient public market for tens of thousands of companies.

Eighth, a number of the firms restored something of the traditional integration of the planning system by having customers and suppliers hold joint ownership in them. Indeed, in the case of MOVEN, this was driven by the explicit desire to ensure timely deliveries. The tendency to reestablish the old linkages among firms through ownership will probably be even greater among firms caught up in the mass privatization of 1993–94 whose stock, according to the GKI's rules, cannot be closely held.

Ninth, despite the fact that practically all the firms were incorporated as closed stock companies at the time of the study, practically all of them were eager to bring in outside investment capital, including foreign capital. But this was to happen on the company's own terms. Specifically this meant that outsiders' access to ownership required that they bring something to the table, such as new production technology, equipment, or product lines. By contrast, there was no interest whatsoever in having outside owners who had simply managed to buy shares.

Finally, the managers' motivation for privatization through employee ownership in most of the cases described was driven by the fact that it was the only form of privatization then permitted, rather than a belief in employee ownership per se. They sought independence of their ministerial bosses and of the plan. For them employee ownership was a means—a means that some of them believed in as a good in itself as well—but not the end. The end was independence, being their own bosses, escaping from the shackles imposed by the state plan. Some, like Makharinov, who continues to buy shares of Stroipolymer from his employees, see employee ownership as a stage on the road to a private market economy in which many employees own shares in their firms—which he sees as good—but many do not. Others, like Vrachev, have taken pains to encompass all new employees in the ownership structure.

Obviously the firms examined here are atypical in a variety of ways. As pioneers of privatization, they privatized in spite of the predominant system, not because of it. Given the number of hurdles for early privatizers, there was a considerable degree of natural selection of those which succeeded. The mass privatization that followed was, in its nature, not selective. Early privatization demanded innovative general directors to drive the process, and the exceptional performance of these firms in the first years of employee ownership probably reflects the competence and leadership ability of their general directors more than their new ownership form. But at least in these firms, employee ownership was compatible with an adjustment to the market, increased production, and increased investment. Had the rest of the Russian economy performed as well as this sector did, perhaps economic reform would be perceived as a success by ordinary Russians.

EMPLOYEE OWNERSHIP IN THE
POSTPRIVATIZATION PERIOD

Despite the ideological opposition to employee ownership by the Yeltsin reform team, by July 1994 the Russian economy was characterized by the most substantial degree of employee ownership in the world. Practically every firm of any size which had been privatized had at least a significant minority employee share, and two-thirds or more were majority owned by managers and workers.

What does the future hold for this experiment in converting state ownership into direct employee ownership?

The conclusion of the voucher privatization program on July 1, 1994, clearly marked the end of the first phase of Russia's transition from state to private ownership. The replacement of voucher privatization and sale to employees with cash sales of shares to outside interests suggests that the growth in employee ownership will cease. It will also guarantee an end to ordinary Russians' participation in the purchase of national assets.[9]

Employee ownership is likely to recede in the voucher privatization sector, where it now predominates. Current rules strictly circumscribe work collectives' efforts to limit resale of stock to employees only and to preserve the relatively high degree of dispersal of property ownership achieved in voucher privatization. As a result, there is a clear tendency toward concentration of ownership in the hands of a few managers and their outside associates in firms already privatized.

Still, as a consequence of the overwhelming popular support for employee ownership in the sector already privatized, it seems likely that employee ownership will continue to play a significant role as a form of ownership for some years to come and that it will continue to be a subject of immense political debate. At the core of this debate is a choice between two alternative visions of Russia's economic future.

The one is development toward a textbook process of capitalist accumulation. This includes increasing concentrations of ownership and disparities of income, the high (and heartless) efficiency of the capitalist market economy, and—presumably—a Western style interventionist welfare state to ameliorate the consequences of what otherwise would be rising poverty and cyclical collapses.

The other is development toward a "popular capitalism" of broadly shared ownership among most employees, and a market economy that is modified within the firm by a social partnership between management and workers that implies greater economic egalitarianism and greater paternalism, but also higher productivity and quality. It also implies far more of a welfare function for the firm than is typical in the United States or Western

Europe. There are some parallels in this partnership model to the Japanese experience, although that does not involve worker ownership.

The preference of the Russian government and its Western advisers is for the first alternative. The implementation rules for privatization and for stock sales in postprivatization firms which were established by the GKI are designed to encourage the concentration of ownership in fewer hands. These rules make it difficult for work collectives to keep ownership within the hands of current and retired employees. Pending legislation would force even the pioneering privatized firms examined in this volume to open their ownership structures to outsiders and would block them from keeping ownership among employees as they have sought to do.[10] Furthermore, as labor mobility increases as a consequence of layoffs and bankruptcies, many employees will find that the shares they had purchased are those of their former employer, not their current one.

Under these rules the current system of widely dispersed ownership of firms privatized through July 1994 will evolve toward increasingly concentrated ownership as managers purchase their employees' shares or as outsiders do the same. This route, already taken by a significant number of firms, leads to the "propertization" of the old managerial nomenklatura: solidifying their previous institutional privileges by giving them legal rights of ownership as well. This has also happened in some of the early privatizing firms discussed in this book; by the spring of 1994, for instance, general director Boris Makharinov at Stroipolymer owned in excess of 20 percent of that firm's stock. Judging from Joseph Blasi's survey of some two hundred larger enterprises privatizing under the 1993 rules, a similar occurrence is likely to be extremely common in their ranks.[11] While the government formally opposed this result during the 1992–94 privatization program, many of its implementation regulations encouraged it by preventing the work collective from limiting the concentration of ownership both during the closed subscription process and subsequently. Similarly, Yeltsin's decree preventing employees from controlling more than one-third of the board of directors, regardless of ownership proportion, has permitted many general directors to solidify their control by enabling them to handpick outside directors to serve on the board.

Nurturing Employee Ownership

The alternative route of development is to nurture employee ownership as a basis for an efficient market economy and widely shared property ownership. In the United States, certainly, employee-owned firms have proven to be highly efficient and competitive; as discussed in Chapter 14, there is substantial evidence that they are more productive than their conventionally owned competitors. The Russian evidence discussed in Part

II suggests that the same was true in Russia, at least among firms which privatized early. One can certainly discuss the relative importance of leadership, managerial competence, and ownership form in explaining these results, but in any case it is clear that employee ownership is compatible with improved economic efficiency.

It is also obvious from both American and Russian experience that a formal change in ownership does not automatically create a culture of ownership among employees. Changing employee attitudes is a long-term process, but it can be speeded up by internal company education, communications, and employee participation. That requires mass employee education in the rights and responsibilities of ownership, in the fundamentals of business operations in a market economy, and in understanding company financial reports. Creating a psychology of ownership among Russian workers is even more difficult than it is in American plants, but some of the early privatizing firms succeeded admirably—in part because the high aspirations of their employees provided fertile soil for education. Unfortunately, this sort of education and training is fully as foreign an idea to the Russian government and Western aid agencies as it would have been to the old Gosplan bureaucracy.

Maintaining the new system of dispersed property ownership will require more than just education. First, it requires a mechanism for welcoming new employees into ownership. Second, it requires additional mechanisms for employee influence on and control of management. Blasi (1994c) found that less than 5 percent of companies privatized under the voucher program had any rank-and-file employee representatives on their boards. Outside directors handpicked by top managers will not provide that check on abuse of power, nor will inside management directors. Third, effective employee ownership requires a mechanism for establishing company procedures for creating an internal market for company stock with an honest valuation. This means accepting that there will not be efficient secondary markets for the stock of more than a few hundred Russian firms within the foreseeable future. Therefore, legalizing the mechanisms used in the West to ensure value for minority shareholders in closely held companies (e.g., right of first refusal or buy-sell agreements) is crucial. It is simply an illusion in the current privatization program that an efficient public market will develop spontaneously for the shares of thousands of smaller firms. This market has never developed in the West, even after four hundred years of limited liability firms. Yet illusions in Russia tend to have a life of their own.

Economics as a Cultural System

The choice of the former of these two alternative visions seems based more upon an ideological construction of economic life and less upon economic realities and their sociopolitical consequences. The course chosen by Gaidar and Chubais under the tutelage of the International Monetary Fund (IMF), the World Bank, and some handpicked Western advisers is premised upon the assumption that creating capitalist market economies calls primarily for freeing *homo economicus*–economic man–from the tyranny of the state. Change the institutions–dismantle the plan, abolish price controls, enshrine private property at the center of the economic system, protect foreign investment–and the paradise of a Western market economy will appear spontaneously. The only snake in this Garden of Eden is an excessively accommodative monetary policy.

Both in the Russian government and among its Western advisers there seems to be an absence of any recognition that Western market economies are in fact immensely complicated cultural systems in which norms and values regulate economic behavior more than do contracts and governments. That intrinsically conservative and customary economic culture is supplemented by a complex web of law and regulatory institutions to channel the creativity of entrepreneurship (and of avarice and greed) into socially acceptable channels. The two, which make up an organic whole, have grown up together during the two centuries of political and economic struggle since the onset of the industrial revolution, and they differ significantly from nation to nation. Despite the global marketplace there are immense differences among the American, English, German, Italian, and Swedish variants of capitalist market economies and Western interventionist welfare states. To propose to implement the American model in Germany or the German model in America would be recognized as an act of hubris even by the IMF, and those economic cultures have far more in common with each other than do those of Russia and the West.

Obviously, the same problem pertains in importing foreign experience to Russia and expecting it to have an outcome comparable to that in its country of origin. Arkady I. Volsky, the industrialist leader, summed it up succinctly during one debate about the utility of the Swedish model in Russian economic reform: "The problem with the Swedish model is, we don't have enough Swedes" (*New York Times*, August 2, 1992).

Thus, despite the immense attractiveness of Western models of managed capitalism, which ameliorate the negative distributive consequences of market capitalism with the security net of the welfare state and mitigate its cyclical crises with well-honed tools of state intervention, there seems to be little evidence that the path chosen by the Russian government's economic reform team and its Western advisers will lead there in the foreseeable future. Rather, that path seems so far to have slashed production, dramatically reduced macroeconomic efficiency below the depressingly inadequate levels of the planned economy, and cut living standards for four-fifths of the population. The elderly, women, the unskilled, and children are the particular victims. Better schooled in Marxism than in market economics, Russians talk of being condemned to repeat the "primitive stage of capitalist accumulation."

Unfortunately, that primitive capitalist accumulation is not taking place in the hands of a new, productive entrepreneurial class. Rather, it is concentrated in the hands of the old political and managerial elite—the old nomenklatura—with some admixture of organized crime and nouveau riche speculators. The relatively modest but endemic corruption of the latter part of the "years of stagnation" under Brezhnev has blossomed as a growth sector throughout the contracting economy. There is a frightening possibility that Yeltsin's economic reform team will ultimately succeed only in combining the worst of the old Soviet system with the worst of Western capitalism.

Even without the corruption factor, the reformers' "shock therapy" of price increases, tight money, unpaid wages, collapsing production, and rising unemployment yielded more shock than therapy. By 1993, Russians were asking each other, "What have Yeltsin and Gaidar succeeded in doing in merely a year which Lenin, Stalin, Khrushchev, Brezhnev, and Gorbachev never could do in seven decades?" The bitter punchline: "Make communism look attractive."

None of this bodes well for the longevity of Russian democracy. Economic reform won overwhelming popular support in its beginnings, and the process continues to enjoy significant support. But that is because of the supposition that it can lead to a social partnership of shared prosperity in the firm and the community, not to palaces for the few and despair for the many. The dramatic success of Vladimir V. Zhirinovsky's bizarrely misnamed Liberal Democratic Party in the December 1993 election certainly underscores the necessity for real economic improvements in the immediate future.

If one accepts the proposition that market economies that have developed organically are regulated by complex cultural norms and thoughtful government regulations as well as by the laws of supply and demand and Adam Smith's "invisible hand," then what is the prescription in the Russian case? One major piece of it, surely, is to pay attention to empirical Russian experience as a guide. The experience we document of Russian firms which privatized early is instructive not least because the forms of internal organization that they developed reflected spontaneous efforts from below to solve the problems of developing a market economy under distinctively Russian conditions. Pluralism in developing economic organizations has a significant value in itself.

Employee ownership has a clear role to play in the chaotic process of Russian economic reform. It is not the only road to economic reform, but it is part of the solution. It appeals to ingrained cultural values including more of a collectivist ethos among workers and more paternalism among managers than many Western advisers are willing to admit. While in the aggregate such employee-owned firms may be less entrepreneurial than newly started firms with more concentrated ownership, the evidence from Part II suggests that employee ownership can be both dynamic and productive. Under Russian circumstances democratic employee-owned firms will unquestionably continue to burden themselves with kindergartens, worker housing, children's camps, and subsidized meals for pensioners. That reflects both the traditional responsibility of enterprises for social welfare and the lack of such amenities in the public sector. It need not lead to greater problems in competitiveness at the level of the firm than does the differential provision of health insurance and retirement benefits among American companies. Moreover, it offers a far higher likelihood of a successful social partnership within firms and municipalities than the alternative of "primitive capitalist accumulation" does. In a time of chaos, a modicum of social stability has much to recommend it.

It has been observed many times that the Russian political culture is characterized by the weakness of civil society and the unquestionable primacy of the state. To impatient reformers at the top, the people are always a problem, not a solution; they are seen as backward, uninformed, and patently incapable of governing themselves. They cannot be trusted to proceed with their own ideas of how change should come about. Therefore, they have to be forced. Sadly enough, many Russian citizens continue to underestimate their own capacity for self-government. Yet our research has persuaded us that Russian workers can effectively wield economic power as owners of their own enterprises. It is an important finding at this rare and crucial juncture in Russian history when Russia's vast riches are, once again, up for grabs. Plainly speaking, ordinary Russians *can* be much more than onlookers and victims of the vast economic changes sweeping Russia. It is our great hope that they *will* choose to do so, despite the burden of their authoritarian past.

NOTES

1. Price liberalization began in January 1992 and led to inflation of 2,600 percent in that year (Russian Federation, State Committee for the Management of State Property 1992: 9). Tight monetary policy was a core prescription from the International Monetary Fund (IMF), and Western stabilization aid was made contingent on its implementation. In practice, however, the need for a liberal credit policy to keep the economy functioning warred with the government's acceptance of the IMF position, and the actual governmental policy veered between following wildly accommodative policies and choking the money supply to the extent that the banking system ran out of cash and firms had to resort to paying their employees in commodities. Similarly, structural reform was impeded by

practical considerations, in particular by the absence of any mechanism to handle the mass unemployment that would result.

2. Majority employee ownership required a two-thirds vote in favor by the work collective. Payment turned out to be nominal because prices were based on depreciated asset values and the government's adjustment factor failed to meet inflation, but the government had not expected the degree of inflation that occurred. The first firms to privatize under these rules paid far more in real terms than the last.

3. David Ellerman argues that this is the general situation in postsocialist economies that had carried out earlier decentralizing economic reforms within the socialist system. These reforms created quasi-private property rights. The consequence in Poland and Slovenia as well as Russia has been a general conflict between workers and managers who were the beneficiaries of these rights, on the one hand, and the neoliberal reform programs of the first postsocialist governments, on the other. Ellerman concludes that "democratic governments must face a choice. They cannot have fast, efficient privatization and at the same time undo the past reforms by disenfranchising the early reform constituencies (largely managers and workers) of their quasi-private rights" (Ellerman 1993: 275).

4. "Perhaps the 'Wall Street' obsession has more of an anthropological than an economic explanation," Ellerman (1993: 273) suggests. Russian author Vladimir Sorokin complained that while the myth of communism has been destroyed, "It has been displaced by a new myth—the myth of the market" (Remnick 1994: 60).

5. Tradability ensured that the voucher program had a significant inflationary impact as vouchers were converted to cash to buy goods for family survival in the economic crisis that was well under way when voucher distribution began in the fall of 1992; the result was a quick concentration of voucher ownership. While vouchers were denominated with a nominal value of 10,000 rubles (and they could be exchanged in closed employee subscriptions for property valued at about 6,000 per voucher in 1991 rubles), market prices in current rubles per voucher ranged from a low of 3,600 rubles in the summer of 1993 to 42,000 rubles in March 1994. Market prices never approached the real value of the assets which the voucher could purchase.

6. Of these, 10 percent bought shares of their employer; 8 percent, those of other firms. In addition, 12 percent said that they had given their vouchers away, and 12 percent had not yet disposed of them at the time of the Public Opinion Foundation poll for the news program "Itogi." The sample size was 1,201 spread across Russia, and the Public Opinion Foundation reported the margin of error to be plus or minus 3 percent. *Moscow Times*, weekly ed., June 12, 1994, 43.

7. Mikhail Kharshan, president of First Voucher Investment Fund, one of the largest funds, estimated that 600 of the 650 will fail, while Alexander Deryabin, president of the International Stock Market Institute, was even more pessimistic: "For about 95 percent of the funds, bankruptcy is just a matter of time." *Moscow Times,* weekly ed., June 5, 1994, 40, 41.

8. This seems to fulfill the low expectations Russian citizens held of the program. When Lynn Nelson and Irina Kuzes (1994a: 62) surveyed four thousand Russians in Moscow, Ekaterinburg, Voronezh, and Smolensk in 1993, only 20 percent thought that the public benefited from the voucher program. By contrast, 82 percent thought the mafia and crime groups benefited, and 76 percent thought government officials benefited.

9. This is clearest in the case of bankruptcy, where a single investor can buy the firm at a price not less than 70 percent of the company's charter capital revalued by a factor of 12. An estimated 1,500 firms employing more than one thousand each are supposed to be slated for bankruptcy. However, investors must also pay all of the firm's debts—a requirement that reduces the interenterprise nonpayment crisis, but makes the purchase

of such firms less attractive. It also remains to be seen whether such general bankruptcy will be permitted politically. Since the new bankruptcy law was approved in March 1993, only fifty companies have faced bankruptcy proceedings. Cf. *Moscow Times,* weekly ed., June 12, 1994, 38.

10. Pending measures would prohibit "closed companies"–that is, closely held companies–with more than fifty employees and force the existing ones to open themselves to outside investors wishing to buy stock from employees.

11. Blasi's survey found that while top managers held an average of only 8.6 percent of shares and other employees held 55 percent, their ideal was 40 percent ownership by top management and 32 percent ownership by other employees (Blasi 1994a: 2, 9).

Bibliography

BOOKS, ARTICLES, AND CONFERENCE PAPERS

Adam, Jan. 1991. *Economic Reforms and the Welfare Systems in the USSR, Poland and Hungary.* New York: St. Martin's Press.

Arbatov, Georgi A. 1992. "A Neo-Bolshevik Brand of Capitalism." *International Herald Tribune*, May 12.

Azrael, Jeremy R. 1966. *Managerial Power and Soviet Politics.* Cambridge, MA: Harvard University Press.

Bell, Daniel. 1988. *Bringing Your Employees into the Business: An Employee Ownership Handbook for Small Business.* Kent, OH: Kent Popular Press. Appeared in Russian as *Vovlechenie vashikh rabotnikov v biznes: Rykovodstvo po sobstvennosti rabotnikov dlya kompanii malogo biznesa.* Voronezh: Tip Tayms, 1994.

Bernstein, David, and William J. Perry. 1993. "Defense Conversion: A Strategic Imperative for Russia." *Stanford Journal of International Affairs* 2(2): 109–136.

Bernstein, David, and Katherine Smith. 1992. *Collaborative Project on Soviet Defense Conversion: Status Report on Conversion after July 1991 Delegation.* Stanford, CA: Center for International Security and Arms Control.

Birman, A. M. 1963. *Nekotorie problemi nauki o sotsialisticheskom khoziaistvovanii.* Moscow: Ekonizdat.

Blasi, Joseph R. 1988. *Employee Ownership: Revolution or Ripoff?* Cambridge, MA: Ballinger.

———. 1992. "What Should the Role of Employee Ownership in Russian Privatization Be? Some Lessons from the U.S. Experience." Paper presented at the Gorbachev Foundation conference, Moscow, July.

———. 1994a. "The Impact of Privatization on the Enterprise and the Impact of the Enterprise on Reform." Paper presented at a conference on conversion of the defense industry in Russia and Eastern Europe, Bonn, Germany, August 10–13.

———. 1994b. "Privatized Enterprises in Russia: Organizational Trends and Problems." Paper presented at the National Center for Employee Ownership annual conference, Cleveland, OH, April 5.

———. 1994c. "Privatizing Russia–A Success Story." *New York Times,* June 30, A23.

Blasi, Joseph R., and Douglas L. Kruse. 1991. *The New Owners: The Mass Emergence of Employee Ownership in Public Companies and What It Means to American Business.* New York: Harper Business.

Bruce, James B., and Clawson, Robert W. 1977. "A Zonal Analysis Model for Comparative Politics: A Partial Soviet Application." *World Politics* 24(2): 177–215.

Bureau of National Affairs. 1987. *Employee Ownership Plans: How 8,000 Companies and 8,000,000 Employees Invest in Their Future.* Washington, DC: Bureau of National Affairs.

Campbell, Robert W. 1961. "Marx, Kantorovich and Novozhilov." *Slavic Review* 20(10): 403–412.

———. 1968. "Economic Reform in the U.S.S.R." *American Economic Review* 58(5): 547–558.

Clarke, Simon. 1992. "Privatisation and Development of Capitalism in Russia." *New Left Review* 196: 3–27.

Clarke, Simon, Peter Fairbrother, Vadim Borisov, and Petr Bizyukov. 1994. "The Privatisation of Industrial Enterprises in Russia: Four Case-Studies." *Europe-Asia Studies* 46(2): 179–214.

Clawson, Robert W. 1969. "The Politics of Industrial Reform in the Soviet Union: 1957–65." Ph.D. diss., University of California, Los Angeles.

Conquest, Robert. 1961. *Power and Policy in the USSR.* New York: St. Martin's Press.

Conte, Michael. 1992. "Does Employee Ownership Affect Performance: A Review of 20 Years of the Major Research." University of Baltimore, School of Business. Manuscript.

Conte, Michael, and Arnold Tannenbaum. 1978. "Employee Ownership: Is the Difference Measurable?" *Monthly Labor Review* 101 (July): 23–28.

———. 1980. *Employee Ownership.* Ann Arbor: University of Michigan, Survey Research Center.

Coordinating Committee for Economic Democracy. 1992. "Razvitie sobstvennosti rabotnikov v Rossii." Report to the conference on "Privatization Through Employee Ownership," Moscow, July 1.

Covey, Stephen R. 1989. *The Seven Habits of Highly Effective People: Restoring the Character Ethic.* New York: Simon and Schuster. Forthcoming in Russian.

Dahl, Robert. 1982. *Dilemmas of Pluralist Democracy.* New Haven: Yale University Press.

———. 1985. *A Preface to Economic Democracy.* Berkeley: University of California Press.

Deming, W. Edwards. 1982. *Out of the Crisis.* Cambridge, MA: MIT Center for Advanced Engineering Study.

DePree, Max. 1989. *Leadership Is an Art.* New York: Doubleday.

Derber, Milton. 1970. *The American Idea of Industrial Democracy.* Urbana: University of Illinois Press.

———. 1977. "Collective Bargaining: The American Approach to Industrial Democracy." *Annals of the American Academy of Political and Social Science* 431: 83–94.

Dobb, Maurice. 1948. *Soviet Economic Development since 1917.* New York: International Publishers.

Ellerman, David. 1993. "Privatization in Post-Socialist Economies." *Human Systems Management* 12: 271–279.

"Employee Ownership Index." 1994. *Journal of Employee Ownership Law and Finance* 6(1): 99.

Fedorovich, M. 1963. "Forsirovat primenenie matematiki v ekonomike." *Voprosi ekonomiki* (1): 95–106.

Foreign Broadcast Information Service–USR–92–115. 1992.

Frydman, Roman, Andrzej Rapaczynski, John S. Earle. 1993. *The Privatization Process in Russia, Ukraine and the Baltic States.* Budapest: Central European University Press.

Grossman, Gregory. 1963. "The Soviet Economy." *Problems of Communism* 12(2): 32–40.

———. 1976. *Value and Plan: Economic Calculation and Organization in Eastern Europe.* Westport, CT: Greenwood.

Hanna, David P. 1988. *Designing Organizations for High Performance.* Reading, MA: Addison Wesley.

Hendley, Kathryn. 1992. *Steps on the Road to Privatization: A Preliminary Report on the Saratov Aviation Plant.* Stanford, CA: Center for International Security and Arms Control.

Hewett, Edward A. 1988. *Reforming the Soviet Economy.* Washington, DC: Brookings Institution.

Higgins, Michael, and David Binns. 1994. "The Role of Employee Ownership in Russian Privatization." Paper presented at a conference on conversion of the defense industry in Russia and Eastern Europe, Bonn, Germany, August 10–13.

Hudiburg, John. 1991. *Winning with Quality: The FPL Story.* White Plains, NY: Quality Resources.

Kelso, Louis, with Mortimer Adler. 1958. *The Capitalist Manifesto.* New York: Random House.

Kelso, Louis, with Patricia Hetter. 1968. *How to Turn Eighty Million Workers into Capitalists on Borrowed Money.* New York: Random House.

Keremetsky, Jacob, and John Logue. 1991. *Perestroika, Privatization and Worker Ownership in the USSR.* Kent, OH: Kent Popular Press.

Khrushchev, N. S. 1957a. *Pravda,* March 30.

———. 1957b. *Pravda,* May 8.

———. 1962. *Pravda,* November 20.

Kishinets, Elena. 1991. "Turning the Ignition On." *Dvigatel (Engine),* March 29.

Koroyed, A., and I. Kugukalo. 1957. *Pravda,* April 4.

Kosygin, Alexei. 1965. *Pravda,* September 28.

Liberman, E. G. 1962. *Pravda,* September 9.

Logue, John. 1991a. "Democratic Theory and Atheoretical Democracy: Reflections on Building Democratic Enterprises in the American Economy." In *Managing Modern Capitalism: Industrial Renewal and Workplace Democracy in the United States and Western Europe,* edited by M. Donald Hancock, John Logue, and Bernt Schiller, 313–339. Westport, CT: Greenwood.

———. 1991b. "Kollektivnaya sobstvennost rabotnikov (obzor amerikanskogo opita)." *SSHA: Ekonomika, politika, ideologiya* 10: 34–48.

Logue, John, and Cassandra Rogers. 1989. *Employee Stock Ownership Plans in Ohio: Impact on Company Performance and Employment.* Kent, OH: NOEOC.

Logue, John, and Karen Thomas. 1994. *Employee Ownership: A Competitiveness Strategy in Northeast Ohio's Manufacturing Sector.* Urban Policy Monograph Series on Regional Competitiveness and Cooperation, no. 10. Akron, OH: Inter-Institutional Urban Research Consortium.

Long, Richard J. 1978. "The Effects of Employee Ownership on Organizational Identification, Employee Job Attitudes and Organizational Performance." *Human Relations* 31: 29–48.

McFaul, Michael, and David Bernstein. 1992. *Industrial Demilitarization, Privatization, Economic Reform, and Investment in Russia: Analysis and Recommendations.* Stanford, CA: Center for International Security and Arms Control.

Mamutov, V. M. 1961. *Prava rukovoditelei predpriiatii i organizatsii sovnarkhozov, ministerstv i vedomosti v reshenii khozyaistvennikh voprosov.* Moscow: Gosiurizdat.

———. 1964. *Kompetentsiia gosudarstvennikh organov v reshenii khozyaistvennikh voprosov promishlennosti.* Moscow: Gosiurizdat.

Marsh, Thomas, and Dale McAllister. 1981. "ESOPs Tables." *Journal of Corporation Law* (spring): 551–623.

Nekrasova, Idlena M., et al. 1986. *Flagman stankostroeniya: Stranitsi istorii zavoda "Krasny Proletary" imeni A. I. Efremova.* Moscow: Moskovsky Rabochy.

Nelson, Lynn D., and Irina Y. Kuzes. 1994a. "Evaluating the Russian Voucher Privatization Program." *Comparative Economic Studies* 36(1): 55–67.

———. 1994b. *Property to the People: The Struggle for Radical Economic Reform in Russia.* Armonk, NY: M. E. Sharpe.

Nove, Alec. 1961. *The Soviet Economic System.* New York: Praeger Publishers.

———. 1972. *An Economic History of the USSR.* New York: Pelican Books.

Quarrey, Michael. 1986. *Employee Ownership and Corporate Performance.* Arlington, VA: National Center for Employee Ownership.

Remnick, David. 1994. "Exit the Saints." *The New Yorker,* July 18, 50–60.

Rosen, Corey, and Katherine Klein. 1983. "Job Creating Performance of Employee-Owned Firms." *Monthly Labor Review* (August): 15–19.

Rosen, Corey, Katherine Klein, and Karen Young. 1986. *Employee Ownership in America: The Equity Solution.* Lexington, MA: D. C. Heath.

Russell, R., A. Hochner, and S. Perry. 1979. "Participation, Influence and Worker Ownership." *Industrial Relations* 18: 330–341.

Russian Federation. 1991. "Fundamental Provisions of the Program for Privatization of State-Owned and Municipal Enterprises in the Russian Federation for 1992." Approved by Decree No. 341 of the President of the Russian Federation on December 29, 1991.

———. 1992. "State Program of Privatization of State and Municipal Enterprises of the Russian Federation for 1992." Approved by Resolution No. 2 980-1 of the Supreme Soviet of the Russian Federation, June 11, 1992.

———. State Committee for the Management of State Property. 1992. *Annual Report, 1992.*

Schroeder, Gertrude E. 1968. "Soviet Economic 'Reforms': A Study in Contradictions." *Soviet Studies* 20(7): 462–477.

———. 1970. "Soviet Economic Reform at an Impasse." *Problems of Communism* 20(4): 38–40.

———. 1985. "The Slowdown in Soviet Industry, 1976–1982." *Soviet Economy* 1(1): 42–74.

Seliunin, Valilii. 1988. *Pravda,* May 8.

Simmons, John. 1991. "Seven Soviet Myths." *Nezavisimaya Gazeta,* July 27.

———. 1992a. "After the Employee Ownership Debate." *Rossiskaya Gazeta,* September 13.

———. 1992b. "Privatization from the Bottom Up." *Rossiskaya Gazeta,* May 30.

Simmons, John, and John Logue. 1992. "The 13 Myths of Russian Privatization." *Izvestia,* April 1.

Simmons, John, and William Mares. 1983. *Working Together.* New York: Knopf. Appeared in Russian as *Kak stat sobstvennikom: Amerikanskii opit uchastiya rabotnikov v sobstvennosti i upravlenii.* Moscow: Argumenti i Fakti, 1993.

Smiley, Robert W., Jr., and Ronald J. Gilbert. 1989. *Employee Stock Ownership Plans: Business Planning, Implementation, Law and Taxation.* New York: Prentice Hall. Annual updates.

Stack, Jack. 1992. *The Great Game of Business.* New York: Doubleday. Forthcoming in Russian.

Sutela, Pekka. 1994. "Insider Privatisation in Russia: Speculations on Systemic Change." *Europe-Asia Studies* 46(3): 417–436.

Swearer, Howard. 1963. "The Dynamics of Administrative Reform in the Soviet Union." University of California, Los Angeles. Manuscript.

Ulam, Adam B. 1976. *A History of Soviet Russia.* New York: Praeger Publishers.

United States General Accounting Office. 1987. *Employee Stock Ownership Plans: Little Evidence of Effects on Corporate Performance.* Washington, DC: General Accounting Office.

Varvarov, Valery N. 1991. "Materiali analiza raboti predpriyaty Kontserna v usloviyakh kollektivno-dolevoi formi sobstvennosti." BUTEK, Moscow. Manuscript.

Vrachev, Vadim G. 1992. "Sobstvennost rabotnikov delaet iz zavoda-bankrota uspeshnoe predpriyatie." In *Materiali rossisko-amerikanskoy konferentsy "Privatizatsiya cherez sobstvennost rabotnikov,"* 56–64. Moscow. Conference paper printed in conference book.

———. 1993. "AO 'VIKA': Kazansky Elektromekhanichesky Zavod." In *Opit razvitiya form aktsionernoy sobstvennosti rabotnikov: Materiali tretey nauchno-prakticheskoy konferentsy privatizirovannikh predpriyaty,* 11–20. Moscow: Foundation for Russia's Economic Reform.

Wagner, Ira. 1984. *The Performance of Publicly Traded Employee Ownership Companies.* Arlington, VA: National Center for Employee Ownership.

World Bank and European Bank for Reconstruction and Development Study Team. 1992. "Mass Privatization in Russia." Moscow, March 23. Unpublished working document.

Yampolskaia, Ts. A. 1965. *Obshchestvennie organizatsii i razvitie sovetskoi sotsialisticheskii gosudarstvennosti.* Moscow: Gosiurizdat.

Zaleski, E. 1967. *Planning in the Soviet Union, 1962–1966.* Chapel Hill: University of North Carolina Press.

Zaslavskaia, Tatiana. 1985. *Izvestia,* June 1.

NEWSPAPERS AND MAGAZINES

The following publications are for 1991–1994.

Economist.
Ekonomicheskiye i Sotsialnyie Peremeny: Monitoring Obshchestvennogo Mneniya.
Finansovye izvestia.
Izvestia.
Journal of Commerce.
Kommersant.
Los Angeles Times.
Manchester Guardian Weekly.
Moscow News.
Moscow Times.
New York Times.
Nezavisimaya Gazeta.
Ogonyok.
Radio Free Europe-Radio Liberty Daily Report.
Rossiskaya Gazeta.

Index

About the Contributors

DAVID BINNS is the associate director of the Foundation for Enterprise Development, a private, nonprofit foundation which promotes enterprise development through employee ownership and participation. Binns served previously as executive director of the ESOP Association, the national trade association representing the interests of companies with Employee Stock Ownership Plans (ESOPs) and professionals providing advisory services to ESOP companies. He is a frequent speaker and writer on issues related to employee ownership and enterprise development.

ROBERT W. CLAWSON, emeritus professor of political science at Kent State University, has written widely on issues of Soviet economic and military development. He is the former director of the Lemnitzer Center for NATO Studies at Kent State University.

DAVID HANNA is a team leader at the Covey Leadership Center and a senior associate of Participation Associates. He is the former manager of organizational development at Procter and Gamble. He is the author of *Designing Organizations for High Performance* (1988).

YAKOV KEREMETSKY is a senior researcher at the Institute for the Study of the United States and Canada of the Russian Academy of Sciences. His books include *Trade Unions of the United States in the Struggle Against Capital* (1970), *The Class Struggle as an Agent of Social Change* (1984),

Political Consciousness of the U.S. Working Class (1991), all in Russian, and *Perestroika, Privatization and Worker Ownership in the USSR* (with John Logue, 1991). In recent years, his research has focused on the process of privatization and changing forms of ownership and management in Russia, and he has done consulting for the Foundation for Economic Reform of Russia.

YURI I. KIRILLOV, educated at the Moscow Technological College of Machine Tool Building, began work at Krasny Proletary in 1974 as a young technology specialist and worked his way up through the production technology side of the machine tool business. He supervised the construction of the company's new Moscow plant in 1983–86, designing both its production and management systems. He was elected general director of Krasny Proletary in 1988.

JOHN LOGUE is professor of political science at Kent State University and director of the Northeast Ohio Employee Ownership Center. He has written widely on various aspects of industrial democracy and employee ownership in the United States and Scandinavia. His most recent book, edited with Don Hancock and Bernt Schiller, is *Managing Modern Capitalism: Industrial Renewal and Workplace Democracy in the United States and Western Europe* (Greenwood/Praeger, 1991).

OLGA MAIBORODA is the director of ECOS, the first nongovernmental environmental organization in Sochi, Russia. She received her B.A. in English and foreign literature from Volgograd State University and her M.A. in American literature from Kent State University. In 1991–93, she worked with the Northeast Ohio Employee Ownership Center's Russian privatization program.

SERGEY PLEKHANOV is a visiting professor of political science at York University (Toronto) while on leave from the Institute for the Study of the United States and Canada of the Russian Academy of Sciences. After years of research and writing on American politics and society (published works include *Right Wing Extremism and U.S. Foreign Policy, Modern American Political Consciousness* [coauthored], and numerous chapters and articles), Plekhanov became actively involved in the struggles for democratic reforms in the USSR. In 1991–92, he was founding chairman of the Coordinating Committee for Economic Democracy, a group of Russian industrialists, academics, and politicians advocating privatization through employee ownership.

JOHN SIMMONS is president of Participation Associates and a former staff member of the World Bank. Together with William Mares, Simmons authored *Working Together* (1983), which has appeared in a revised Russian translation as *How to Become an Owner: America's Experience with Employee Participation in Management and Ownership* (1993). He is the past president of the board of directors of the Association for Quality and Participation, and is adjunct professor of management at the Kellogg School of Management, Northwestern University.

VICTOR B. SUPYAN is head of the Center of Social-Economic Studies and Projects of the Institute for the Study of the United States and Canada of the Russian Academy of Sciences. He is the author of *The American Labor Force in the Conditions of the New Phase of Technological Progress* (in Russian) (1990) and *Utilization of the Labor Force in the United States* (in Russian) (1982), as well as numerous articles and book chapters in the fields of the labor market, human resources management, privatization, and technological change.

OLEG TIKHONOV has been a research associate at the Institute for the Study of the United States and Canada of the Russian Academy of Sciences since 1984. His primary fields of research are U.S. federal tax policy, private pensions, and Employee Stock Ownership Plans. Recent works include *The Contemporary U.S. Tax System* (in Russian) (1990).

VALERY N. VARVAROV is the director of the Privatization and Enterprise Reform Program at Russia's Economic Reform Foundation. He has been directly involved in assisting state enterprises to privatize as employee-owned companies since 1989, when he was director for human resources at BUTEK. He was previously a director of the Institute of Economics and Administration of the machine industry, and he has written on management issues and employee ownership.

ISBN 0-313-28748-1

EAN

9 780313 287480

HARDCOVER BAR CODE